Cold War
Biographies

Cold War
Biographies
Volume 1: A-J

Sharon M. Hanes
and Richard C. Hanes

Lawrence W. Baker,
Project Editor

THOMSON
★
GALE

Cold War: Biographies

Sharon M. Hanes and Richard C. Hanes

Project Editor
Lawrence W. Baker

Editorial
Matthew May, Diane Sawinski

Permissions
Margaret Chamberlain, Shalice Shah-Caldwell

Imaging and Multimedia
Lezlie Light, Mike Logusz, Dave Oblender, Kelly A. Quin

Product Design
Pamela A. E. Galbreath, Jennifer Wahi

Composition
Evi Seoud

Manufacturing
Rita Wimberley

LIBRARY OF CONGRESS CATALOGING-IN-PUBLICATION DATA

Hanes, Sharon M.

  Cold War : biographies / Sharon M. Hanes and Richard C. Hanes ; Lawrence W. Baker, editor.

    v. cm. — (UXL Cold War reference library)

Includes bibliographical references and index.

Contents: v. 1. A–J. Dean G. Acheson. Konrad Adenauer. Salvador Allende. Clement R. Attlee. Ernest Bevin. Leonid Brezhnev. George Bush. James F. Byrnes. Jimmy Carter. Fidel Castro. Chiang Kai-shek. Winston Churchill. Clark M. Clifford. Deng Xiaoping. John Foster Dulles. Dwight D. Eisenhower. Mikhail Gorbachev. Andrey Gromyko. W. Averell Harriman. Ho Chi Minh. J. Edgar Hoover. Lyndon B. Johnson — v. 2. K–Z. George F. Kennan. John F. Kennedy. Nikita Khrushchev. Kim Il Sung. Jeane Kirkpatrick. Henry Kissinger. Helmut Kohl. Aleksey Kosygin. Igor Kurchatov. Douglas MacArthur. Harold Macmillan. Mao Zedong. George C. Marshall. Joseph R. McCarthy. Robert S. McNamara. Vyacheslav Molotov. Richard M. Nixon. J. Robert Oppenheimer. Ayn Rand. Ronald Reagan. Condoleezza Rice. Andrey Sakharov. Eduard Shevardnadze. Joseph Stalin. Margaret Thatcher. Josip Broz Tito. Harry S. Truman. Zhou Enlai.

  ISBN 0-7876-7663-2 (alk. paper) — ISBN 0-7876-7664-0 (v. 1 : alk. paper) — ISBN 0-7876-7665-9 (v. 2 : alk. paper)

  1. Cold War—Biography—Juvenile literature. 2. History, Modern—1945–1989—Juvenile literature. 3. Biography—20th century —Juvenile literature. [1. Cold War—Biography. 2. History, Modern—1945–1989. 3. Biography—20th century.] I. Hanes, Richard Clay, 1946– . II. Baker, Lawrence W. III. Title. IV. Series.

  D839.5.H36 2003
  909.82'5'0922—dc22   2003018989

Contents

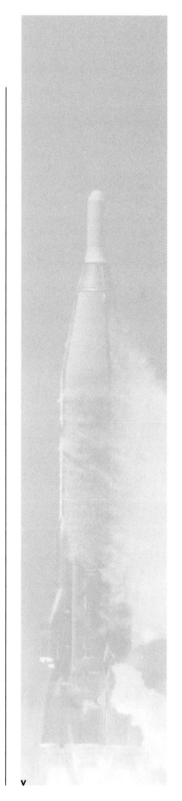

Volume 2

Introduction

Sometimes single events alter the course of history; other times, a chain reaction of seemingly lesser occurrences changes the path of nations. The intense rivalry between the United States and the Soviet Union that emerged immediately after World War II (1939–45) followed the second pattern. Known as the Cold War, the rivalry grew out of mutual distrust between two starkly different societies: communist Soviet Union and the democratic West, which was led by the United States and included Western Europe. Communism is a political and economic system in which the Communist Party controls all aspects of citizens' lives and private ownership of property is banned. It is not compatible with America's democratic way of life. Democracy is a political system consisting of several political parties whose members are elected to various government offices by vote of the people. The rapidly growing rivalry between the two emerging post–World War II superpowers in 1945 would dominate world politics until 1991. Throughout much of the time, the Cold War was more a war of ideas than one of battlefield combat. Yet for generations, the Cold War affected almost every aspect of American life and those who lived in numerous other countries around the world.

The global rivalry was characterized by many things. Perhaps the most dramatic was the cost in lives and public funds. Millions of military personnel and civilians were killed in conflicts often set in Third World countries. This toll includes tens of thousands of American soldiers in the Korean War (1950–53) and Vietnam War (1954–75) and thousands of Soviet soldiers in Afghanistan. National budgets were stretched to support the nuclear arms races, military buildups, localized wars, and aid to friendly nations. On the international front, the United States often supported oppressive but strongly anticommunist military dictatorships. On the other hand, the Soviets frequently supported revolutionary movements seeking to overthrow established governments. Internal political developments within nations around the world were interpreted by the two superpowers—the Soviet Union and the United States—in terms of the Cold War rivalry. In many nations, including the Soviet-dominated Eastern European countries, basic human freedoms were lost. New international military and peacekeeping alliances were also formed, such as the United Nations (UN), the North Atlantic Treaty Organization (NATO), the Organization of American States (OAS), and the Warsaw Pact.

Effects of the Cold War were extensive on the home front, too. The U.S. government became more responsive to national security needs, including the sharpened efforts of the Federal Bureau of Investigation (FBI). Created were the Central Intelligence Agency (CIA), the National Security Council (NSC), and the Department of Defense. Suspicion of communist influences within the United States built some individual careers and destroyed others. The national education priorities of public schools were changed to emphasize science and engineering after the Soviets launched the satellite *Sputnik,* which itself launched the space race.

What would cause such a situation to develop and last for so long? One major factor was mistrust for each other. The communists were generally shunned by other nations, including the United States, since they gained power in Russia in 1917 then organized that country into the Soviet Union. The Soviets' insecurities loomed large. They feared another invasion from the West through Poland, as had happened through the centuries. On the other hand, the West was highly suspicious of the harsh closed society of Soviet communism. As a result, a move by one nation would bring a response by the other. Hard-liners on both sides believed long-term coexistence was not feasible.

A second major factor was that the U.S. and Soviet ideologies were dramatically at odds. The political, social, and economic systems of democratic United States and communist Soviet Union were essentially incompatible. Before the communist (or Bolshevik) revolution in 1917, the United States and Russia competed as they both sought to expand into the Pacific Northwest. In addition, Americans had a strong disdain for Russian oppression under their monarchy of the tsars. Otherwise, contact between the two growing powers was almost nonexistent until thrown together as allies in a common cause to defeat Germany and Japan in World War II.

It was during the meetings of the allied leaders in Yalta and Potsdam in 1945 when peaceful postwar cooperation was being sought that the collision course of the two new superpowers started becoming more evident. The end of World War II had brought the U.S. and Soviet armies face-to-face in central Europe in victory over the Germans. Yet the old mistrusts between communists and capitalists quickly dominated diplomatic relations. Capitalism is an economic system in which property and businesses are privately owned. Prices, production, and distribution of goods are determined by competition in a market relatively free of government intervention. A peace treaty ending World War II in Europe was blocked as the Soviets and the U.S.-led West carved out spheres of influence. Western Europe and Great Britain aligned with the United States and collectively was referred to as the "West"; Eastern Europe would be controlled by the Soviet Communist Party. The Soviet Union and its Eastern European satellite countries were collectively referred to as the "East." The two powers tested the resolve of each other in Germany, Iran, Turkey, and Greece in the late 1940s.

In 1949, the Soviets successfully tested an atomic bomb and Chinese communist forces overthrew the National Chinese government, and U.S. officials and American citizens feared a sweeping massive communist movement was overtaking the world. A "red scare" spread through America. The term "red" referred to communists, especially the Soviets. The public began to suspect that communists or communist sympathizers lurked in every corner of the nation.

Meanwhile, the superpower confrontations spread from Europe to other global areas: Asia, Africa, the Middle East, and Latin America. Most dramatic were the Korean and Vietnam wars, the Cuban Missile Crisis, and the military standoffs in Berlin, Germany. However, bloody conflicts erupted in many other areas as the United States and Soviet Union sought to expand their influence by supporting or opposing various movements.

In addition, a costly arms race lasted decades despite sporadic efforts at arms control agreements. The score card for the Cold War was kept in terms of how many nuclear weapons one country had aimed at the other. Finally, in the 1970s and 1980s, the Soviet Union could no longer keep up with the changing world economic trends. Its tightly controlled and highly inefficient industrial and agricultural systems could not compete in world markets while the government was still focusing its wealth on Cold War confrontations and the arms race. Developments in telecommunications also made it more difficult to maintain a closed society. Ideas were increasingly being exchanged despite longstanding political barriers. The door was finally cracked open in the communist European nations to more freedoms in the late 1980s through efforts at economic and social reform. Seizing the moment, the long suppressed populations of communist Eastern European nations and fifteen Soviet republics demanded political and economic freedom.

Through 1989, the various Eastern European nations replaced long-time communist leaders with noncommunist officials. By the end of 1991, the Soviet Communist Party had been banned from various Soviet republics, and the Soviet Union itself ceased to exist. After a decades-long rivalry, the end to the Cold War came swiftly and unexpectedly.

A new world order dawned in 1992 with a single superpower, the United States, and a vastly changed political landscape around much of the globe. Communism remained in China and Cuba, but Cold War legacies remained elsewhere. In the early 1990s, the United States was economically burdened with a massive national debt, the former Soviet republics were attempting a very difficult economic transition to a more capitalistic open market system, and Europe, starkly divided by the Cold War, was reunited once again and sought to establish a new union including both Eastern and Western European nations.

Reader's Guide

Cold War: Biographies presents biographies of fifty men and women who participated in or were affected by the Cold War, the period in history from 1945 until 1991 that was dominated by the rivalry between the world's superpowers, the United States and the Soviet Union. These two volumes profile a diverse mix of personalities from the United States, the Soviet Union, China, Great Britain, and other regions touched by the Cold War. Detailed biographies of major Cold War figures (such as Fidel Castro, Winston Churchill, Mikhail Gorbachev, John F. Kennedy, Nikita Khrushchev, and Joseph R. McCarthy) are included. But Cold War: Biographies also provides biographical information on lesser-known but nonetheless important and fascinating men and women of that era. Examples include nuclear physicist Igor Kurchatov, the developer of the Soviet atomic bomb; U.S. secretary of state George C. Marshall, a former Army general who unveiled the Marshall Plan, a major U.S. economic aid program for the war-torn countries of Western Europe; Kim Il Sung, the communist dictator of North Korea throughout the Cold War; and Condoleezza Rice, the top U.S. advisor on the Soviet Union when the Cold War ended in November 1990.

Cold War: Biographies also features sidebars containing interesting facts about people and events related to the Cold War. Within each full-length biography, boldfaced cross-references direct readers to other individuals profiled in the two-volume set. Finally, each volume includes photographs and illustrations, a "Cold War Timeline" that lists significant dates and events of the Cold War era, and a cumulative subject index.

U•X•L Cold War Reference Library

Cold War: Biographies is only one component of the three-part U•X•L Cold War Reference Library. The other two titles in this set are:

- *Cold War: Almanac* (two volumes) presents a comprehensive overview of the period in American history from the end of World War II until the fall of communism in Eastern Europe and the Soviet Union and the actual dissolution of the Soviet Union itself. Its fifteen chapters are arranged chronologically and explore such topics as the origins of the Cold War, the beginning of the nuclear age, the arms race, espionage, anticommunist campaigns and political purges on the home fronts, détente, the Cuban Missile Crisis, the Berlin Airlift and the Berlin Wall, the Korean and Vietnam wars, and the ending of the Cold War. The *Almanac* also contains more than 140 black-and-white photographs and maps, "Words to Know" and "People to Know" boxes, a timeline, and an index.

- *Cold War: Primary Sources* (one volume) tells the story of the Cold War in the words of the people who lived and shaped it. Thirty-one excerpted documents provide a wide range of perspectives on this period of history. Included are excerpts from presidential press conferences; addresses to U.S. Congress and Soviet Communist Party meetings; public speeches; telegrams; magazine articles; radio and television addresses; and later reflections by key government leaders.

- A cumulative index of all three titles in the U•X•L Cold War Reference Library is also available.

Acknowledgments

Kelly Rudd and Meghan O'Meara contributed importantly to *Cold War: Biographies*. Special thanks to Catherine

Filip, who typed much of the manuscript. Much appreciation also goes to copyeditors Christine Alexanian, Taryn Benbow-Pfalzgraf, and Jane Woychick; proofreader Wyn Hilty; indexer Dan Brannen; and typesetter Marco Di Vita of the Graphix Group for their fine work.

Dedication

To Aaron and Kara Hanes, that their children may learn about the events and ideas that shaped the world through the latter half of the twentieth century.

Comments and suggestions

We welcome your comments on *Cold War: Biographies* and suggestions for other topics to consider. Please write: Editors, *Cold War: Biographies,* U•X•L, 27500 Drake Rd., Farmington Hills, Michigan 48331-3535; call toll free: 1-800-877-4253; fax to 248-699-8097; or send e-mail via http://www.gale.com.

Cold War Timeline

September 1, 1939 Germany invades Poland, beginning World War II.

June 30, 1941 Germany invades the Soviet Union, drawing the Soviets into World War II.

December 7, 1941 Japan launches a surprise air attack on U.S. military installations at Pearl Harbor, Hawaii, drawing the United States into World War II.

November 1943 The three key allied leaders—U.S. president Franklin D. Roosevelt, British prime minister **Winston Churchill**, and Soviet premier **Joseph Stalin**—meet in Tehran, Iran, to discuss war strategies against Germany and Italy.

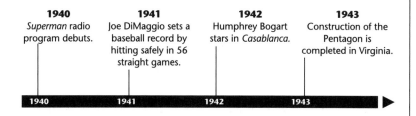

1940	**1941**	**1942**	**1943**
Superman radio program debuts.	Joe DiMaggio sets a baseball record by hitting safely in 56 straight games.	Humphrey Bogart stars in *Casablanca*.	Construction of the Pentagon is completed in Virginia.

| 1940 | 1941 | 1942 | 1943 |

August-October 1944 An international conference held at Dumbarton Oaks in Washington, D.C., creates the beginning of the United Nations.

February 1945 The Yalta Conference is held in the Crimean region of the Soviet Union among the three key allied leaders, U.S. president Franklin D. Roosevelt, British prime minister Winston Churchill, and Soviet premier Joseph Stalin to discuss German surrender terms, a Soviet attack against Japanese forces, and the future of Eastern Europe.

April-June 1945 Fifty nations meet in San Francisco to write the UN charter.

April 12, 1945 U.S. president Franklin D. Roosevelt dies suddenly from a brain hemorrhage, leaving Vice President **Harry S. Truman** as the next U.S. president.

April 23, 1945 U.S. president Harry S. Truman personally criticizes Soviet foreign minister **Vyacheslav Molotov** for growing Soviet influence in Eastern Europe, setting the tone for escalating Cold War tensions.

May 7, 1945 Germany surrenders to allied forces, leaving Germany and its capital of Berlin divided into four military occupation zones with American, British, French, and Soviet forces.

July 16, 1945 The United States, through its top-secret Manhattan Project, successfully detonates the world's first atomic bomb under the leadership of nuclear physicist **J. Robert Oppenheimer.**

July-August 1945 The Big Three—U.S. president Harry S. Truman, British prime minister Winston Churchill, and Soviet premier Joseph Stalin meet in Potsdam, Ger-

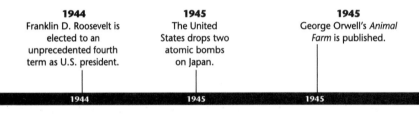

1944	**1945**	**1945**
Franklin D. Roosevelt is elected to an unprecedented fourth term as U.S. president.	The United States drops two atomic bombs on Japan.	George Orwell's *Animal Farm* is published.
1944	1945	1945

many, to discuss postwar conditions. On August 2, newly elected **Clement R. Attlee** replaces Churchill.

August 14, 1945 Japan surrenders, ending World War II, after the United States drops two atomic bombs on the cities of Hiroshima and Nagasaki.

November 29, 1945 Josip Broz Tito assumes leadership of the new communist government in Yugoslavia.

December 1945 U.S. secretary of state **James F. Byrnes** travels to Moscow to make a major effort to establish friendly relations with the Soviets, making agreements regarding international control of atomic energy and the postwar governments of Bulgaria, Hungary, and Japan; the agreements proved highly unpopular in the United States.

January 12, 1946 Nuclear physicist J. Robert Oppenheimer is awarded the "United States of America Medal of Merit" for his leadership on the Manhattan Project.

February 9, 1946 Soviet leader Joseph Stalin delivers the "Two Camps" speech, declaring the incompatibility of communist Soviet Union with the West.

February 22, 1946 U.S. diplomat **George F. Kennan** sends the "Long Telegram" from Moscow to Washington, D.C., warning of the Soviet threat.

March 5, 1946 Former British prime minister Winston Churchill delivers the "Iron Curtain Speech" at Westminster College in Fulton, Missouri.

September 1946 Clark M. Clifford, special counsel to U.S. president Harry S. Truman, coauthors an influential secret report titled "American Relations with the Soviet Union," warning of the threat of Soviet aggression

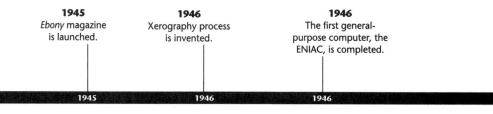

1945
Ebony magazine
is launched.

1946
Xerography process
is invented.

1946
The first general-
purpose computer, the
ENIAC, is completed.

1945   1946   1946

and calling for a policy of containment of further communist expansion.

September 6, 1946 U.S. secretary of state James F. Byrnes announces in a major speech that it is now U.S. policy to reestablish an independent Germany, something the Soviets strongly opposed; many consider this speech the end of the wartime alliance between the West and the Soviet Union.

October 7, 1946 W. Averill Harriman begins a stint as secretary of commerce, a position in which Harriman greatly influences later passage of the Marshall Plan, a plan to rebuild European economies devastated by World War II.

December 2, 1946 The United States, Great Britain, and France merge their German occupation zones to create what would become West Germany.

February 1947 After British foreign minister **Ernest Bevin** announces the withdrawal of long-term British support for Greece and Turkey, he approaches the U.S. government to seek its expansion in its international commitment to European security.

March 12, 1947 U.S. president Harry S. Truman announces the Truman Doctrine, which states that the United States will assist any nation in the world being threatened by communist expansion.

June 5, 1947 U.S. secretary of state **George C. Marshall** announces the Marshall Plan, an ambitious economic aid program to rebuild Western Europe from World War II destruction.

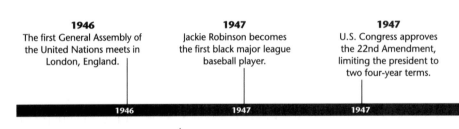

1946
The first General Assembly of the United Nations meets in London, England.

1947
Jackie Robinson becomes the first black major league baseball player.

1947
U.S. Congress approves the 22nd Amendment, limiting the president to two four-year terms.

1946   1947   1947

July 1947 U.S. diplomat George F. Kennan introduces the containment theory in the "X" article in *Foreign Affairs* magazine.

July 26, 1947 Congress passes the National Security Act, creating the Central Intelligence Agency (CIA) and the National Security Council (NSC).

October 1947 Actor **Ronald Reagan** and author **Ayn Rand** testify before the House Un-American Activities Committee (HUAC), a congressional group investigating communist influences in the United States.

December 5, 1947 The Soviets establish the Communist Information Bureau (Cominform) to promote the expansion of communism in the world.

February 25, 1948 A communist coup in Czechoslovakia topples the last remaining democratic government in Eastern Europe.

March 14, 1948 Israel announces its independence as a new state in the Middle East.

June 24, 1948 The Soviets begin a blockade of Berlin, leading to a massive airlift of daily supplies by the Western powers for the next eleven months.

January 21, 1949 At the beginning of his second term of office, President Harry S. Truman appoints **Dean G. Acheson** secretary of state.

April 4, 1949 The North Atlantic Treaty Organization (NATO), a military alliance involving Western Europe and the United States, comes into existence.

May 5, 1949 The West Germans establish the Federal Republic of Germany government.

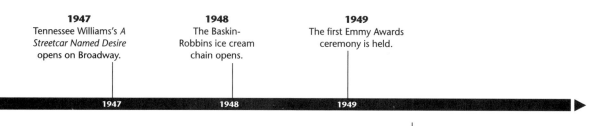

1947
Tennessee Williams's *A Streetcar Named Desire* opens on Broadway.

1948
The Baskin-Robbins ice cream chain opens.

1949
The first Emmy Awards ceremony is held.

1947   1948   1949

May 12, 1949 The Soviet blockade of access routes to West Berlin is lifted.

May 30, 1949 Soviet-controlled East Germany establishes the German Democratic Republic.

August 1949 Konrad Adenauer becomes the first chancellor of West Germany in the first open parliamentary elections of the newly established Federal Republic of Germany (FRG).

August 29, 1949 Under the leadership of Soviet nuclear physicist **Igor Kurchatov,** the Soviet Union conducts its first successful atomic bomb test at the Semipalatinsk Test Site in northeastern Kazakhstan.

October 1, 1949 Communist forces under **Mao Zedong** gain victory in the Chinese civil war, and the People's Republic of China (PRC) is established, with **Zhou Enlai** its leader.

January 1950 Former State Department employee Alger Hiss is convicted of perjury but not of spy charges.

February 3, 1950 Klaus Fuchs is convicted of passing U.S. atomic secrets to the Soviets.

February 9, 1950 U.S. senator **Joseph R. McCarthy** of Wisconsin publicly claims in a speech in Wheeling, West Virginia, to have a list of communists working in the U.S. government.

March 1, 1950 Chiang Kai-shek, former leader of nationalist China, which was defeated by communist forces, establishes the Republic of China (ROC) on the island of Taiwan.

April 7, 1950 U.S. security analyst Paul Nitze issues the secret National Security Council report 68 (NSC-68), calling

1949
Arthur Miller's *Death of a Salesman* opens on Broadway in New York City.

1950
The first Xerox copy machine is produced.

1950
The comic strip *Peanuts* debuts in U.S. newspapers.

1949   1950   1950

for a dramatic buildup of U.S. military forces to combat the Soviet threat.

June 25, 1950 North Korean communist leader **Kim Il Sung** launches his armed forces against South Korea in an attempt to reunify Korea under his leadership, leading to the three-year Korean War.

October 24, 1950 U.S. forces push the North Korean army back to the border with China, sparking a Chinese invasion one week later and forcing the United States into a hasty retreat.

April 11, 1951 U.S. president Harry S. Truman fires General **Douglas MacArthur,** the U.S. military commander in Korea, for publicly attacking the president's war strategy.

April 19, 1951 General Douglas MacArthur delivers his farewell address to a joint session of Congress.

June 21, 1951 The Korean War reaches a military stalemate at the original boundary between North and South Korea.

September 1, 1951 The United States, Australia, and New Zealand sign the ANZUS treaty, creating a military alliance to contain communism in the Southwest Pacific region.

October 25, 1951 Winston Churchill wins reelection as British prime minister over Clement R. Attlee.

October 3, 1952 Great Britain conducts its first atomic weapons test.

November 1, 1952 The United States tests the hydrogen bomb on the Marshall Islands in the Pacific Ocean.

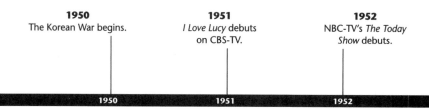

1950
The Korean War begins.

1951
I Love Lucy debuts
on CBS-TV.

1952
NBC-TV's *The Today
Show* debuts.

1950   1951   1952

November 4, 1952 Former military general **Dwight D. Eisenhower** is elected U.S. president.

March 5, 1953 After leading the Soviet Union for thirty years, Joseph Stalin dies of a stroke; Georgy Malenkov becomes the new Soviet leader.

June 27, 1953 An armistice is signed, bringing a cease-fire to the Korean War.

August 12, 1953 The Soviet Union announces its first hydrogen bomb test.

May 7, 1954 The communist Viet Minh forces of **Ho Chi Minh** capture French forces at Dien Bien Phu, leading to a partition of Vietnam and independence for North Vietnam under Ho's leadership.

June 29, 1954 Nuclear physicist J. Robert Oppenheimer's security clearance is not renewed due to his opposition of the development of the hydrogen bomb; his stance leads anticommunists to question his loyalty to the United States.

September 8, 1954 The Southeast Asia Treaty Organization (SEATO) is formed.

December 2, 1954 The U.S. Senate votes to censure U.S. senator Joseph R. McCarthy of Wisconsin after his communist accusations proved to be unfounded.

January 12, 1955 U.S. secretary of state **John Foster Dulles** announces the "New Look" policy, promoting massive nuclear retaliation for any hostile actions.

February 8, 1955 Nikolai Bulganin replaces Georgy Malenkov as Soviet premier.

May 14, 1955 The Warsaw Pact, a military alliance of Soviet-controlled Eastern European nations, is established;

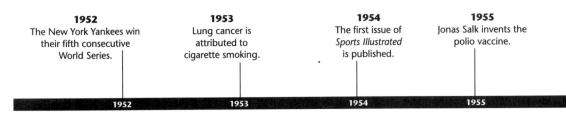

1952
The New York Yankees win their fifth consecutive World Series.

1953
Lung cancer is attributed to cigarette smoking.

1954
The first issue of *Sports Illustrated* is published.

1955
Jonas Salk invents the polio vaccine.

1952   1953   1954   1955

the countries include Albania, Bulgaria, Czechoslovakia, East Germany, Hungary, Poland, and Romania.

November 22, 1955 Under the guidance of nuclear physicist **Andrey Sakharov**, the Soviets detonate their first true hydrogen bomb at the Semipalatinsk Test Site; Sakharov would be awarded several of the Soviet Union's highest honors.

February 24, 1956 Soviet leader **Nikita Khrushchev** gives his "Secret Speech," attacking the past brutal policies of the late Soviet leader Joseph Stalin.

October 31, 1956 British, French, and Israeli forces attack Egypt to regain control of the Suez Canal.

November 1, 1956 In Hungary, the Soviets crush an uprising against strict communist rule, killing many protestors.

January 10, 1957 **Harold Macmillan** becomes the new British prime minister.

February 1957 Soviet leader Nikita Khrushchev appoints **Andrey Gromyko** foreign minister, replacing Vyacheslav Molotov; Gromyko will hold the position for the next twenty-eight years.

March 7, 1957 The Eisenhower Doctrine, offering U.S. assistance to Middle East countries facing communist expansion threats, is approved by Congress.

October 5, 1957 Shocking the world with their new technology, the Soviets launch into space *Sputnik,* the first man-made satellite.

1958 FBI director J. Edgar Hoover (1895–1972) writes *Masters of Deceit,* a book that educates the public about the threat of communism within the United States.

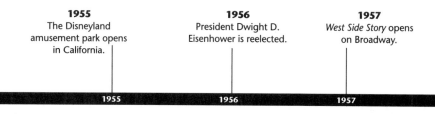

1955
The Disneyland amusement park opens in California.

1956
President Dwight D. Eisenhower is reelected.

1957
West Side Story opens on Broadway.

1955   1956   1957

March 27, 1958 Nikita Khrushchev replaces Nikolai Bulganin as Soviet premier while remaining head of the Soviet Communist Party.

November 10, 1958 Soviet leader Nikita Khrushchev issues an ultimatum to the West to pull out of Berlin, but later backs down.

January 2, 1959 Revolutionary **Fidel Castro** assumes leadership of the Cuban government after toppling pro-U.S. dictator Fulgencio Batista y Zaldivar.

September 17, 1959 Soviet leader Nikita Khrushchev arrives in the United States to tour the country and meet with U.S. president Dwight D. Eisenhower.

May 1, 1960 The Soviets shoot down a U.S. spy plane over Russia piloted by Francis Gary Powers, leading to the cancellation of a planned summit meeting in Paris between Soviet leader Nikita Khrushchev and U.S. president Dwight D. Eisenhower.

November 8, 1960 U.S. senator **John F. Kennedy** of Massachusetts defeats Vice President **Richard M. Nixon** in the presidential election.

January 1961 Robert S. McNamara becomes secretary of defense in the new Kennedy administration, a position he would hold until 1968 throughout the critical years of the Vietnam War.

March 1, 1961 U.S. president John F. Kennedy establishes the Peace Corps.

April 15, 1961 A U.S.-supported army of Cuban exiles launches an ill-fated invasion of Cuba, leading to U.S. humiliation in the world.

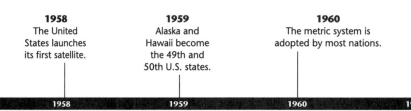

1958
The United States launches its first satellite.

1959
Alaska and Hawaii become the 49th and 50th U.S. states.

1960
The metric system is adopted by most nations.

| 1958 | 1959 | 1960 | 1961 |

June 3, 1961 U.S. president John F. Kennedy meets with Soviet leader Nikita Khrushchev at a Vienna summit meeting to discuss the arms race and Berlin; Kennedy comes away shaken by Khrushchev's belligerence.

August 15, 1961 Under orders from Soviet leader Nikita Khrushchev, the Berlin Wall is constructed, stopping the flight of refugees from East Germany to West Berlin.

October 1962 The Cuban Missile Crisis occurs as the United States demands the Soviets remove nuclear missiles from Cuba.

1963 Longtime U.S. diplomat W. Averell Harriman heads the U.S. team for negotiating with the Soviet Union the Limited Test Ban treaty, which bans above-ground testing of nuclear weapons.

January 1, 1963 Chinese communist leaders Mao Zedong and Zhou Enlai denounce Soviet leader Nikita Khrushchev's policies of peaceful coexistence with the West; the Soviets respond by denouncing the Chinese Communist Party.

August 5, 1963 The first arms control agreement, the Limited Test Ban Treaty, banning above-ground nuclear testing, is reached between the United States, Soviet Union, and Great Britain.

November 22, 1963 U.S. president John F. Kennedy is assassinated in Dallas, Texas, leaving Vice President **Lyndon B. Johnson** as the new U.S. president.

August 7, 1964 U.S. Congress passes the Gulf of Tonkin Resolution, authorizing U.S. president Lyndon B. Johnson to conduct whatever military operations he thinks appropriate in Southeast Asia.

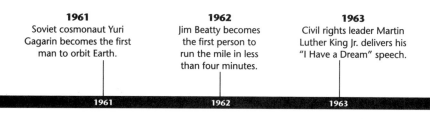

1961
Soviet cosmonaut Yuri Gagarin becomes the first man to orbit Earth.

1962
Jim Beatty becomes the first person to run the mile in less than four minutes.

1963
Civil rights leader Martin Luther King Jr. delivers his "I Have a Dream" speech.

1961   1962   1963

October 15, 1964 Soviet leader Nikita Khrushchev is removed from Soviet leadership and replaced by **Leonid Brezhnev** as leader of the Soviet Communist Party and **Aleksey Kosygin** as Soviet premier.

October 16, 1964 China conducts its first nuclear weapons test.

November 3, 1964 Lyndon B. Johnson is elected U.S. president.

March 8, 1965 U.S. president Lyndon B. Johnson sends the first U.S. ground combat units to South Vietnam.

June 23, 1967 U.S. president Lyndon B. Johnson and Soviet premier Aleksey Kosygin meet in Glassboro, New Jersey, to discuss a peace settlement to the Vietnam War.

January 23, 1968 Forces under the orders of North Korean communist leader Kim Il Sung capture a U.S. spy ship, the USS *Pueblo,* off the coast of North Korea and hold the crew captive for eleven months.

January 31, 1968 Communist forces inspired by the leadership of the ailing Ho Chi Minh launch the massive Tet Offensive against the U.S. and South Vietnamese armies, marking a turning point as American public opinion shifts in opposition to the Vietnam War.

July 15, 1968 Soviet leader Leonid Brezhnev announces the Brezhnev Doctrine, which allows for the use of force where necessary to ensure the maintenance of communist governments in Eastern European nations.

August 20, 1968 The Warsaw Pact forces a crackdown on a Czechoslovakia reform movement known as the "Prague Spring."

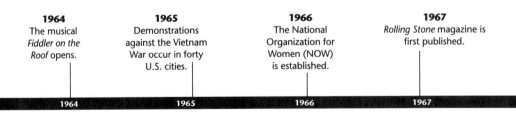

1964 The musical *Fiddler on the Roof* opens.

1965 Demonstrations against the Vietnam War occur in forty U.S. cities.

1966 The National Organization for Women (NOW) is established.

1967 *Rolling Stone* magazine is first published.

1964   1965   1966   1967

August 27, 1968 Antiwar riots rage in Chicago's streets outside the Democratic National Convention.

November 5, 1968 Richard M. Nixon defeats Vice President Hubert Humphrey in the U.S. presidential election.

March 18, 1969 The United States begins secret bombing of Cambodia to destroy North Vietnamese supply lines.

July 20, 1969 The United States lands the first men on the moon.

October 15, 1969 Former West Berlin mayor Willy Brandt is elected chancellor of West Germany.

April 16, 1970 Strategic arms limitation talks, SALT, begin.

April 30, 1970 U.S. president Richard M. Nixon announces an invasion by U.S. forces of Cambodia to destroy North Vietnamese supply camps.

May 4, 1970 Four students are killed at Kent State University as Ohio National Guardsmen open fire on antiwar demonstrators.

November 3, 1970 Salvador Allende becomes president of Chile.

October 20, 1971 West German chancellor Willy Brandt is awarded the Nobel Peace Prize for seeking greater political and military stability in Europe.

October 25, 1971 The People's Republic of China (PRC) is admitted to the United Nations as the Republic of China (ROC) is expelled.

February 20, 1972 U.S. president Richard M. Nixon makes an historic trip to the People's Republic of China to discuss renewing relations between the two countries.

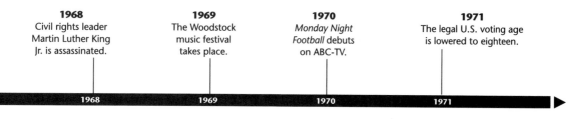

1968
Civil rights leader Martin Luther King Jr. is assassinated.

1969
The Woodstock music festival takes place.

1970
Monday Night Football debuts on ABC-TV.

1971
The legal U.S. voting age is lowered to eighteen.

1968　　1969　　1970　　1971

May 26, 1972 U.S. president Richard M. Nixon travels to Moscow to meet with Soviet leader Leonid Brezhnev to reach an agreement on the strategic arms limitation treaty, SALT I.

January 27, 1973 After intensive bombing of North Vietnamese cities the previous month, the United States and North Vietnam sign a peace treaty, ending U.S. involvement in Vietnam.

June 27, 1973 Soviet leader Leonid Brezhnev journeys to Washington, D.C., to meet with U.S. president Richard M. Nixon to pursue détente.

August 22, 1973 U.S. national security advisor **Henry Kissinger** is nominated by U.S. president Richard M. Nixon to also serve as secretary of state.

September 11, 1973 Chilean president Salvador Allende is ousted in a coup and is replaced by pro-U.S. dictator Augusto Pinochet Ugarte.

May 16, 1974 Helmut Schmidt becomes the new West German chancellor.

June 27, 1974 U.S. president Richard M. Nixon travels to Moscow for another summit conference with Soviet leader Leonid Brezhnev.

August 9, 1974 Under threats of impeachment due to a political scandal, U.S. president Richard M. Nixon resigns as U.S. president and is replaced by Vice President Gerald R. Ford.

September 4, 1974 George Bush is sent as an envoy to the People's Republic of China.

1972 The Watergate scandal begins.

1973 U.S. troops pull out of Vietnam.

1974 Hank Aaron passes Babe Ruth as baseball's all-time home run hitter.

1972   1973   1974

November 23, 1974 U.S. president Gerald R. Ford and Soviet leader Leonid Brezhnev meet in the Soviet city of Vladivostok.

1975 Nuclear physicist Andrey Sakharov receives the Nobel Peace Prize for his brave opposition to the nuclear arms race in the Soviet Union.

April 30, 1975 In renewed fighting, North Vietnam captures South Vietnam and reunites the country.

August 1, 1975 Numerous nations sign the Helsinki Accords at the end of the Conference on Security and Cooperation in Europe.

January 27, 1976 George Bush is confirmed by the U.S. Senate as the director of the Central Intelligence Agency (CIA).

September 9, 1976 Mao Zedong dies and Hua Guofeng becomes the new leader of the People's Republic of China.

November 2, 1976 Former Georgia governor **Jimmy Carter** defeats incumbent U.S. president Gerald R. Ford in the presidential election.

December 16, 1976 U.S. president-elect Jimmy Carter names Zbigniew Brzezinski as the new national security advisor.

June 16, 1977 Soviet leader Leonid Brezhnev is elected president of the Soviet Union in addition to leader of the Soviet Communist Party.

December 25, 1977 Israeli prime minister Menachim Begin and Egyptian president Anwar Sadat begin peace negotiations in Egypt.

February 24, 1978 Deng Xiaoping is elected head of the Chinese Communist Party.

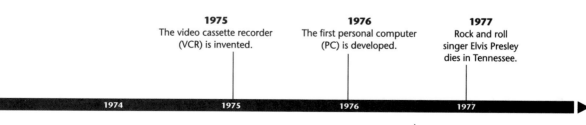

1975
The video cassette recorder (VCR) is invented.

1976
The first personal computer (PC) is developed.

1977
Rock and roll singer Elvis Presley dies in Tennessee.

1974   1975   1976   1977

September 17, 1978 Israeli prime minister Menachim Begin and Egyptian president Anwar Sadat, meeting with U.S. president Jimmy Carter at Camp David, reach an historic peace settlement between Israel and Egypt.

January 1, 1979 The United States and the People's Republic of China (PRC) establish diplomatic relations.

January 16, 1979 The shah of Iran is overthrown as the leader of Iran and is replaced by Islamic leader Ayatollah Ruhollah Khomeini.

May 4, 1979 Margaret Thatcher becomes the new British prime minister.

June 18, 1979 U.S. president Jimmy Carter and Soviet leader Leonid Brezhnev sign the SALT II strategic arms limitation agreement in Vienna, Austria.

July 19, 1979 Sandinista rebels seize power in Nicaragua with Daniel Ortega becoming the new leader.

November 4, 1979 Islamic militants seize the U.S. embassy in Tehran, Iran, taking U.S. staff hostage.

December 26, 1979 Soviet forces invade Afghanistan to prop up an unpopular pro-Soviet government, leading to a decade of bloody fighting.

January 1980 Nuclear physicist Andrey Sakharov is seized by the secret police, sentenced, and sent into exile to the closed city of Gorky for the next six years.

April 24, 1980 An attempted military rescue of American hostages in Iran ends with eight U.S. soldiers dead.

August 14, 1980 The Solidarity labor union protests the prices of goods in Poland.

November 4, 1980 Former California governor Ronald Reagan is elected president of the United States.

1978
Pope John Paul II
begins reign as
the leader of the
Catholic Church.

1979
The Three Mile Island
nuclear reactor accident
occurs in Pennsylvania.

1980
Former Beatle John
Lennon is murdered.

1978   1979   1980

January 20, 1981 Iran releases the U.S. hostages as Ronald Reagan is being sworn in as the new U.S. president.

January 29, 1981 U.S. president Ronald Reagan appoints **Jeane Kirkpatrick** as U.S. representative to the United Nations where she acts a key architect of Reagan's strong anticommunist position early in his presidency.

October 1, 1982 Helmut Kohl is elected West German chancellor.

November 12, 1982 Yuri Andropov becomes the new Soviet leader after the death of Leonid Brezhnev two days earlier.

March 8, 1983 U.S. president Ronald Reagan calls the Soviet Union the "Evil Empire."

March 23, 1983 U.S. president Ronald Reagan announces the Strategic Defense Initiative (SDI).

September 1, 1983 A Soviet fighter shoots down Korean Airlines Flight 007 as it strays off-course over Soviet restricted airspace.

October 25, 1983 U.S. forces invade Grenada to end fighting between two pro-communist factions.

February 13, 1984 Konstantin Chernenko becomes the new Soviet leader after the death of Yuri Andropov four days earlier.

May 2, 1984 Nuclear physicist Andrey Sakharov begins a hunger strike.

February 1985 The United States issues the Reagan Doctrine, which offers assistance to military dictatorships in defense against communist expansion.

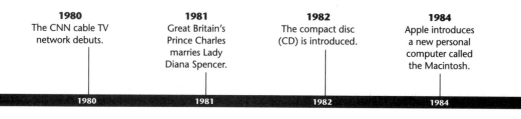

1980	**1981**	**1982**	**1984**
The CNN cable TV network debuts.	Great Britain's Prince Charles marries Lady Diana Spencer.	The compact disc (CD) is introduced.	Apple introduces a new personal computer called the Macintosh.

1980   1981   1982   1984

March 11, 1985 Mikhail Gorbachev becomes the new Soviet leader after the death of Konstantin Chernenko the previous day.

July 2, 1985 Eduard Shevardnadze is named the new foreign minister by Soviet leader Mikhail Gorbachev, replacing Andrey Gromyko.

October 11–12, 1986 Soviet leader Mikhail Gorbachev and U.S. president Ronald Reagan meet in Reykjavik, Iceland, and agree to seek the elimination of nuclear weapons.

October 17, 1986 Congress approves aid to Contra rebels in Nicaragua.

November 3, 1986 The Iran-Contra affair is uncovered.

June 11, 1987 Margaret Thatcher wins an unprecedented third term as British prime minister.

December 8–10, 1987 U.S. president Ronald Reagan and Soviet leader Mikhail Gorbachev meet in Washington to sign the Intermediate Nuclear Forces Treaty (INF), removing thousands of missiles from Europe.

February 8, 1988 Soviet leader Mikhail Gorbachev announces the decision to begin withdrawing Soviet forces from Afghanistan.

May 29, 1988 U.S. president Ronald Reagan journeys to Moscow for a summit meeting with Soviet leader Mikhail Gorbachev.

November 8, 1988 U.S. vice president George Bush is elected president of the United States.

January 11, 1989 The Hungarian parliament adopts reforms granting greater personal freedoms to Hungarians, including allowing political parties and organizations.

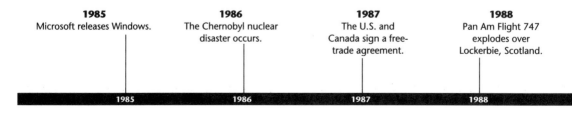

1985	**1986**	**1987**	**1988**
Microsoft releases Windows.	The Chernobyl nuclear disaster occurs.	The U.S. and Canada sign a free-trade agreement.	Pan Am Flight 747 explodes over Lockerbie, Scotland.

| 1985 | 1986 | 1987 | 1988 |

January 18, 1989 The labor union Solidarity gains formal acceptance in Poland.

March 26, 1989 Open elections are held for the new Soviet Congress of People's Deputies, with the communists suffering major defeats; Boris Yeltsin wins the Moscow seat.

May 11, 1989 Soviet leader Mikhail Gorbachev announces major reductions of nuclear forces in Eastern Europe.

June 3–4, 1989 Chinese communist leaders order a military crackdown on pro-democracy demonstrations in Tiananmen Square, leading to many deaths.

June 4, 1989 The first Polish free elections lead to major victory by Solidarity.

October 7, 1989 The Hungarian communist party disbands.

October 23, 1989 Massive demonstrations begin against the East German communist government, involving hundreds of thousands of protesters and leading to the resignation of the East German leadership in early November.

November 10, 1989 East Germany begins dismantling the Berlin Wall; Bulgarian communist leadership resigns.

November 24, 1989 Czechoslovakia communist leaders resign.

December 1, 1989 Soviet leader Mikhail Gorbachev and U.S. president George Bush, assisted by **Condoleezza Rice** of the National Security Council, begin a three-day meeting on a ship in a Malta harbor to discuss rapid changes in Eastern Europe and the Soviet Union.

December 20, 1989 Lithuania votes for independence from the Soviet Union.

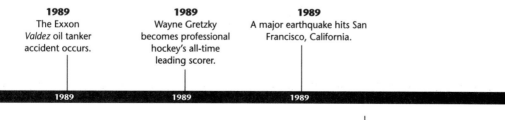

1989	**1989**	**1989**
The Exxon *Valdez* oil tanker accident occurs.	Wayne Gretzky becomes professional hockey's all-time leading scorer.	A major earthquake hits San Francisco, California.
1989	1989	1989

December 22, 1989 Romanian communist leader Nicolae Ceausescu is toppled and executed three days later.

March 1990 Lithuania declares independence from Moscow.

March 14, 1990 Mikhail Gorbachev is elected president of the Soviet Union.

March 18, 1990 Open East German elections lead to a major defeat of Communist Party candidates.

May 29, 1990 Boris Yeltsin is elected president of the Russian republic.

May 30, 1990 Soviet leader Mikhail Gorbachev begins a summit meeting with U.S. president George Bush in Washington, D.C.

June 1990 Russia declares independence as the Russian Federation.

October 15, 1990 Soviet leader Mikhail Gorbachev is awarded the Nobel Peace Prize for his reforms that ended the Cold War.

November 14, 1990 Various nations sign the Charter of Paris for a New Europe, ending the economic and military division of Europe created by the Cold War.

July 1, 1991 The Warsaw Pact disbands.

August 19, 1991 Soviet communist hardliners attempt an unsuccessful coup of Soviet leader Mikhail Gorbachev, leading to the banning of the Communist Party in Russia and other Soviet republics.

August 20–September 9, 1991 The various Soviet republics declare their independence from the Soviet Union, including Estonia, Latvia, Lithuania, Ukraine, Belorussia, Moldovia, Azerbaijan, Uzbekistan, Kirgizia, and Tadzhikistan.

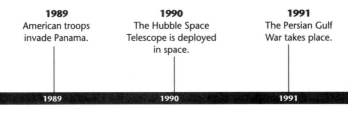

1989
American troops invade Panama.

1990
The Hubble Space Telescope is deployed in space.

1991
The Persian Gulf War takes place.

1989   1990   1991

October 3, 1991 East and West Germany reunite as one nation.

December 8, 1991 Russia, Ukraine, and Belorussia create the Commonwealth of Independent States organization as an alliance replacing the Soviet Union.

December 25, 1991 Mikhail Gorbachev resigns as the Soviet president, and the Soviet Union ceases to exist.

January 28, 1992 In his State of the Union Address, U.S. president George Bush declares victory in the Cold War.

1991
Clarence Thomas
becomes a U.S.
Supreme Court justice.

1992
Hurricane Andrew
causes $15 billion
in damage
in Florida.

1991   1992

Cold War
Biographies

Dean G. Acheson

Born April 11, 1893
Middletown, Connecticut
Died October 12, 1971
Sandy Spring, Maryland

U.S. secretary of state, lawyer, and author

S ecretary of State Dean Acheson played a critical role in developing U.S. foreign policy as the post–World War II (1939–45) rivalry with the Soviet Union was taking shape. He firmly believed in maintaining a position of strength through military might while seeking solutions through diplomacy. His influence would last throughout the Cold War (1945–91). The Cold War was an intense political and economic rivalry between the United States and the Soviet Union.

Early influences

Dean Gooderham Acheson was born on April 11, 1893, in Middletown, Connecticut. His father, Edward Campion Acheson, was born in Britain but left home at age sixteen to journey to Canada, where he joined the military. He married Eleanor Gooderham, daughter of a wealthy Canadian family, and moved to New England. There he became an Episcopal minister and later the Episcopal bishop of Connecticut. Having a comfortable middle-class upbringing, young Dean attended the exclusive Groton preparatory

"The Truman administration's 1947 assumption of responsibility in the eastern Mediterranean, the 1948 grandeur of the Marshall Plan, ... the NATO defense of Europe in 1949, and the intervention in Korea in 1950—all these constituted expanding action in truly historic mold."

Dean G. Acheson.
Reproduced by permission of AP/Wide World Photos.

school, graduating in 1911. He then attended Yale University and went on to Harvard Law School. At Harvard, Acheson studied under future U.S. Supreme Court justice Felix Frankfurter (1882–1965). While in law school, Acheson married Alice Stanley, a graduate of the prestigious Wellesley College, in May 1917. They would have three children.

Following graduation from Harvard in 1918, Acheson moved to Washington, D.C., to become a law clerk for Supreme Court justice Louis D. Brandeis (1856–1941). Brandeis became a highly influential person in Acheson's intellectual life. After two years with Brandeis, Acheson joined the highly respected Washington law firm of Covington, Burling, and Rublee in 1921. As a young lawyer, Acheson made a striking impression: He was a stylish dresser with tailored suits and a handkerchief. He was very quick intellectually but had a sarcastic wit that the press would later interpret as arrogance. He was impatient with slower thinkers.

After participating in the successful presidential campaign of Franklin D. Roosevelt (1882–1945; served 1933–45) in 1932, Acheson became undersecretary of the treasury in early 1933. However, he resigned six months later in protest over Roosevelt's monetary policies and returned to his job in the law firm.

Beginning of an influential public career

With a world war looming, President Roosevelt appointed Acheson assistant secretary of state for economic affairs in 1940. In that position, Acheson promoted an active U.S. role in combating Germany's push to dominate Europe, the same strategy he would later recommend for dealing with the Soviet Union. He persuaded Roosevelt to adopt the Lend-Lease program, which provided aging U.S. warships to Britain in exchange for the use of military bases in various British colonies around the world. Also under this program, $39 billion in aid would go to countries battling Germany, primarily Great Britain and the Soviet Union. Acheson's role in postwar economic matters would be even larger: At an international meeting held at Bretton Woods, New York, he was instrumental in establishing the International Monetary Fund and the International Bank for Reconstruction and Development

(World Bank). Both became major funding institutions for nations recovering from the destruction of World War II and for developing nations worldwide.

President Roosevelt died suddenly of a cerebral hemorrhage (bleeding in the brain) on April 12, 1945. Roosevelt's successor, Vice President **Harry S. Truman** (1884–1972; see entry), appointed Acheson undersecretary of state, first under **James F. Byrnes** (1879–1972; see entry) and later under **George C. Marshall** (1880–1959; see entry). Both Truman and Acheson had straightforward, realistic approaches to foreign policy, so they built a strong working relationship. In his first several months in office, Truman relied heavily on Acheson to guide him on foreign policy. During this time, Acheson encouraged Truman to drop the atomic bombs on Japan in August 1945 to end World War II. Acheson also developed a plan for international control of atomic energy programs through the United Nations. It was called the Baruch Plan, after American financier Bernard Baruch (1870–1965), the U.S. representative on the UN Atomic Energy Commission who presented the plan to the United Nations. However, Baruch had insisted on substantial changes to the plan that Acheson strongly opposed. The Soviets also rejected the proposal.

Cold War architect

Soviet military intimidation in 1946 in Iran, Turkey, and Greece began to convince Acheson that friendly cooperation would not be possible. The Soviet Union operated under a communist form of government. Communist economic theory calls for the elimination of private property and privately owned businesses so that goods produced and wealth accumulated can be shared equally by all. This system threatened the U.S. economy, which relies on free trade and competition to thrive; accumulation of wealth and private property is one of the chief goals of American business. Because of the conflict between U.S. and Soviet economic goals, Acheson advised Truman to strongly oppose the Soviet Union's efforts to expand its influence.

In a meeting with congressional leaders at the White House, Acheson presented some alarming news about Soviet intentions. He claimed that if Greece and Turkey fell to Soviet influence, all of Western Europe could be next. (Western Europe includes Austria, Belgium, Denmark, France, Germany, Italy, Liechtenstein, Luxembourg, the Netherlands, Norway, Portugal, Spain, Sweden, Switzerland, and the United Kingdom.) Acheson then developed a speech for Truman to give to Congress on March 12, 1947. The historic speech outlined what is now called the Truman Doctrine, stating that it was in America's interest to stop communist expansion anywhere in the world. This marked the first time the United States adopted a policy of direct involvement in the internal affairs of foreign nations threatened by communism. This policy would guide the United States throughout the rest of the Cold War.

The next step for Acheson was to design an economic recovery plan for Western Europe. Acheson believed that the region was vulnerable to growing communist influence because it had been economically weakened by World War II. He contended that the economic prosperity of Europe was directly related to the well-being of the United States. In a speech on June 5, 1947, Secretary of State Marshall formally introduced the proposed economic recovery plan, which became known as the Marshall Plan. It provided $12 billion over a four-year period to restore industry and expand trade in Western Europe. Having achieved his key goals, Acheson resigned as undersecretary on June 30 and returned to private law practice. However, after only eighteen months, he would get the call to public service once again.

Secretary of State

On January 21, 1949, at the beginning of his second term of office, President Truman appointed Acheson secretary of state. Acheson turned once again to the defense of Europe. Having addressed Europe's economic strength through the Marshall Plan, Acheson next wanted to build Europe's military strength. Toward this end, he promoted creation of the North Atlantic Treaty Organization (NATO) in the spring of 1949. NATO was a peacetime alliance of Western European nations, Canada, and the United States, and a key factor in the attempt to contain communism. Under Acheson's guidance, the part of Germany that was occupied by U.S., British, and French

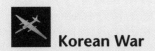

Korean War

The Korean War (1950–53) dominated Dean Acheson's term as secretary of state. In fact, some people accused Acheson of being responsible for the war. In January 1950, in his first month as secretary, Acheson gave a speech to the National Press Club. During the speech, he stated that South Korea was outside what he considered the U.S. defense perimeter. Critics claimed Acheson's comment made North Korea think that the United States would not respond if North Korea attacked the south.

When North Korean forces invaded South Korea on June 25, 1950, Acheson instantly became President Harry Truman's key war advisor. That same day, he went before an emergency session of the United Nations (UN) Security Council to obtain resolutions condemning the attack and calling for a military response. The United States would spearhead the war effort with the assistance of several other nations. Acheson was lucky: Because the Soviet Union was boycotting the UN at the time (protesting the organization's exclusion of the People's Republic of China), Soviet representatives were not present to veto the resolutions.

On June 30, U.S. troops under the command of General **Douglas MacArthur** (1880–1964; see entry) arrived in Korea. Though North Korea had pushed deep into the south, MacArthur's strategy of splitting North Korean forces by invading farther up the Korean coast worked. North Korean forces were put on the run as the largely American force pushed all the way north to the border with the People's Republic of China (PRC). Acheson hoped MacArthur would crush the North Korean forces for a decisive victory. However, contrary to expectations, on November 25, the PRC entered the war in support of North Korea. The PRC sent three hundred thousand troops into North Korea, routing U.S. forces. U.S. soldiers retreated into South Korea and finally were able to battle to a stalemate at the original boundary between North and South Korea. Acheson later commented that the PRC attack was his worst moment in public life. Acheson had to support Truman's decision to remove General MacArthur from his command in April 1951 for not following orders. The war would drag on until June 1953, months after Acheson had returned to private life.

military forces became an independent government, the Federal Republic of Germany, more commonly called West Germany. The new nation was established in June 1949.

However, by June, Cold War events began turning more ominous. First, communist forces led by **Mao Zedong** (1893–1976; see entry) finally overthrew the Chinese government after years of civil war. Then in August, the Soviet Union tested an atomic bomb, surprising U.S. officials, who had thought the Soviets were far behind them in research and development. The United States was no longer the only nation with atomic weapons. In reaction, Acheson promoted development of the much more powerful hydrogen bomb, despite objections by other key advisors. Acheson also guided a study of foreign policy written by policy analyst Paul H. Nitze (1907–). Known as National Security Council Memorandum 68 (NSC-68), the study reflected Acheson's "get tough" approach to stopping the expansion of Soviet influence. The report called for substantial increases in military spending. It was not immediately well received by Congress because of its costs, but the North Korean invasion of South Korea (see box) on June 25, 1950, spurred Congress to adopt it.

Acheson recommended a military counterattack against North Korean forces. Meanwhile, he suspected that the Soviet Union might try to attack Western Europe while the United States was preoccupied with Korea, so he took steps to try to prevent this: He tried unsuccessfully to lobby Europe to rearm Germany; however, he did manage to increase the number of U.S. troops in Europe. He also appointed the highly popular World War II general **Dwight D. Eisenhower** (1890–1969; see entry) supreme commander of NATO. The army and air force grew dramatically as Acheson sought to triple the U.S. defense budget. In addition, Acheson established new U.S. military bases in Morocco, Libya, Saudi Arabia, and Japan, and provided support to the French in Vietnam, where they were fighting communist rebel forces.

While Acheson was busily serving as chief advisor to Truman regarding the Korean War, he had to deal with continual attacks from U.S. senator **Joseph R. McCarthy** (1908–1957; see entry) of Wisconsin and his supporters, who accused Acheson of being "soft on communism." They made these accusations because the communists had gained ground in China and Eastern Europe during the late 1940s, while Acheson was secretary of state. McCarthy also charged that communists had infiltrated Acheson's State Department. Critics constantly pressured Acheson to resign. To escape from public pressure, Acheson took refuge on his eighteenth-century Maryland farm, where he made furniture by hand.

An active life after public service

In January 1953, President Dwight D. Eisenhower entered the White House and Acheson's time as secretary of state came to a close. Though retired, Acheson remained active in foreign policy for years. He was a leading critic of Eisenhower and Eisenhower's secretary of state, **John Foster Dulles** (1888–1959; see entry), especially of their heavy reliance on nuclear deterrents. Acheson served as an informal advisor to Presidents **John F. Kennedy** (1917–1963; served 1961–63; see entry) and **Lyndon B. Johnson** (1908–1973; served 1963–69; see entry), continuing to advocate tough positions against Soviet actions. For example, he urged Kennedy to bomb the newly discovered Soviet missile sites during the Cuban Missile Crisis in October 1962. (Kennedy chose a less aggressive but successful course of blockading Cuba.) Acheson also supported U.S. military action in Vietnam until 1968, when he became convinced the war was no longer winnable. At that time, he advised President Johnson to begin scaling

Advisor Dean Acheson (center, with white mustache) counsels President Lyndon B. Johnson (right, with pillow behind head). Others at the table include U.S. ambassador to the UN George Ball (far left) and Secretary of State Dean Rusk (smoking pipe). *Photograph by Yoichi R. Okamoto. Reproduced by permission of the Lyndon Baines Johnson Library Collection.*

down U.S. involvement. President **Richard M. Nixon** (1913–1994; served 1969–74; see entry) and his national security advisor, **Henry Kissinger** (1923–; see entry), called on Acheson in 1969 for advice.

Acheson wrote many books and articles on foreign policy and politics in his later years. He won the Pulitzer Prize in history for his 1969 book *Present at the Creation: My Years in the State Department.* On October 12, 1971, Acheson died suddenly of a stroke while working at his desk on his Sandy Spring, Maryland, farm. He was seventy-eight.

For More Information

Books

Acheson, Dean. *Present at the Creation: My Years in the State Department.* New York: Norton, 1969.

Acheson, Dean. *Sketches from Life of Men I Have Known.* New York: Harper, 1961.

Brinkley, Douglas. *Dean Acheson: The Cold War Years, 1953–1971.* New Haven, CT: Yale University Press, 1992.

Isaacson, Walter, and Evan Thomas. *The Wise Men: Six Friends and the World They Made: Acheson, Bohlen, Kennan, Harriman, Lovett, McCloy.* New York: Simon and Schuster, 1986.

Web Site

"Oral History Interview with Dean Acheson." *Truman Presidential Museum and Library.* http://www.trumanlibrary.org/oralhist/acheson.htm (accessed on August 20, 2003).

Konrad Adenauer

Born January 5, 1876
Cologne, Germany
Died April 19, 1967
Rhoendorf, West Germany

West German chancellor

Konrad Adenauer was the first chancellor of West Germany, officially known as the Federal Republic of Germany (FRG). He held the office from 1949 to 1963, taking West Germany from postwar military occupation to national independence. This was a critical period for reestablishing governmental relations with other nations and for encouraging economic recovery after Germany's defeat in World War II (1939–45). Adenauer's period of leadership coincided with the early years of the Cold War (1945–91). The Cold War was an intense political and economic rivalry between the United States and the Soviet Union that lasted from 1945 to 1991.

Adenauer, a staunch anticommunist, created strong economic and military ties with the democratic West (Western Europe and the United States). Through his fourteen years of leadership, postwar West Germany established sound foreign and domestic policies and made an astonishing economic recovery. Adenauer was the longest-serving democratically elected leader in modern German history.

"There is no doubt that the construction of a competent Federal Government effectively from a standing start was one of the greatest of Adenauer's formidable achievements."
— *Historian Charles Williams*

Konrad Adenauer. *Courtesy of the Library of Congress.*

An early start in politics

Konrad Adenauer was born in January 1876 to a middle-class Roman Catholic family in the city of Cologne, Germany. His father, Johann Konrad Adenauer, was a Prussian soldier and government worker who insisted on college educations for his three sons. After graduating from high school in 1894, Konrad Adenauer studied political science and law in college. Following graduation from the University of Bonn in 1900, he passed the German bar exam and briefly worked in the Cologne prosecutor's office as a lawyer. Adenauer joined a private law firm in 1902 and through this job became acquainted with politically influential Cologne residents. The head of his law firm was the leader of the Central Party in Cologne, a nationwide Catholic-oriented political party. The Central Party's power base was in several regions of Germany that had large Catholic populations, including the Rhineland, where Cologne was located. Adenauer advanced further into the political life of Cologne, and in 1904 he married Emma Weyer, daughter of a wealthy and prominent family. Her uncle was mayor of Cologne. Konrad and Emma would have three children.

Interested in holding political office, Adenauer won his first public position in 1906 on Cologne's city council. By 1909, Adenauer had become an assistant to his wife's uncle, the mayor. When World War I (1914–18) broke out, Adenauer took charge of managing Cologne's food supply, an important responsibility in such a large city. During the war, Adenauer suffered two personal traumas: In October 1916, his wife died from lingering complications of childbirth. Then in March 1917, Adenauer was in a serious car accident and received severe facial injuries. Numerous surgeries permanently changed the appearance of his face.

Mayor of Cologne

While recovering in the hospital, Adenauer won election as mayor of Cologne in September 1917. At only forty-one years of age, he was mayor of the third-largest city in Germany. In August 1919, Adenauer remarried. With his new wife, Auguste Zinsser, he had four children. Serving as mayor of Cologne for sixteen years, Adenauer gained prominence as a political representative of the Rhineland's regional interests and a leading Central Party member. Adenauer was a very hardworking, reserved person who could be very forceful. Cologne prospered under his leadership, and he was popular with the voters. There was public pressure for him to run in the 1921 and 1926 elections for chancellor of the national German government—the Weimar Republic—which was established after Germany's defeat in World War I. However, he chose not to run for chancellor and, instead, won reelection as mayor of Cologne in 1929.

Adenauer was one of the early opponents of Adolf Hitler (1889–1945), the leader of the Nazi Party (known primarily for its brutal policies of racism) in Germany. In February 1933, two months after Hitler gained power in Germany, Adenauer was forced to flee Cologne with his family because he had refused to raise the Nazi flag on city buildings when Hitler came for a visit. Adenauer was arrested in 1934 and again in 1944, narrowly avoiding execution. His wife would later die from injuries she sustained while being questioned about his whereabouts. Between 1933 and 1945, Adenauer remained out of politics and kept out of sight, sometimes staying in a religious monastery.

Creating a new Germany

When Cologne was liberated from Nazi control in March 1945, Adenauer temporarily regained his mayor position. However, conflicts with officials of the British-occupied zone of Germany led him to depart once again in October 1945. Adenauer harbored a disdain for the British throughout the rest of his political career. He turned his attention to national politics and helped form a new political party, the Christian Democratic Union (CDU). Hoping to gain wider appeal than the Central Party, the CDU sought support from both Catholics and Protestants. Adenauer became head of the party in the British-occupied zone of Germany in 1946, at age seventy. By 1949, he served as head of the party for all of West Germany. The CDU was so strong that it essentially governed West Germany while West Germany remained under Allied occupation forces. In his leadership position, Adenauer played a key role in deciding the future direction of West Germany. He helped draft the West German constitution, completed in May 1949. The new country would be democratic and capitalist and strongly allied with the West. By 1949, Germany was formally divided into two countries: West Germany became the Federal Republic of Germany (FRG); East Germany became the German Democratic Republic (GDR) and aligned itself with the communist bloc, or group, of countries led by the Soviet Union.

West Germany held its first parliamentary elections in August 1949. Victorious, Adenauer became the first chancellor of postwar West Germany. Adenauer was vehemently anticommunist and believed the best alliance for his country was with the United States. Adenauer planned to lead West Germany through major steps of economic development and rearmament, or building up its military supplies, all the while hoping that communist rule in East Germany would eventually come to an end. As he put his plan into action, he became recognized as a major European statesman. Ultimately, he hoped to reunite West and East Germany.

A plan for independence

The first step in his plan came in 1950: Adenauer believed Germany needed a renewed relationship with France to begin building a strong, unified Europe. However, after suffering through two world wars in the past forty years, both of which Germany began, the French population was fearful of the Germans. In forging foreign ties, Adenauer had to overcome the horrible legacy of Hitler. France responded to his overtures with the Schuman Plan. This was an economic plan that proposed having West Germany and France pool their coal and steel resources, both critically needed by West Germany for its rebuilding. Adenauer was very pleased. It was a first step toward European integration. It was also the first formal acceptance of the West German government by a foreign nation.

Next, Adenauer sought to build a European defense alliance, called the European Defense Community (EDC). However, France rejected the proposal. Adenauer was dismayed by this rejection. When Adenauer threatened to join an alliance with the Soviet Union for defense, Western European countries and the United States invited West Germany to join the North Atlantic Treaty Organization (NATO). NATO was a re-

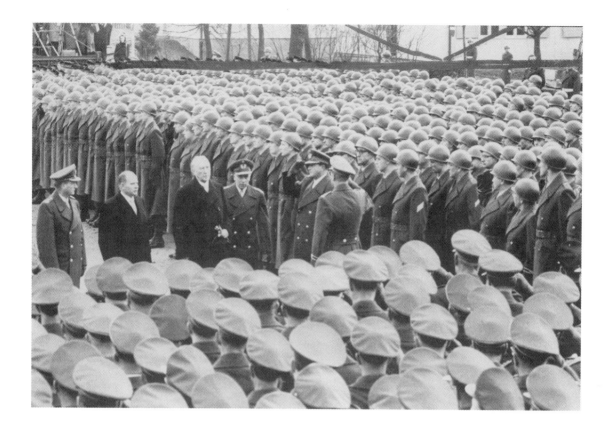

German chancellor Konrad Adenauer reviews his troops in 1956. *Reproduced by permission of the Corbis Corporation.*

cently formed defense alliance including Western European countries, the United States, and Canada. West Germany joined NATO in 1955. To reduce France's fears about Germany, Adenauer agreed to limit the size of the West German military, and Britain agreed to station fifty thousand troops in West Germany for fifty years, for military defense purposes. France feared a remilitarized Germany after suffering through two wars with Germany already in the twentieth century. In May 1952, Adenauer had signed a treaty to formally end military occupation of West Germany in May 1955, meaning Germany could now make its own political decisions.

Perhaps in a last-ditch effort to derail Western European integration involving West Germany, the Soviet Union proposed a plan for reunifying East and West Germany. Though that was one of Adenauer's ultimate goals, he did not trust the Soviets and believed they were simply trying to impede West Germany's growing attachments to the West; he thought they would eventually seek to gain control of West

Germany, just as they had done in East Germany. Adenauer wanted German reunification, but only on his own terms. He endured substantial criticism from the West German population for favoring Western alliances over Soviet reunification proposals.

Membership in NATO gave West Germany a higher status. Quickly, the Soviets invited Adenauer to Moscow for talks to establish formal relations. He went to Moscow in September 1955. Until 1966, the Soviet Union was the only nation to officially recognize both East and West Germany. The United States would not recognize East Germany until 1974. The Soviets also agreed to return German prisoners of war from World War II, who had been held for over a decade.

The next step for Adenauer was formation of the European Economic Community, more commonly known as the Common Market, in March 1957. The Common Market created much stronger economic ties between the European countries. Having achieved military and economic alliances for West Germany, Adenauer rose to the pinnacle of his popularity. At eighty-one years of age, he won reelection in a landslide. His CDU party held a strong majority in the West German government.

An aging leader

When Charles de Gaulle (1890–1970) returned to power in France in 1958, Adenauer renewed his efforts to strengthen ties with France. Discussions between the two leaders began in September 1958. In 1963, the two countries signed the Franco-German Friendship Treaty. The treaty called for military cooperation and much closer coordination on foreign policy decisions.

A Cold War crisis came to Adenauer's doorstep in 1961, when Soviet leader **Nikita Khrushchev** (1894–1971; see entry) ordered the construction of the Berlin Wall. Khrushchev wanted to stop the steady flow of residents from the communist East Germany into the democratic West Germany. Adenauer chose not to contest construction of the wall, bringing considerable criticism from the West German population. As a result, Adenauer's political party, the CDU,

Willy Brandt

Konrad Adenauer led West Germany through its initial years, establishing its place in the world community of nations. He looked toward the United States for protection from potential Soviet communist expansion. Serving as West German chancellor from 1969 to 1974, Willy Brandt (1913–1992) continued to expand West Germany's international influence by seeking to ease tensions with Eastern Europe and the Soviet Union.

Like Adenauer, Brandt (born Karl Herbert Frahm) fled from the Nazis in 1933. After World War II, Brandt returned to German politics. He was elected to the first West German legislature in 1949. Brandt then served as mayor of West Berlin from 1957 to 1966.

In the late 1960s, Brandt introduced a new policy called Ostopolitik, which recognized East Germany and territorial changes that occurred at the conclusion of World War II, including the new boundaries of Poland. Brandt signed nonaggression agreements with the Soviet Union and Poland in 1970. He also recognized the territorial gains the Soviet Union had made in

Willy Brandt. *Reproduced by permission of Getty Images.*

Eastern Europe during World War II. Later agreements would ease travel restrictions between East and West Germany. In 1971, Brandt received the Nobel Peace Prize for easing Cold War tensions. After leaving office in 1974, he became a leader in the European antinuclear movement in the early 1980s. He lobbied against U.S. escalation of a new nuclear arms race and placement of new nuclear missiles in Europe.

lost strength in the West German government in the September 1961 elections. Now eighty-five years old, Adenauer refused to step down as chancellor, despite increasing pressure. In 1963, his last year as chancellor, Adenauer accompanied U.S. president **John F. Kennedy** (1917–1963; served 1961–63; see entry) on Kennedy's famous visit to the Berlin Wall. However, by that time, Adenauer was considered out of touch with the younger generations and with changing international relations. He finally resigned in October 1963 but remained chairman of the CDU party until March 1966. Much of his time, however, was spent writing a four-volume set of memoirs, tending his rose garden, and painting. Adenauer died on April 19, 1967, at the age of ninety-one. His funeral drew worldwide tributes unprecedented for a German leader.

For More Information

Books

Adenauer, Konrad. *Memoirs.* 4 vols. Chicago: H. Regnery, 1966–68.

Hiscocks, Richard. *The Adenauer Era.* Philadelphia, PA: Lippincott, 1966.

McGhee, George C. *At the Creation of a New Germany: From Adenauer to Brandt, an Ambassador's Account.* New Haven, CT: Yale University Press, 1989.

Wighton, Charles. *Adenauer: A Democratic Dictator.* London: Muller, 1963.

Williams, Charles. *Adenauer: The Father of the New Germany.* New York: J. Wiley, 2000.

Salvador Allende

Born July 26, 1908
Valparaíso, Chile
Died September 11, 1973
Santiago, Chile

Chilean president

> "I am a militant socialist, a man who has realized that unity alone held out the hope of victory for the people."

Salvador Allende made history by being the first democratically elected socialist head of state in the Western Hemisphere. Socialism is an economic and political system in which the government owns most means of production and profits are shared with everyone. Trained as a doctor, Allende devoted most of his life to improving the lives of working-class Chileans. He wanted to create a true republic of the working class, in which democracy ruled—a country dedicated to their health, welfare, and development. He wanted to show that a peaceful road to socialism existed.

Allende's unique background allowed him to play a crucial role in the creation of the Popular Unity Coalition that brought him to power. He was able to unify traditional and revolutionary political parties to create a group to govern Chile. But in doing so, he touched off a frenzy of concern in the Western world. The United States and other Western countries worried that Chile's socialism provided an opportunity for communist countries, especially the Soviet Union, to gain a foothold in the Americas. Communism is a governmental system in which a single political party, the Commu-

Salvador Allende. *Reproduced by permission of the Corbis Corporation.*

17

nist Party, controls nearly all aspects of society. In a communist economy, private ownership of businesses and property is prohibited so that the goods produced and the wealth accumulated can be shared equally by all.

Early life

Salvador Allende Gossens was born on July 26, 1908, into an upper-middle-class family in Valparaíso, Chile. His father, Salvador Allende Castro, was a lawyer. His mother, Laura Gossens, was a teacher and stressed a freethinking family atmosphere. Allende's family had a long tradition of service to the country. At sixteen years of age, following his education in Chile's public schools, Salvador Allende volunteered for military service. He went on to earn an officer's rank in the army reserves.

His family also had a long tradition of participation in radicalism, in which extreme change in politics is advocated. His father and uncle were part of the reformist efforts (mass changes) of the Radical Party in the nineteenth and early twentieth centuries. Allende was exposed to radical ideas and concepts early in life. When his father died, Salvador Allende declared that he would dedicate his life to the social struggle, or concerns related to such issues as health and employment, of the people of Chile.

After his discharge from the military, Allende went on to study medicine at the University of Chile. He was a good student and held several leadership positions while in school. He was president of the student medical center, vice chairman of the student federation, and a delegate to the university council. He married Hortensia Bussy and had three daughters.

Allende's education was not restricted to medicine. He began reading the works of political philosopher Karl Marx (1818–1883) and writings by former Soviet leader Vladimir Lenin (1870–1924). Allende became convinced that a socialist revolution would solve Chile's social and economic problems. He did not, however, agree with the rigidity of the Soviet Union's communist policies. While in school, Allende helped found the Chilean Socialist Party as a socialist alternative to the Communist Party's support for the Soviet Union.

Allende's education was interrupted by frequent suspensions from school and at least two arrests, all of which stemmed from his political activities. Allende was protesting the dictatorship of General Carlos Ibáñez del Campo (1877–1960). Allende was awarded a doctorate in medicine in 1937, but because of his political activism and his outspokenness, he found that potential employers were wary of offering him high-level medical positions. He ended up in a series of lower-level jobs.

Political life

Though Allende's medical career never really blossomed, his political career began to take off. He served as secretary general of the Socialist Party of Chile in 1933. In 1937, he was elected to Chile's Chamber of Deputies, the lower house of Chile's congress. While in congress, Allende introduced many bills addressing issues of public health, social welfare, and women's rights. He developed a reputation as a champion of the poor.

Allende served as Chile's minister of health from 1939 to 1943, during which time he focused on the social causes of poor health. Allende knew that individual decisions always affected personal health, but he believed that social factors, such as poverty, access to health care, and the living conditions of each person, also played a role. He tried to address these factors through changes in health insurance and industrial safety laws. While he was minister of health, he published a book, *The Medical-Social Reality in Chile*.

In 1945, Allende was elected to Chile's Senate, the upper house of Chile's congress. Allende served three eight-year terms in the Senate, which included stints as vice president and then president of the Senate. He also unsuccessfully ran for president of Chile a number of times. He was suspended from the Socialist Party for a while in 1952 because of his support for the Communist Party of Chile, which was outlawed at that time. In 1956, he served as the first president of the Popular Revolutionary Action Front (FRAP), a communist-socialist coalition, or group. In 1970, Allende was finally successful in his bid for the presidency and became the first popularly elected socialist head of state in the Americas.

Allende's Journeys in the Communist World

In 1958, Salvador Allende visited Cuba and began lifelong friendships with **Fidel Castro** (1926–; see entry), who became president of communist Cuba in 1959, and revolutionary Che Guevara (1928–1967). Later, as a senator in Chile, Allende visited communist North Vietnam and was hosted by North Vietnamese leader **Ho Chi Minh** (1890–1969; see entry). Allende also visited North Korea and East Germany, two more countries that had communist governments.

Allende continued to emphasize that he did not want violent revolution in Chile, but his visits and friendships in the communist world frightened many people, both inside and outside of Chile. Chileans worried that Allende did not seem to recognize the repression and lack of civil rights that were common under communist governments. Still, Allende asserted that he believed in democratic evolution, not revolution. When Allende was elected as president of Chile, his friend Guevara sent him a note saying that Allende was seeking change through political means, while Guevara sought it through revolution.

President-Elect Allende

In Chile, there were numerous political parties. To elect a president, various parties often had to cooperate with one another and agree to vote for one person. A candidate needed at least a plurality (most votes) to make the runoff election in which to seek a majority. By the late 1960s, Allende was considered past his prime as a politician. However, he was also recognized as the only person who could bring together the groups necessary to win the election. Allende was able to unite the Socialist Party with the Radical Party, the Communist Party, the Christian Democrats, and other reform parties in Chile to craft a coalition—called the Popular Unity Coalition—that was able to garner enough support to win the election.

Allende won plurality (36 percent), but since he did not receive a majority of votes, he had to participate in a runoff in a second election to gain a majority. In the runoff, Allende won. However, the 36 percent in the initial balloting represented only a tiny percentage of Chile's total population. Since the number of votes Allende received represented less than half the voters, the Chilean congress had to confirm his victory in the runoff election. Confirmation was not guaranteed, and much negotiation took place.

Finally, the Chilean congress agreed to confirm Allende as president in exchange for his support of some changes to Chile's constitution. The changes reflected the concerns of many Chileans that Allende's socialist affiliations would lead to a deterioration in the people's rights, similar to that seen in the Soviet Union. Allende instituted major changes in the economic system, such as wage increases for low-paid workers while freezing prices of goods. He also nationalized companies, such as copper mines, owned by U.S. citizens without compensating for losses; pushed for collective farms; and nationalized many local businesses. Allende supported the constitutional amendments guaranteeing freedom of assembly, freedom of the press, and other basic freedoms. He became president in 1970.

Chilean president Salvador Allende waves to supporters. *Reproduced by permission of the Corbis Corporation.*

Cold War fears

Allende had run for president on a platform, or political program, of moderate reform. He advocated agricultural reform, which usually meant the redistribution of land from large landowners to people with no land. He also supported labor reform, social welfare programs, and liberal economic programs. One of his more controversial proposals involved Chile's copper mines. These were very important to Chile's economy. Copper mining and production made up a huge part of Chile's exports each year—about 75 percent. But companies based in the United States controlled the copper mines. Allende and many other Chileans believed that the copper mines should be controlled by Chile. Allende proceeded to nationalize ownership of the copper mines.

The United States did not want Allende to be Chile's president. U.S. president **Richard M. Nixon** (1913–1994; served 1969–74; see entry) was strongly anticommunist and did not believe that Chile should have a socialist government. When Allende was elected, Nixon did not send him the customary greeting of congratulations. Nixon feared that Chile would be only the first of the South American governments to fall to communism, that Chile would pave the way for others. Allende added to Nixon's fears when he resumed diplomatic ties with communist Cuba within ten days of taking office.

Immediately following Allende's election, many of the wealthier people in Chile sent their money out of the country. They were afraid that Allende would take their money and give it to poor people. In addition, about fifteen thousand people left Chile. Trying to calm his nation's fears, Allende said that 98 percent of Chileans had nothing to fear from his government, but many people worried that they were part of the 2 percent that would be affected.

Rumors spread of a violent response to Allende's election. Some people were pushing the military to take control of Chile and overthrow Allende. The move to overthrow Allende was coming from reactionary people in Chile. Reactionary opinions involve a former, and sometimes outdated, political policy. Allende said that his supporters would answer force with force.

Allende tried to alleviate U.S. fears of a communist government in the Americas by promising that Chile would never permit its military bases to be used against the United States. The United States was not convinced and began pressuring other countries to reduce or eliminate trade with

Chile, thereby seriously hurting its economy. However, because conservative Chileans were affiliated with the military, the United States continued to send money and equipment to the Chilean military.

Deterioration

In the early 1970s, the world was in the midst of a recession, or reduced economic activity. Chile was no exception. Inflation, or increasing consumer prices, was high, and jobs were scarce. There were shortages of the basic items required for living, and food was rationed. The Chilean people became more and more frantic about the economic situation.

Allende tried to respond, but the U.S. economic blockade made it difficult. In addition, he instituted some programs that frightened the Chilean people. For example, he started a neighborhood surveillance program and applied pressure on opposition newspapers to quiet the voices critical of his programs. For many Chileans, Allende's programs seemed too much like the confining programs of the Soviet Union. Allende lost even more support by appearing to be soft on crime, which continued to escalate.

In 1972 and 1973, general strikes, or work stoppages, crippled the Chilean economy. Workers and shopkeepers were upset with the inflation and lack of goods, and they protested by refusing to work. The economy began to collapse. The country was falling apart, but the military, fortified by U.S. contributions, was strong.

The coup

On September 11, 1973, the military put into action a plan to overthrow President Allende. The military surrounded Allende's palace; inside, Allende, his daughter Beatriz, and his supporters waited. Allende's daughter was a fervent supporter of the far left, or liberal, component of the Socialist Party. Some historians have suggested that Allende's decision to nationalize businesses was partially driven by a wish not to disappoint her. Allende made one final speech affirming his belief in the Chilean people, and then died. It was never determined whether he shot himself or was killed by an assassin.

The coup was very violent. Several thousand people were killed or injured in the overthrow of Allende. Allende was buried in an unmarked grave, reportedly so that the grave site would not become a shrine. In 1990, he was reburied with honor. Allende became a hero for many liberals. With his commitment to workers' rights and the welfare of the poor, as well as his unwillingness to bow to pressure from the United States, he inspired many liberals in America. Allende's stature only grew when accusations surfaced that the United States, specifically the Central Intelligence Agency (CIA), had engineered his downfall. For the political right, or conservatives, Allende continued to stand for the threat of communism.

For More Information

Books

Alegria, Fernando. *Allende.* Translated by Frank Janney. Stanford, CA: Stanford University Press, 1994.

Allende Gossens, Salvador. *Salvador Allende Reader: Chile's Voice of Democracy.* Edited by James D. Cockcroft. New York: Ocean Press, 2000.

Boorstein, Edward. *Allende's Chile: An Inside View.* New York: International Publishers, 1977.

Davis, Nathaniel. *The Last Two Years of Salvador Allende.* Ithaca, NY: Cornell University Press, 1985.

Kaufman, Edy. *Crisis in Allende's Chile: New Perspectives.* New York: Praeger, 1988.

Petras, James F., and Morris Morley. *The United States and Chile: Imperialism and the Overthrow of the Allende Government.* New York: Monthly Review Press, 1975.

Sigmund, Paul E. *The United States and Democracy in Chile.* Baltimore, MD: Johns Hopkins University Press, 1993.

Clement R. Attlee

Born January 3, 1883
Putney, England
Died October 8, 1967
London, England

British prime minister

Clement Attlee was Britain's top leader from 1945 to 1951. Both before and after serving as prime minister, Attlee headed the British Labour Party, from 1935 to 1940 and from 1951 to 1955. The rise of the Labour Party made the British government a two-party system; the second party was the Conservative Party. Attlee substantially changed Britain's economic and political role in the world by dismantling the British Empire and bringing socialism, in the form of a national welfare system, to Britain. Socialism is a system in which the government owns or controls all means of production and all citizens share in the work and products. Operated by the national government, a national welfare system provides financial help and other forms of assistance to poor and needy citizens.

Attlee's tenure as his nation's leader occurred when the Cold War was just beginning. The Cold War was an intense political and economic rivalry between the United States and the Soviet Union that lasted from 1945 to 1991. During the Cold War, the United States ran a democratic system of government, which consists of several political parties

"On a personal level, Attlee had a shyness ... which is unique in modern British politics. A small number of people are like this in all walks of life, yet none but Clem Attlee has ever become prime minister. His shyness camouflaged his ability." — *Author Robert Pearce*

Clement R. Attlee. *Courtesy of the Library of Congress.*

whose members are elected to various government offices by vote of the general population. The United States operates under a capitalist economic system. This means prices, production, and distribution of goods are determined by competition in a market relatively free of government interference. In contrast, the Soviet Union ran a communist governmental system led, in which a single political party, the Communist Party, control almost all aspects of society. In a communist economy, private ownership of property and business is prohibited so that goods produced and wealth accumulated can be shared equally by all. The low-key Attlee had to develop Britain's early Cold War policies and provide leadership to a nation greatly weakened by two world wars.

Dedication to the poor

Clement Richard Attlee was born in January 1883 in Putney, England, the fourth son of a devoutly religious family. His father, Henry Attlee, was a prosperous London lawyer, and his mother, Ellen Watson, was educated as well. Raised in a comfortable middle-class neighborhood, Clement was educated at Haileybury College boarding school and then Oxford University. He studied law at Inner Temple and set up his own law office in 1905. That same year, he began volunteer work for a boys club at a settlement house in London's impoverished East End. Settlement houses were private organizations established in poor neighborhoods in the late nineteenth century to provide assorted social services to nearby residents. Attlee moved into the house in 1907, serving as a house manager.

Greatly influenced by the poverty of London's East End, he developed socialist political beliefs and a commitment to social reform. Attlee joined a socialist organization, the Fabian Society, in 1907, and in 1908 he became politically active in the Independent Labour Party. In 1909, he abandoned his law career for politics and would continue living in the London slums until 1923. During this period, Attlee lectured in social sciences at Ruskin College and Oxford University and later was appointed as a lecturer at the London School of Economics. Attlee was fully dedicated to improving the lives of Britain's working class.

Political career takes off

At the outbreak of World War I (1914–18), Attlee joined the British army and served in France and Africa. He attained the rank of major, a title he would continue to use when his military service was over. After the war, he returned to teach at the London School of Economics. However, his political career soon began. In 1919, he was elected mayor of Stepney of East London and became a member of the London Labour Party's executive committee. In 1922, Attlee won election to Parliament. He also married Violet Millar of Hampstead that year; they would have four children.

Despite his liberal politics, Attlee was very conservative in his lifestyle and mannerisms. He was strongly family-oriented and showed little egotism or flamboyant behavior. Some even regarded him as colorless. Attlee did not have notable public speaking skills; he was to the point and used few words. However, he was known for his witty one-liners. An excellent administrator, Attlee much preferred working behind the scenes.

Through the 1920s, Attlee moved up in Parliament to undersecretary for war in 1924 and various other cabinet positions through 1930. In 1931, Attlee resigned from Parliament to become deputy leader of the Labour Party. He was elected Labour Party leader in October 1935. The Labour Party rose to prominence in opposition to the well-established Conservative Party, and thus a two-party political system in Britain was born.

Attlee strongly opposed Prime Minister Neville Chamberlain's appeasement policies toward Nazi Germany. (Appeasement meant giving in to Germany's demands; the Nazi Party was known primarily for its brutal policies of racism.) Attlee proposed taking action against Germany's military expansion in Europe. Chamberlain (1869–1940) was a member of the Conservative Party, which opposed most Labour Party beliefs, but when war broke out in 1939, Chamberlain asked Attlee to be part of a wartime coalition, or partnership. Attlee refused and blocked all Labour Party participation, leading to Chamberlain's resignation in May 1940. **Winston Churchill** (1874–1965; see entry), also of the Conservative Party, replaced Chamberlain.

Though he belonged to a different political party, Churchill shared Attlee's views regarding Germany. Churchill appointed Attlee to his five-member War Cabinet to perform various duties. By 1942, Attlee was deputy prime minister. While Churchill focused on the war, Attlee took care of the home front. Under Attlee's leadership, the British government took control of every aspect of the economy to support the war effort.

Britain's war effort was successful. With the Allies poised to defeat Germany, Attlee represented Britain at the United Nations organizational meeting in April 1945 in San Francisco, California. Also at that time, Attlee and other Labour Party members pulled out of Churchill's wartime coalition government, forcing a general election for prime minister in July; Attlee and Churchill were the two candidates. With the election votes still being counted, both Attlee and Churchill traveled to the Potsdam Conference in Germany, a postwar meeting of the victorious Big Three war allies: the United States, Great Britain, and the Soviet Union. While at the conference, Attlee learned he had won in a landslide, so he then took over for Churchill in the discussions.

A changing Britain

After World War II (1939–45), Attlee embarked on a dramatic change of British government policies, both at home in Britain and in foreign relations. He had hoped to transform Britain's government-controlled wartime economy into a peacetime socialist economy. However, because the defeated Germany was no longer a threat, wartime aid from the United States abruptly stopped. This left the British economy in shambles. For many Britons, hardships immediately after the war were worse than they had been during the war. Shortages grew worse: Civilians were restricted from using gasoline, and even potatoes, a staple food, were rationed. In an effort to increase industrial productivity as well as support increased social services, Attlee began to curtail British foreign commitments; this allowed him to reduce the military budget and brought soldiers back into the civilian workforce. In 1945 and 1946, Attlee nationalized, or placed under the control of the national government, basic British industries such as gas, electricity, coal, railways, civil aviation, roads, and the Bank of England. These industries were losing large amounts of money at the time, so opposition to Attlee's plan was minimal. With the British economy near collapse, the United States provided a $937 million loan in 1945, shortly after the surrender of Germany. Even with this help, Attlee had to maintain strict, wartime-like measures, such as banning gasoline for civilian use and rationing potatoes; high taxes; and wage and price controls to boost the British economy. Because of the persistent hardships, Attlee's public support steadily dwindled as the middle class switched allegiance to the Conservative Party.

In 1947, Attlee nationalized more of the economy, including the iron and steel industries. This was an unpopular move with both labor and industry because they were losing ownership of their industries to the state. Attlee also made other major changes in 1947 by greatly expanding social services to Britons. He extended social insurance and established a national health care system called the National Health Service.

A diminished world role

The dramatic changes in domestic policies directly influenced Attlee's foreign policy. In order to increase industrial productivity and to pay for the expanded social services and subsidize, or financially support, the nationalized industries at home, Attlee had to make cuts in foreign commitments. He began to dismantle the British Empire, which included colonies around the world. In its place he established the British Commonwealth of Nations, an alliance of Britain and its former colonies. Attlee granted independence to Jordan in 1946 and gave India its independence in 1947. In recognition of ethnic differences in the region, he created Pakistan from part of British-controlled India. Attlee also ended British control of Egypt and Palestine.

Besides trimming Britain's colonies from the budget, Attlee ended foreign aid to other countries. In February 1947, he ended financial aid to Greece and Turkey. At the time, the Greek government was fighting a communist-supported revolt, and Turkey was under pressure from the Soviet Union to allow the Soviets access to the Mediterranean Sea. Alarmed by Britain's withdrawal from these two countries, the United States quickly decided to replace Britain in the area. On March 12, 1947, President **Harry S. Truman** (1884–1972; served

British prime minister Clement R. Attlee (bottom right) consults with U.S. president Harry S. Truman. Secretary of State Dean Acheson (left) and Secretary of Defense George C. Marshall stand behind them. *Reproduced by permission of Getty Images.*

1945–53; see entry) sought economic aid for Greece and Turkey from Congress and announced the Truman Doctrine. The doctrine stated that the United States would provide assistance to countries combating communist aggression.

A major goal of Attlee's foreign policy was to draw the United States into a much greater role in protecting Europe from Soviet Communist expansion. U.S. aid for Greece and Turkey was the first step. Next would come the Marshall Plan

British Atomic Bomb Program

While serving as Great Britain's prime minister, Clement Attlee had to make a key decision: to commit his nation to the nuclear arms race. During World War II, British, Canadian, and U.S. atomic scientists worked together to develop an atomic bomb as part of the top-secret Manhattan Project. In 1942, Britain's prime minister, Winston Churchill, reached a secret agreement with the United States about sharing technical atomic bomb information. Just after replacing Churchill as prime minister in July 1945, Attlee was informed of the atomic bomb project. The United States dropped two atomic bombs on Japan in August 1945, ending World War II. Attlee suddenly had to deal with the nuclear age.

Attempting to avoid a nuclear arms race, Attlee desperately tried to develop agreements with the United States and the Soviet Union to ban atomic bombs. Unsuccessful in his attempts, Attlee gave British scientists the go-ahead in late September 1945 to conduct atomic energy research for civilian use. He still held back on the decision about atomic bomb production.

Others, including his foreign minister, **Ernest Bevin** (1881–1951; see entry), wanted Attlee to push ahead on the bomb.

Attlee was also trying to obtain the previously promised atomic secrets from the United States. However, shortly after World War II, Congress had passed a law prohibiting the United States from sharing scientific information about the bomb. President Harry S. Truman still privately indicated to Attlee that he would honor the earlier agreement. But when Britain formally requested assistance in April 1946, Truman refused to cooperate. It was clear that Britain would have to develop an atomic bomb on its own. By late 1946, unable to achieve any arms control agreements, Attlee knew it was time for Britain to produce its own bomb. He believed Britain needed the bomb to maintain a level of prestige with the United States. In January 1947, he secretly decided to move forward with development of the atomic bomb. Britain conducted its first successful test in 1952, joining the United States and the Soviet Union as one of the world's nuclear powers.

in mid-1947, a program that provided long-term economic assistance to Western Europe and Britain, and the North Atlantic Treaty Organization (NATO) in 1949. NATO was a peacetime alliance of the United States and eleven other nations, and a key factor in the attempt to contain communism. Britain also became more aggressive against Soviet threats of expansion. Attlee approved the development of Britain's own atomic bomb program, and he began rearming Britain by taking money from social programs.

In 1950, Attlee supported a military response to the communist North Korean invasion of South Korea. This conflict soon mushroomed into the Korean War (1950–53). Attlee's decision proved highly unpopular among Britons and led to his final political demise. Postwar economic problems in Britain had gradually eroded his popular support. U.S. loans in 1945 and the Marshall Plan of 1947 were not enough to sustain the British economy or Attlee's popularity. In October 1951, Attlee resigned as prime minister, and Churchill won the position for a second time. In December 1955, after suffering a stroke, Attlee resigned as leader of the Labour Party.

An honored life

Attlee received numerous awards for his dedicated service to Great Britain during difficult times. In 1951, he received the Order of Merit, and in 1955 he was knighted and granted an earldom, an honor that gave him a seat in the House of Lords, the upper house of British parliament. He was one of only four prime ministers in British history to receive these honors. He spent much time writing and giving lectures until he was disabled in 1966 by another stroke. He died in London in October 1967.

For More Information

Books

Attlee, Clement R. *As It Happened.* London: W. Heinemann, 1954.

Beckett, Francis. *Clem Attlee.* London: Richard Cohen Books, 1997.

Brookshire, Jerry H. *Clement Attlee.* New York: Manchester University Press, 1995.

Pearce, Robert D. *Attlee.* New York: Longman, 1997.

Ernest Bevin

Born March 9, 1881
Winsford, Cheshire, England
Died April 14, 1951
London, England

British foreign minister

Immediately following the end of World War II (1939–45) in Europe, a general election was held in Great Britain for prime minister, Britain's top leadership position. **Clement R. Attlee** (1883–1967; see entry), leader of the Labour Party, defeated wartime hero **Winston Churchill** (1874–1965; see entry) for the office. After his election, Attlee asked Ernest Bevin to be his foreign secretary. According to Mark Stephens's 1985 book *Ernest Bevin: Unskilled Labourer and World Statesman, 1881–1951,* Attlee wanted "a heavy tank," not "a sniper."

Such was the hard-nosed, up-front character of Ernest Bevin. As British foreign minister from 1945 to 1951, Bevin had a major role in developing British foreign policy during the Cold War's early years. The Cold War was an intense political and economic rivalry between the democratic United States and the communist Soviet Union that lasted from 1945 to 1991.

The rise of a leader

Ernest Bevin was born on March 9, 1881, to a poor mother, Diana Mercy Bevin, in Winsford, Cheshire, England.

"Unintelligent people always look for a scapegoat."

Ernest Bevin. *Courtesy of the Library of Congress.*

33

He was the youngest of seven children. He never knew his father. His mother did domestic work and sometimes served as the village midwife, a person who helps mothers during childbirth. She died of cancer when he was eight. Orphaned, Ernest lived with a stepsister and her husband for awhile, and then left school at age eleven to seek work. He worked at various unskilled jobs until becoming a delivery driver, using a horse-drawn cart to deliver mineral water in the town of Bristol. He held the job for eleven years, until he was twenty-nine years old.

By 1908, Bevin's life had begun to take shape. He became involved in labor issues and married Florence Townley, the daughter of a Bristol wine taster. They had one child. Bevin's career took off in 1910, when he joined the Dockers' Union while they were on strike (a work stoppage in protest of low wages or unsatisfactory working conditions) in Bristol. He organized a new branch of the union for truck drivers. The expanded membership helped the dockworkers win their strike. Greatly enthused by his quick success, Bevin became a full-time labor organizer and exhibited great skill in negotiating and recruiting. Through his energetic leadership, working conditions on the docks improved, and he received increasing recognition. By 1914, Bevin was a national organizer for the Dockers' Union. During World War I (1914–18), he mobilized transport workers and unions to support Britain's war effort. By 1920, he was a top official in the dockworkers' union.

Bevin was an unusual character. He ate and drank excessively at times and smoked heavily. Short and stocky, he lumbered about awkwardly. He had poor table manners, and he spoke with poor grammar in a gravelly voice. But Bevin also had natural skills and behavioral traits that made him an effective negotiator in labor disputes and later in foreign policy conferences. His success in bitter negotiations with employers was attributed to his ruthless demeanor. He was abrupt, boastful, and self-righteous. His forceful character led to poor relations with the press and professional politicians. Yet surprisingly, he could be a very effective and impassioned orator at times, and above all, he was very imaginative.

Despite his outward arrogance, he inspired strong loyalty, obedience, and even affection in union members during his labor days and later among the British people in general.

Witnessing Bevin's twenty-five years as a union leader convinced newly elected prime minister Clement Attlee that Bevin had an ideal personality for dealing with the tough Soviet premier **Joseph Stalin** (1879–1953; see entry) and other Soviet leaders. Some historians even claim Bevin's tough approach contributed to the beginning of the Cold War. Bevin battled growing Soviet influence by taking an early hardline position against Stalin and organizing alliances in opposition to the perceived Soviet threat, which became increasingly real as positions became cemented.

A major step in Bevin's labor career came in 1922, when he combined many small local unions into one, the Transport and General Workers' Union. Bevin led this trade union—the world's largest—until 1940. In 1937, Bevin was also elected chairman of the Trades Union Congress (TUC). The TUC is a national organization of British trade unions that was founded in 1868. Bevin had become one of the most powerful union leaders in Britain. As Nazi leader Adolf Hitler (1889–1945) rose to power in Germany through the 1930s, Bevin used his position to vigorously argue for rearming Britain so Britain could challenge the growing German threat.

Acknowledging Bevin's prominence in British labor circles, Winston Churchill, Britain's prime minister during World War II, appointed Bevin to the five-person War Cabinet in May 1940. Bevin's position was minister of labor and national service. He was charged with the daunting task of mobilizing British troops through unpopular measures such as a military draft, meaning certain citizens would be eligible to serve in the military if required, and restrictions on trade union activities, including strikes. The Emergency Powers Act of 1940 gave Bevin the power to shift the workforce between the armed forces, the war industry, and civilian needs. As World War II progressed, his mobilization program proved an incredible success.

Foreign minister

In July 1945, Bevin traveled with Churchill and Attlee to Potsdam, Germany, for a postwar meeting of leaders from the United States, Great Britain, and the Soviet Union. The key purpose of the meeting was to determine the fate of Ger-

Problems in Palestine

Great Britain had assumed control of Palestine, a region on the east coast of the Mediterranean inhabited by Arab peoples who had been under British colonial rule, in October 1918 at the end of World War I. Immediately following World War II, increased Jewish immigration into the area became a major concern. Persecuted during the war by German Nazi troops, many Jews fled Europe, hoping to find safety and better economic conditions in Palestine. Jews are believers of Judaism who trace their descent from Hebrews of the ancient biblical kingdom of Israel. Arabs are the inhabitants who occupy Southwest Asia and Northern Africa, including Saudi Arabia, Yemen, Oman, and Egypt. Bevin faced the difficult task of maintaining good relations with the Arabs while dealing with the desire of Jews to establish a homeland for the many thousands fleeing Europe and the Soviet Union, where they faced religious persecution as well. Bevin hoped Britain could maintain a dominant role in the Middle East, and he knew that would require good relations with the various Arab states. Therefore, because the Arab peoples were alarmed by the growing influx of Jews in the region, Bevin opposed Jewish immigration and the creation of an independent Jewish state in Palestinian territory. There were few Jews in the region to begin with, but with growing numbers, Arabs feared the Jews would create their own country, which they did; Arabs held a strong anti-Israel position, that Jews should be removed entirely from the Middle East region.

Bevin proposed a federated Jewish-Arab state, but negotiations on this proposal collapsed by 1948. A federated state would be similar in appearance to the United States, where a single central government exists but separate states under it control affairs within their borders. In an effort to gain independence and drive the British out of the region, Jewish terrorists, or radical rebels, began striking against British troops many, which had been defeated in the war. While the meeting was taking place, Attlee learned he had defeated Churchill in the general elections for prime minister. Attlee then appointed Bevin foreign minister of the new British government. Though Bevin had no experience in foreign affairs, Attlee believed Bevin's toughness and long experience as a negotiator was needed. Bevin officially took office on July 26, 1945. Immediately, while at Potsdam, Bevin confronted the Soviets on their efforts to place a new postwar communist government in Poland. The Soviets backed off and promised to allow general elections. However, they did not fulfill the in the area, leading to bloody clashes. On July 22, 1946, ninety-one people were killed when Zionists bombed British government and military offices. (Zionists were members of the Jewish movement to establish the state of Israel. They wanted to reestablish themselves in their biblical homeland and be safe from persecution in Europe and Russia.) Bevin turned to the United States for assistance, but President Harry S. Truman took a decidedly pro-Israel position. Against the advice of his advisors, Truman recognized Israel within hours of its establishment, thus creating much ill will with Arab countries in the region. Israel had been carved out of Arab lands with force. However, Truman was facing reelection in a tough political race and needed the support of the strong and wealthy pro-Israel lobby in the United States. With the increasing violence in Palestine, the British public was becoming less and less supportive of keeping British troops in the area. In frustration, Bevin decided to completely withdraw Britain, including eighty thousand British soldiers, from the region. Giving up on long-term British influence in the region, Bevin announced that Britain's withdrawal would be completed by May 15, 1948.

Meanwhile, fighting became more intense between Israelis and Palestinians as the Zionists made territorial gains. On the same day that the last British commissioner departed, Israel declared independence. Within hours, U.S. president Truman extended formal recognition. Immediately, armies from Syria, Iraq, Egypt, and Transjordan launched attacks against the newly formed country. Fighting continued through the remainder of 1948. Finally, Israel secured control of the region, and the fighting stopped. The failure to reach a peaceful settlement in British-controlled Palestine is considered the greatest failure of British foreign policy during the Cold War. Bevin was greatly criticized for his handling of the situation.

promise, and this deception would influence Bevin's decisions on other postwar issues. By 1946, Bevin came to the conclusion that the communist Soviets were intent on taking over all of Europe, including Great Britain.

The Potsdam Conference also established a council of foreign ministers to sign a peace treaty with Germany. Bevin hosted the first council meeting in London in September 1945, but it was unproductive. As it turned out, there would be no peace treaty until 1990, after the collapse of communism in Eastern Europe.

Foreign policy

Addressing the growing Soviet threat, Bevin proclaimed economic restoration and the defense of Western Europe as his top priorities. Because the British economy had been severely weakened by World War II, Bevin began trying to shift European defense responsibilities to the United States. The first occasion came in February 1947 when Britain withdrew its longstanding financial support from Greece and Turkey. At the time, the Greek government was fighting a civil war against communist rebel forces. Turkey was under pressure from the Soviets to share its access to the Mediterranean Sea. Bevin approached the United States, asking U.S. leaders to fill the gap left by Britain and to make commitments to European security. President **Harry S. Truman** (1884–1972; served 1945–53; see entry) immediately took up the challenge. The resulting Truman Doctrine, a U.S. pledge to assist governments being threatened by communist expansion or rebellion, came in March.

Bevin next argued for economic aid for Europe in general. The United States responded in July with the Marshall Plan, a massive program of economic aid to Western European countries, including Britain. Bevin helped create the Organization for European Economic Cooperation in April 1948 to coordinate dispersal of U.S. aid under the Marshall Plan.

True to his roots in organized labor, Bevin believed unity was strength, and he applied this belief to foreign affairs. After securing U.S. economic involvement in Europe's postwar reconstruction, Bevin sought a U.S. military commitment to European security. First, Bevin established the Brussels Treaty in March 1948, a defense pact between Britain, France, Belgium, Luxembourg, and the Netherlands. Next, Bevin sought to dramatically expand this alliance; his efforts led to the creation of the North Atlantic Treaty Organization (NATO) in April 1949. NATO included the United States, Canada, and the Western European nations. Thanks in part to Bevin, NATO would bring a long period of peace to the European continent.

Bevin also pursued aggressive steps for Britain itself. He sought to rearm Britain and pursue a program to develop an atomic bomb. When the Soviets blockaded West Berlin in 1948, Bevin had the Royal Air Force take part in the massive airlift led by the United States to supply the shut-out West

Berliners with food and other essentials. Bevin even allowed the United States to station its bombers at a British air base. However, donating large amounts of British food and supplies to Germany via the airlift was not a popular cause among the British population, because they themselves were suffering from shortages. Furthermore, Britain's economic problems were worsened by increased military spending.

Bevin and the East

Despite cooperative efforts such as the airlift, Bevin did not always see eye to eye with the United States on foreign policy issues. For example, under Bevin's guidance, Britain formally recognized the communist People's Republic of China (PRC) in January 1950. Communist forces had waged a long civil war against the Chinese government in the 1930s and 1940s. They finally won in 1949 and established the PRC. The overthrown government leaders fled to the island of Taiwan and established the Republic of China (ROC). Immediately, the United States officially recognized the ROC as the only legitimate government of China; nevertheless, Bevin and Britain stood by the PRC. They did this because the PRC represented most of the Chinese population and President **Chiang Kai-shek** (1887–1975; see entry) had not been popular with the Chinese people. Bevin also believed that differences between the communist Chinese and Soviet Union would eventually surface, and he wanted Britain to be able to take advantage by increasing ties with China further at the time of the split. The United States did not recognize the Communist PRC until 1979.

British foreign minister Ernest Bevin signs a document in his office in 1947. *Reproduced by permission of the Corbis Corporation.*

Bevin did support the U.S. decision to militarily respond to North Korea's invasion of South Korea, which occurred on June 25, 1950. Bevin readily committed British troops to a United Nations military force dominated by the United States. However, Bevin strongly opposed the desire by U.S. general **Douglas MacArthur** (1880–1964; see entry) to invade the PRC, a plan MacArthur announced after successfully pushing the communist North Korean forces back north, all the way to the border with the PRC. In fact, Bevin's protest contributed to MacArthur's dismissal by President Truman. Bevin's commitment of British troops to the Korean War (1950–53) was unpopular with the British public and ultimately led to the end of the Labour Party's control of the British government. The Conservative Party candidate Winston Churchill replaced Clement Attlee as prime minister in the fall of 1951.

With his health failing, Bevin orchestrated one last feat in foreign affairs in 1950. He arranged for a $5 billion aid package to Southeast Asian countries, called the Colombo Plan, to help fend off communist expansion. Bevin resigned on March 9, 1951, his seventieth birthday, and died five weeks later. Though not versed in international relations to begin with, Bevin is regarded as one of the best foreign ministers in British history.

For More Information

Bullock, Alan. *The Life and Times of Ernest Bevin.* 3 vols. London: Heinemann, 1960–83.

Stephens, Mark. *Ernest Bevin: Unskilled Labourer and World Statesman, 1881–1951.* Stevenage, Herts.: SPA Books, 1985.

Weiler, Peter. *Ernest Bevin.* New York: St. Martin's Press, 1993.

Leonid Brezhnev

Born December 19, 1906
Kamenskoye, Ukraine
Died November 10, 1982
Moscow, Russia

General secretary of the Soviet Communist Party

When chosen to succeed **Nikita Khrushchev** (1894–1971; see entry) as the leader of the Soviet Communist Party, Leonid Brezhnev was fifty-eight years old. Says author John L. Keep, in *A History of the Soviet Union, 1945–1991: Last of the Empires,* Brezhnev was "sturdily built, beetle-browed … a cheerful and sociable man who treated others courteously and had considerable charm. There was also a darker, more devious side to his character."

Apparently Brezhnev showed both his tough side and his charm early in his career in the Communist Party. He moved up through the party ranks swiftly while tackling challenging assignments. He would travel to rural areas to impose Soviet rule on peasants and replace local leaders with the Communist Party system. Unfortunately, little is known of this early period of Brezhnev's life. When he was later chosen to succeed Khrushchev, Brezhnev was probably considered by most as a short-term, safe choice. However, Brezhnev proved to be a long-term stabilizing force in the Communist Party. The party bureaucracy would flourish under his eighteen years of steady leadership (1964–82) during the Cold War.

"Whatever else may divide us, Europe is our common home; a common fate has linked us through the centuries, and it continues to link us today."

Leonid Brezhnev. *Reproduced by permission of Getty Images.*

The Cold War was a prolonged conflict between the democratic, capitalist United States and the communist Soviet Union, the world's two superpowers; the battle lasted from 1945 to 1991. The weapons of this conflict were words—propaganda and threats. Communism is a political and economic system in which the Communist Party controls nearly all aspects of citizens' lives. In a communist economy, private ownership of property is banned. This system is not compatible with American political and economic values, in which a capitalist system allows property to be privately owned. Production, distribution, and prices of goods are determined by competition in an open market that operates with relatively little government intervention. A variety of political parties and public elections give citizens a voice in their government.

Coming of age in a communist state

In December 1906, Leonid Ilyich Brezhnev was born to Russian working-class parents in the mining town of Kamenskoye, Ukraine, later renamed Dniprodzerzhyns'k, Ukraine. Little is known of his childhood until 1921. Then, at age fifteen, he began working in the same steel mill as his father, Ilya Brezhnev. Leonid was only eleven years old when the communists gained control of Russia in the Bolshevik Revolution of 1917. In 1922, the Soviet Union was created, and Brezhnev joined the Young Communist League, known as Komsomol. This membership allowed him to enter a technical school. His studies qualified him as a land surveyor, and beginning in 1927 he held several rural public administrative jobs in the Kursk and Ural regions of the Soviet Union. By 1931, he returned home and began studies at the Dniprodzerzhyns'k Metallurgical Institute. That same year, he joined the Communist Party and married Viktoria Petrovna, a nurse. After graduating in 1935, Brezhnev became an engineer and worked in the Dniprodzerzhyns'k steel mill for two years.

Under the communist regime of Soviet premier **Joseph Stalin** (1879–1953; see entry), Brezhnev's career in the Communist Party flourished. Brezhnev's role in Stalin's Great Terror, which lasted from 1936 to 1938, is not known, but during that period Stalin purged many party leaders. Millions of citizens and leaders were executed or imprisoned. Stalin allowed young communists like Brezhnev to replace those who were purged. Brezhnev held several local positions and brought Soviet rule to various rural regions; in 1937, he was elected deputy mayor of Dniprodzerzhyns'k.

In 1938, Nikita Khrushchev, the future leader of the Soviet Union, became first secretary of the Ukrainian Communist Party, and Brezhnev became one of his close associates. Brezhnev built friendships and political alliances quite easily. By 1939, he was secretary (leader) of the regional Communist Party organization in Dniprodzerzhyns'k. After Germany's invasion of the Soviet Union in June 1941 during World War II (1939–45), Brezhnev served in the Soviet military. He was a political officer in charge of recruiting soldiers into the Communist Party and maintaining morale among troops. Toward the end of the war, Brezhnev played a role in the Sovietization of Czechoslovakia and Romania. Sovietization was the practice of bringing a region under Soviet control by taking over ownership of factories and farmlands and establishing a ruling Communist Party structure. In 1946, Brezhnev left the military with the rank of major general.

Establishing his party standing

When Brezhnev returned to the Ukraine from the military, Khrushchev made him first secretary of a regional Communist Party committee. In this important position, Brezhnev oversaw reconstruction of industry in a region devastated by the war. Brezhnev's success in this job brought him personal acclaim. By November 1947, he became first secretary of a larger district, his home district of Dniprodzerzhyns'k. He also gained membership to the Central Committee of the Ukrainian Communist Party. The Central Committee was an important administrative body overseeing day-to-day party activities.

In 1950, Brezhnev moved with Khrushchev to Moscow to work on the Central Committee of the Soviet Communist Party. Soon, Khrushchev appointed him first secretary of the Central Committee in the Soviet republic of Moldavia. Brezhnev was to complete the Sovietization of that country by changing private farmland into community-owned farmland and strengthening the Communist Party. Party membership in the region greatly increased because of Brezhnev's efforts.

While he was in Moldavia, Brezhnev formed a strong working relationship with another future Soviet leader, Konstantin Chernenko (1911–1985).

In 1952, because of his connection to Khrushchev and his own success in promoting the communist cause, Brezhnev was elected to membership in the Soviet Central Committee and the Presidium of the Supreme Soviet. The Presidium was the executive body and center of power in the Soviet Communist Party; it sets party policies. When Stalin died in 1953, however, Brezhnev, a longtime Stalin supporter, temporarily lost his lofty seats. He was demoted to a position in the ministry of defense and was in charge of the political aspects of the Soviet navy.

Rise in prominence

Brezhnev's fortunes would shift again when Khrushchev became first secretary of the Soviet Communist Party. He appointed Brezhnev second secretary of the Kazakhstan Communist Party; Kazakhstan was the second largest republic in the Soviet Union. In Kazakhstan, Khrushchev placed Brezhnev in charge of the ambitious Virgin Land program, an effort to convert a vast amount of unused land, some 90 million acres, into grain production. Brezhnev would become first secretary of the Kazakhstan Central Committee in August 1954 after purging the previous first secretary and his supporters.

After some success on the Virgin Land project, which produced a record grain harvest of 33 million tons (30 million metric tons) in 1956, Brezhnev returned to the inner power circles of Moscow, where he would remain the rest of his life. He rose to secretary of the Soviet Central Committee in February 1956 and became a member of the Presidium again in July 1957. In 1960, Brezhnev became the head of state as chairman of the Presidium of the Supreme Soviet. In this position, he became involved in foreign affairs, though Khrushchev remained in charge as general secretary of the Central Committee. By June 1963, Brezhnev resigned from his Presidium position to be second secretary of the Central Committee. He served as Khrushchev's assistant in the day-to-day operations of the Soviet Communist Party. At this point, many considered him the eventual successor to Khrushchev.

An Aging Soviet Leadership

Toward the end of Leonid Brezhnev's long term as the leader of the Soviet Union, the Soviet Communist Party leadership was aging and losing touch with a changing world. Like Brezhnev, many Soviet leaders were in their early youth at the time of the Bolshevik Revolution in 1917, when communists first gained control of the Russian government. They were educated in the new communist education system and joined the Communist Party in the 1930s. After Joseph Stalin's purge of many party leaders during the Great Terror (1936–38), the most promising of this younger generation of communists rose up through the ranks to lead the Communist Party.

Not long after World War II, Brezhnev met Konstantin Chernenko while they were both serving the Communist Party in Moldavia. Chernenko was born to a Russian peasant farming family. Like Brezhnev, he joined the Communist Party in 1931, serving in various propaganda positions, including the one in Moldavia, which began in 1948. (Propaganda is information and ideas that are spread to support a cause.) In 1956, Brezhnev brought Chernenko to Moscow to work for the party's Central Committee. When Brezhnev became leader of the Soviet Union in 1964, he made Chernenko his chief of staff. Chernenko traveled extensively with Brezhnev and was considered by many to be Brezhnev's eventual successor.

However, when Brezhnev died in November 1982, another conservative party leader, Yuri Andropov (1914–1984), was chosen as Soviet leader. Andropov had been an organizer for Komsomol, the Young Communist League, through the 1930s and 1940s until he was brought to Moscow as a promising young leader. Under Brezhnev, Andropov headed the Committee on State Security (KGB) from 1967 to 1982. He replaced Brezhnev as leader of the Soviet Union in 1983. However, Andropov's health declined sharply, and he died only fifteen months later. Andropov was replaced by Chernenko, who would be leader for only one year before he died. Following Chernenko's death, a much younger and more dynamic party leader, **Mikhail Gorbachev** (1931–; see entry) would take over and try to revitalize Soviet society, which had stagnated under the leadership of Brezhnev, Andropov, and Chernenko.

Soviet leadership

By the fall of 1964, Brezhnev's relationship with Khrushchev would dramatically change. On October 14, 1964, Brezhnev helped lead a bloodless coup against Khrushchev, his longtime mentor. (*Coup* is short for coup d'état. Usually carried out by a small group, a coup is an overthrow of an existing leader or government. Sometimes a coup can turn violent.) Other Communist Party leaders were tired of Khrushchev's increasingly independent behavior and unpredictable shifts in policies. They wanted more stability and predictability. They would find that in Brezhnev, who succeeded his former friend as Soviet leader. Whereas Khrushchev was bold and impulsive, Brezhnev was cautious and patient. A collective leadership structure was put in place so power would be shared among a small group of leaders.

Brezhnev became first secretary of the Central Committee, the most powerful of all the positions. **Aleksey Kosygin** (1904–1980; see entry) became chairman of the Council of Ministers. The Council of Ministers controlled Soviet economic and cultural life. By December 1966, Nikolay Podgorny (1903–1983) was named head of state in charge of foreign affairs. Brezhnev was in charge of Communist Party activities; Kosygin was responsible for economic planning; and Podgorny headed foreign affairs. By March 1966, Brezhnev had gained greater dominance, becoming general secretary of the Communist Party. Under Brezhnev's conservative leadership, the vast Soviet bureaucracy gained strength.

Brezhnev brought changes to the Soviet Union. He stopped public attacks on Stalin and his policies, attacks that Khrushchev had begun in 1956. Brezhnev also sought to boost Soviet agricultural productivity. However, with the Communist Party tightly controlling the agricultural industry, progress was limited. Under Brezhnev, the secret police, or KGB, rose in power again after a decline under Khrushchev. Khrushchev had opposed the Stalin regime of force and terror by the secret police; Khrushchev related to the peasants (having been one himself) and thus supported domestic improvements, such as agricultural reforms, that would help the common person. Brezhnev returned the secret police to power to maintain control, but without Stalin's terror. The Soviets again more forcibly repressed dissidents, individuals who disagree with the ideas of those in power. Many prominent writers and artists were deported, exiled, or sent to labor camps and psychiatric wards. The hard-line communists believed the traditional party bureaucracy was being threatened by Khrushchev's reforms; they also felt that too much freedom of expression was creeping into the communist system under Khrushchev, so they tightened controls on behavior and ended the rather mild reforms.

During his rule, Brezhnev and his family continued living modestly, occupying a five-room apartment. However, he did have an affection for luxury cars and owned one of the few Rolls-Royce automobiles in the Soviet Union. Other world leaders would give him luxury cars as gifts. Another affection of Brezhnev's was tobacco, which would contribute to severe health problems later.

One of Brezhnev's key goals was to reach nuclear parity (equal strength in nuclear arms) with the United States by 1970. Through a massive and expensive missile production program, he accomplished this goal. Brezhnev also built a huge navy and maintained the largest army in the world. In addition, the Soviet space program overtook the United States in reaching space exploration goals.

Expanding world influence

Brezhnev became more directly involved in foreign affairs in 1968, when Czechoslovakian leader Alexander Dubcek (1921–1992) proposed giving greater freedoms to Czech citizens, including freedom of the press. Brezhnev approved the use of military force to crush the reform movement and remove Dubcek from office. Brezhnev then unveiled what became known as the Brezhnev Doctrine, stating that the Soviets would intervene in any country where threats to communist rule could threaten other communist countries as well. The Soviets would use this doctrine to justify military intervention in the internal politics of other communist countries under Soviet influence.

Brezhnev also became involved in dealing with China, West Germany, and the United States. Brezhnev had to deal with growing friction between the Soviets and the Chinese communists who controlled the People's Republic of China (PRC). Military skirmishes occurred near the long border between the two countries. Because the PRC's relations with the United States were improving, Brezhnev worried that those two countries might form an alliance against the Soviets. Recognizing the need for strong neighboring allies, Brezhnev sought to ease tensions on the Soviet Union's western border. He wanted to normalize relations between West Germany and the Warsaw Pact. The Warsaw Pact was a de-

Soviet leader Leonid Brezhnev (left) meets with U.S. president Richard Nixon in the Oval Office in June 1973. *Photograph by Wally McNamee. Reproduced by permission of the Corbis Corporation.*

fense alliance composed of Eastern European countries under Soviet control. In 1970 and 1971, Brezhnev built a warm relationship with West German chancellor Willy Brandt (1913–1992; see box in **Konrad Adenauer** entry).

In the early 1970s, efforts at détente (the easing of tensions) with the West brought Brezhnev even more into international relations. Through détente, Brezhnev wanted to curb the arms race and gain access to Western technology that he desperately needed for Soviet industry and agriculture. Once Brezhnev had achieved nuclear parity, he was willing to enter arms control talks. He was eager to cut back military spending to help raise the standard of living in the Soviet Union.

Arms control talks progressed, and in May 1972, Brezhnev hosted U.S. president **Richard M. Nixon** (1913–1994; served 1969–74; see entry) in Moscow for the signing of the Strategic Arms Limitation Treaty, SALT I. This treaty froze production of certain nuclear weapon systems.

Other meetings followed: Brezhnev traveled to Washington, D.C., in June 1973; Nixon again went to Moscow in July 1974; and President Gerald R. Ford (1913–; served 1974–77) went to the Soviet city of Vladivostok in November 1974.

The Helsinki Accords, signed in August 1975, represented the high point of détente. This agreement recognized the postwar territorial boundaries of the European nations. The Soviets had long sought recognition of the political boundaries of Eastern European communist countries and finally achieved it in Helsinki, and again more formally in the treaty ending World War II in 1991. In 1979, Brezhnev would meet with President **Jimmy Carter** (1924–; served 1977–81; see entry) in Vienna, Austria, to sign SALT II, a new Strategic Arms Limitation Treaty. By the mid-1970s, Brezhnev's prestige had substantially risen, and so had the Soviet Union's. In 1976, Brezhnev became marshal of the Soviet Union, the only party leader aside from Stalin to achieve that military rank. In May 1977, Brezhnev became the first Soviet party

U.S. president Gerald Ford (left) meets Soviet leader Leonid Brezhnev for the first time, in the Soviet city of Vladivostok in November 1974. *Reproduced by permission of the Corbis Corporation.*

leader to also be head of state, replacing Podgorny as chairman of the Presidium of the Supreme Soviet.

During the 1970s, Brezhnev also pressed for more Soviet support of national liberation movements and greater support of left-wing governments in Third World countries. Left-wing groups are politically radical elements often seeking change from traditional forms of rule. Third World refers to poor underdeveloped or economically developing nations in Africa, Asia, and Latin America. Many of these countries were seeking independence from the political control of Western European nations. Brezhnev believed such radical movements, as opposed to the traditional oppressive military dictatorships, opened the door for adopting alternative forms of government such as communism. The Soviets' support included that of North Vietnam during the Vietnam War (1954–75). Brezhnev also used his influence to help Nixon negotiate a peace treaty with the North Vietnamese to end the war. He believed this would lead to U.S. public opinion support for signing the SALT I arms agreement. In the Middle East, the Soviets supported Egypt and Syria in a 1973 war with Israel, leading to a direct confrontation with the United States. (The United States, through its strong pro-Israel lobby within the United States itself, provided substantial economic support to Israel.) The Soviets would continue supporting Syria and the Palestine Liberation Organization (PLO) in the Middle East. Brezhnev also supported communist rebels in 1974 in Angola. He provided equipment, Soviet military advisors, and twenty thousand Cuban troops. The rebel forces successfully overthrew the government. In 1977, Brezhnev provided similar support to the Ethiopian government so it could repel attacks by neighboring Somalia, a U.S. ally.

Growing problems in later years

By the end of the 1970s, problems were building for Brezhnev. In 1979, he approved the Soviet invasion of Afghanistan. The Soviets were seeking to support an unpopular communist government against an Islamic movement trying to seize power. The war would drag on for ten years and cost thousands of Soviet lives. The Soviet invasion angered President Carter, and U.S.-Soviet relations cooled. The arrival of President **Ronald Reagan** (1911– ; served 1981–89; see entry) in the White House in January 1981 would lead to even cooler relations. Reagan greatly boosted the U.S. military budget, accelerating the arms race and forcing Brezhnev to increase his military spending in order to keep up. In December 1981, Brezhnev made another move unpopular with the West when he supported the Polish government's suppression of the Solidarity workers union. (The government had officially banned Solidarity as martial law was imposed on Polish citizens.) The union, which represented a strong challenge to communist control, was protesting the rise in food prices and challenging communist authority in Poland.

On the home front, the dramatic arms buildup through the 1960s and 1970s and Soviet military adventures in Third World countries had taken money away from other sectors of the Soviet economy. As a result, agriculture, industrial production of nonwar consumer goods, and health care services declined sharply. Shortages of goods became worse, and the Soviet standard of living declined. Soviet morale sank as lines of people seeking basic necessities grew longer outside Soviet stores. The decline in morale would cause worker production to drop further, in a vicious downward spiral. Widespread rumors of corruption in Brezhnev's government lowered morale even further. Meanwhile, Brezhnev kept tight control of the growing number of Soviet dissidents criticizing communist rule.

By 1982, Brezhnev's health was visibly failing. He had suffered a heart attack in 1974 and was suffering from leukemia (a blood disease) and emphysema (a respiratory disease) by the early 1980s. His public appearances dwindled. Despite increasing feebleness, he stayed in power until his death in November 1982. Brezhnev had led the Soviet Communist Party longer than anyone else would—eighteen years.

For More Information

Books

Breslauer, George W. *Khrushchev and Brezhnev as Leaders: Building Authority in Soviet Politics.* Boston: Allen and Unwin, 1982.

Brezhnev, Leonid I. *Memoirs.* New York: Pergamon Press, 1982.

Dornberg, John. *Brezhnev: Masks of Power.* New York: Basic Books, 1974.

Edmonds, Robin. *Soviet Foreign Policy: The Brezhnev Years.* New York: Oxford University Press, 1983.

Gelman, Harry. *The Brezhnev Politburo and the Decline of Detente.* Ithaca, NY: Cornell University Press, 1984.

Keep, John L. H. *Last of the Empires: A History of the Soviet Union, 1945–1991.* New York: Oxford University Press, 1995.

McNeal, Robert H. *The Bolshevik Tradition: Lenin, Stalin, Khrushchev, Brezhnev.* 2nd ed. Englewood Cliffs, NJ: Prentice-Hall, 1975.

Volkogonov, Dimitri A. *Autopsy for an Empire: The Seven Leaders Who Built the Soviet Regime.* New York: Free Press, 1998.

Web Sites

The Cold War Museum. http://www.coldwar.org (accessed on August 21, 2003).

Jimmy Carter Library and Museum. http://www.jimmycarterlibrary.org (accessed on August 21, 2003).

George Bush

Born June 12, 1924
Milton, Massachusetts

U.S. president, vice president, and CIA director

G eorge Bush was president of the United States as the Cold War came to an end. The Cold War was an intense political and economic rivalry between the United States and the Soviet Union that lasted from 1945 to 1991. In the final years of the Cold War, the world was dramatically changing. Eastern European countries were throwing out their Soviet-controlled communist governments. The Berlin Wall, dividing East and West Berlin, came down, and East and West Germany became one united country. And, stunningly, the Soviet empire collapsed. New independent nations and governments appeared.

"This is America ... a brilliant diversity spread like stars. Like a thousand points of light in a broad and peaceful sky."

Education and war

George Herbert Walker Bush was born to Prescott Bush and Dorothy Walker on June 12, 1924, in Milton, Massachusetts. His father was a prominent Wall Street investment banker and served as U.S. senator from Connecticut from 1952 to 1963. His mother was the daughter of a leading Wall Street banker located in St. Louis, Missouri. George grew up in

George Bush. *Courtesy of the Library of Congress.*

affluent Greenwich, Connecticut, and attended the top private schools, including the Phillips Academy preparatory school in Andover, Massachusetts.

Bush graduated from Phillips in 1942, while World War II (1939–45) was still raging. He joined the U.S. Naval Reserve on his eighteenth birthday and became the youngest naval pilot at the time to complete his training. Bush was a torpedo bomber pilot on aircraft carriers in the Pacific Ocean from 1943 to 1945. He flew fifty-eight combat missions and was shot down twice by the Japanese; once, he was rescued by a U.S. submarine. For bravery in action, he received the Distinguished Flying Cross.

Upon returning from the war, Bush entered Yale University, where he excelled as a student and was captain of the baseball team. While he was still a student, he married Barbara Pierce in January 1945. They would have six children, but one died at the age of three from leukemia. Bush graduated with honors with a degree in economics in 1948.

Texas oil and politics

Rather than following in his father's footsteps, Bush and his family moved to Odessa in west Texas. There, he entered the oil industry business with the help of a family friend. In 1951, Bush established his own company, the Bush-Overbey Oil Development Company; then he founded the Zapata Petroleum Corporation in 1953 and the Zapata Off-Shore Company in 1954.

In 1958, Bush shifted his company's corporate headquarters to the city of Houston, where he became active in the Republican Party. In 1964, he ran for a U.S. Senate seat as part of the newly forming conservative right led by the Republican presidential candidate at the time, Barry Goldwater (1909–1998). This part of the Republican Party opposed civil rights legislation and domestic spending on social programs; it supported U.S. withdrawal from the United Nations (UN) and major cuts in foreign aid. Like Goldwater, Bush was soundly defeated. In 1966, he entered the race for a seat in the U.S. House of Representatives; this time he won. Bush swayed back and forth between conservative and moderate positions on social and economic issues. Then in 1970, he left his seat to run for the Senate again, only to lose once more. He would not run for public office again until 1980.

Public service

During the 1970s, Bush served in various government positions. In February 1971, U.S. president **Richard M. Nixon** (1913–1994; served 1969–74; see entry) appointed Bush to serve as U.S. ambassador to the UN, where Bush became a highly respected representative. In December 1972, Bush left the UN post to become chairman of the Republican National Committee. By early 1973, Nixon and members of his administration became engulfed in the Watergate scandal, which involved the 1972 burglary of the Democratic National Committee offices and a coverup that followed. During this time, Bush sought to minimize the effect of the scandal on the Republican Party. He supported Nixon until August 1974, when he joined others who were calling for Nixon to resign. Nixon resigned on August 9. Vice President Gerald R. Ford (1913–; served 1974–77) was sworn in as the new president. Bush hoped to be selected as Ford's vice president, but Ford chose former New York governor Nelson A. Rockefeller (1908–1979) instead. Ford then appointed Bush as head of the U.S. Liaison Office in Communist China. There Bush served as the top U.S. representative to China for the next two years.

Bush returned to the United States in 1976 to become director of the Central Intelligence Agency (CIA). He was only in that position for a short time before Democrat **Jimmy Carter** (1924–; served 1977–81; see entry) became the next president in January 1977. Bush resigned from the CIA and returned briefly to a private life in Texas as chairman of the First National Bank of Houston.

To Washington, D.C.

In 1979, Bush announced he would seek the Republican nomination for president the following year. However, he was unable to match the popularity of **Ronald Reagan** (1911–; served 1981–89; see entry). When Reagan won the party's nomination in the summer of 1980, he chose Bush as his vice presidential running mate. Reagan handily defeated the incumbent, or current office holder, Jimmy Carter, in the national election that fall, and easily won reelection in 1984. Bush served as vice president for the full eight years of Reagan's presidency.

As vice president, Bush traveled over one million miles to represent the United States at various functions. During his second term of office, a major scandal known as the Iran-Contra Affair erupted. Members of the Reagan administration were illegally selling weapons to Iran in exchange for U.S. hostages held by pro-Iranian rebels in Lebanon. Reagan's representatives were using part of the money from the illegal arms sales to illegally fund contra rebels fighting to overthrow the procommunist Nicaraguan government in Latin America. The United States under Reagan and Bush provided funds to an anticommunist group in Nicaragua known as the contras (short for the Spanish word meaning "counterrevolutionaries"). Bush and Reagan both denied knowledge of these covert, or secret, activities. Several officials were charged and convicted.

In 1988, Bush succeeded in gaining the Republican Party's presidential nomination and won the national election over the Democratic candidate, Massachusetts governor Michael Dukakis (1933–). The national economy was doing well at the time, so President Bush was able to pursue foreign affairs, his preferred focus, rather than dealing as closely with domestic issues.

Cold War ends

By 1989, when Bush took office as U.S. president, the Soviet empire was crumbling. **Mikhail Gorbachev** (1931–; see entry) had become leader of the Soviet Union in 1985. Inheriting a nation in economic disarray, Gorbachev introduced major reforms (perestroika) and greater freedom of expression (glasnost). To achieve sufficient economic stability, Gorbachev had to significantly cut Soviet defense spending. This meant ending the Cold War arms race. Between 1985 and 1988, Gorbachev and President Reagan worked together to dramatically change U.S.-Soviet relations. The two leaders agreed to major cuts in long-range nuclear weapons and eliminated intermediate-range nuclear weapons from Europe.

In December 1988, only a month after Bush won the presidential election, Gorbachev gave a historic speech at the UN. He announced that it was possible for the two superpowers to peacefully coexist and that the Soviets would withdraw five hundred thousand troops and thousands of heavy conventional weapons from Eastern Europe. The announcement stunned the world. A memorable photograph was taken of Reagan, Gorbachev, and President-elect Bush with the Statue of Liberty in the background.

When Bush took office in January 1989, he was hesitant to cooperate as fully with Gorbachev as Reagan had been. He believed Reagan had gone too far too fast in his talks with the Soviet leader. Bush decided to slow down arms control negotiations. In early 1989, however, Bush's secretary of state, James Baker (1930–), established a close working relationship with Soviet foreign minister **Eduard Shevardnadze** (1928–; see entry) through a series of meetings. Soon, events would show Bush that the speed in the changes that were occurring was legitimate.

By the fall of 1989, various Eastern European countries that had been under Soviet communist domination since the end of World War II threw out their communist governments and adopted noncommunist government systems. For the first time, the Soviets did not militarily intervene to save the communist governments. In November 1989, the Berlin Wall—the most striking image of the Cold War—was dismantled and came tumbling down. The stark concrete-and-barbed-wire wall had been built in 1961 between East and West Berlin to keep East Germans living under communist rule from fleeing into West Berlin, which was controlled by the democratic Western powers.

In 1990, the Soviet republics began demanding independence. The Baltic States—Estonia, Latvia, and Lithuania—were the first to break from the Soviet Union. Bush by now had concluded that it was in the best interests of the United States to support Gorbachev in his reforms; otherwise, Gorbachev might lose power, and communist hard-liners could retake the Soviet government. Bush and Gorbachev met on a ship near the European island nation of Malta in the Mediterranean Sea to discuss how to deal with the collapsing Soviet Union; their goal was to avoid political chaos and bloodshed during the transitional time.

In July 1990, Gorbachev agreed to allow Germany to reunify and join the North Atlantic Treaty Organization (NATO) if it desired to. NATO had been a peacetime alliance of the United States and eleven other nations, and a key factor in the attempt to contain communism. Gorbachev also announced that all Soviet troops would be withdrawn from East Germany. West German chancellor **Helmut Kohl** (1930–; see entry) agreed to pay the cost of Soviet troop withdrawal and provide some economic aid to the Soviets. Germany had been split into communist East Germany and democratic West Germany since the end of World War II. By early October 1990, Germany was reunified. In November 1990, Bush met with Gorbachev in Paris, France, to sign a mutual nonaggression pact reducing conventional forces in Europe. This agreement marked the end of the Cold War. In July 1991, they met again, this time in Moscow, where they signed arms control treaties significantly reducing the number of long-range nuclear weapons that the two nations had stockpiled through the years; they also agreed to reduce the number of weapons with multiple nuclear warheads.

In August 1991, Bush traveled to the Ukraine and announced his support for Gorbachev's reforms. He cautioned the Ukrainian people against violent confrontations with the Soviets. Nevertheless, that same month, a group of communist hard-liners attempted to overthrow Gorbachev and reverse his reforms. However, Boris Yeltsin (1931–), president of the new Russian Federation, blocked this attempt, with much public support. Though Gorbachev continued in office, it was now clear he had little power left. The Soviet Union was at an end. Gorbachev resigned as president of the Soviet Union on December 25, 1991, and the Soviet Union ceased to exist. Gorbachev turned control of the Soviet nuclear arsenal, or collection of weapons, over to Yeltsin. Yeltsin was now the most powerful leader in the region.

Bush opened U.S. embassies in the newly independent countries that were no longer part of the Soviet Union. Yeltsin pleaded for U.S. economic aid to help rebuild the Russian economy and introduce a free market system, or economic conditions dictated by open competition. However, the United States was facing huge budget deficits, so there was little public support for Bush to assist the struggling Russian state. The United States did provide some aid, but it was

primarily for humanitarian needs and to help dismantle the nuclear weapons the Soviets had agreed to give up.

Panama and the Persian Gulf War

President Bush also became involved in foreign matters outside Europe and the Soviet Union. In 1989, he ordered a military invasion of Panama to overthrow the corrupt regime of General Manuel Noriega (1934–). Noriega had gained a reputation for brutality and was known to support illegal drug trade; the Bush administration believed Noriega threatened the security of the Panama Canal. The canal was built in 1903 by the United States to improve transportation between the east and west coasts of the United States. At the time, the United States still retained control over the canal and an area surrounding it known as the Canal Zone, though a treaty signed in 1977 by President Carter would give Panama control over the zone beginning on December 31, 1999. The U.S. invasion

U.S. president George Bush (left) signs the Strategic Arms Reduction Talks (START II) Treaty with Russian president Boris Yeltsin. *Photograph by Gennady Galperin. Reproduced by permission of the Corbis Corporation.*

of Panama led to four days of fighting and hundreds of deaths. The Organization of American States, an alliance of Latin American and North American countries dedicated to peacefully resolving conflicts, denounced Bush for the invasion, as did the United Nations General Assembly.

In August 1990, the Middle Eastern country of Iraq invaded and occupied the neighboring nation of Kuwait. Bush first imposed UN-approved trade restrictions on Iraq to force its withdrawal from Kuwait. Bush also sent U.S. forces to Saudi Arabia to protect that nation from possible invasion. When Iraq refused to pull back from Kuwait, Bush pulled together a broad coalition of forces from Western Europe and some Arab states to launch a military campaign against Iraq. The number of U.S. troops in the Persian Gulf region grew to five hundred thousand. The United States launched an air attack on Iraq in January 1991, which was followed by an Allied ground assault, known as Desert Storm, in late February. Iraq's armies were destroyed, and Kuwait was liberated. Bush's approval rating soared to over 90 percent.

A steep decline in popularity

On the domestic front, the U.S. economy had entered a recession, or reduced economic activity, in late 1990, and the economic lull continued into the 1992 election year. Bush's popularity began to slide as he failed to publicly address economic issues. In addition, shortly before the election, a new investigation was released indicating that Bush and Reagan had known more about the Iran-Contra Affair than they had previously admitted. In the fall of 1992, Bush's Democratic challenger, Arkansas governor Bill Clinton (1946–; served 1993–2001), defeated Bush in his reelection bid.

Controversy continued to plague the Bush administration in its final weeks after the election. During this time, Bush sent U.S. troops to Somalia on a mission to feed starving citizens caught in a civil war. However, the marines were caught between the fighting factions, and eighteen U.S. soldiers died. Bush also issued pardons to six former Reagan administration officials, including Secretary of Defense Caspar Weinberger (1917–), who were facing charges in the Iran-Contra Affair.

A quiet retirement

After leaving office in January 1993, Bush returned to Houston, Texas. He maintained little involvement in the Republican Party. Two of his sons carried on the family tradition of public service. His oldest son, George W. Bush (1946–), won election as governor of Texas in 1994 and served for nearly two terms. Another son, Jeb Bush (1953–), became governor of Florida in 1998. In 2000, George W. Bush defeated his Democratic opponent, Vice President Al Gore (1948–), in an exceptionally close presidential election. The Bush family was once again in the White House.

The senior George Bush published an autobiography in 1987 titled *Looking Forward.* In 1998, he coauthored another book, *A World Transformed,* describing world changes through his presidency and afterwards. His wife, Barbara Bush (1925–), published her own memoirs in 1994. In honor of the elder George Bush, the George Bush Presidential Library and Museum was dedicated in November 1997. It is located on the campus of Texas A&M University in College Station, Texas, near Houston.

For More Information

Books

Beschloss, Michael R., and Strobe Talbott. *At the Highest Levels: The Inside Story of the End of the Cold War.* Boston: Little, Brown, 1994.

Bush, Barbara. *Barbara Bush: A Memoir.* New York: Scribner's Sons, 1994.

Bush, George. *Looking Forward.* Garden City, NY: Doubleday, 1987.

Bush, George, and Brent Scowcroft. *A World Transformed.* New York: Knopf, 1998.

Greene, John R. *The Presidency of George Bush.* Lawrence: University Press of Kansas, 2000.

Hurst, Steven. *The Foreign Policy of the Bush Administration: In Search of a New World Order.* New York: Cassell, 1999.

Parmet, Herbert S. *George Bush: The Life of a Lone Star Yankee.* New York: Scribner, 1997.

Web Site

George Bush Presidential Library and Museum. http://bushlibrary.tamu.edu (accessed on August 22, 2003).

James F. Byrnes

Born May 2, 1879
Charleston, South Carolina
Died April 9, 1972
Columbia, South Carolina

U.S. secretary of state, senator,
Supreme Court justice, governor

"Too many people are thinking of security instead of opportunity. They seem more afraid of life than death."

James F. Byrnes. *Reproduced by permission of Getty Images.*

James F. Byrnes was the first American to serve as a U.S. congressman, U.S. senator, Supreme Court justice, secretary of state, and governor. In the early 1940s, he was sometimes called the "assistant president," but by the late 1940s he was a forgotten man in federal government.

Byrnes was at the side of Presidents Franklin D. Roosevelt (1882–1945; served 1933–45) and **Harry S. Truman** (1884–1972; served 1945–53; see entry) as the Cold War was taking shape. The Cold War was an intense political and economic rivalry between the democratic United States and the communist Soviet Union that lasted from 1945 to 1991. Byrnes strove hard to establish a friendship between the Soviet Union and the United States as World War II (1939–45) drew to a close, but he was overcome by the Soviets' aggressive efforts to expand their influence and, as noted in David Robertson's *Sly and Able: A Political Biography of James F. Byrnes,* Truman's frustration over what he viewed as "disastrous compromises." As a result, Byrnes lost influence in the United States and faded from national prominence, but resurfaced as governor of South Carolina.

A self-made man

James Francis Byrnes was born to Irish immigrants in May 1879 in Charleston, South Carolina. His father, for whom he was named, died of tuberculosis, a respiratory disease, only weeks before James was born. His mother, Elizabeth McSweeney Byrnes, was a dressmaker who worked hard to provide for her family. Though his family was needy at times, young James was never deprived. Byrnes attended Catholic school until age fourteen, when he left to become a messenger for a law office. He needed to take this job to help support the family. By age twenty-one, he had become a circuit court stenographer (a type of note taker) in Aiken, South Carolina. Under the fatherly guidance of two judges, Byrnes studied law and successfully passed the South Carolina bar exam three years later in 1903. In 1906, he married Maude Perkins Busch of Aiken. They did not have children. Known by friends as Jimmy, Byrnes won his first public office in 1908, becoming a public prosecutor. In 1911, in a very close race, he won a seat in the U.S. House of Representatives as a Democratic candidate. He served in the House until 1924.

Byrnes was short and thin; he lived modestly but dressed well. Other congressmen considered him tireless and shrewd in diplomacy. He was always thought of as highly ambitious. Byrnes held some extreme personal and political views: He was a white supremacist, one who believes that people of color are naturally inferior to whites. He also actively opposed an antilynching bill in Congress. (Lynching is execution-style murder—often by hanging—carried out by a mob. Lynchings of black Americans frequently occurred in the South.) Despite his vote against antilynching legislation, Byrnes said he opposed the violent tactics of the Ku Klux Klan, a militant white supremacy group that had a large membership in South Carolina. Byrnes was also against women's suffrage, or the right to vote.

While in Congress, Byrnes showed unusual skill in bringing people together to reach compromises and pass legislation. He supported the creation of the federal highway system and became a member of the important House Appropriations Committee after reelection in 1912. Byrnes steadily moved up in prestige in the House and, while working on naval funding, formed a friendship with future president Franklin D. Roosevelt, who was assistant secretary of the navy at the time. In 1924, Byrnes decided to run for the U.S. Senate but lost the Democratic nomination to a longstanding popular figure, Coleman L. Blease (1868–1942). Out of public office, Byrnes moved to Spartanburg, South Carolina, where he practiced law for six years and remained active in civic affairs.

Senator, justice, and administrator

Beginning in 1930, the economic downturn of the Great Depression (1929–41), which began when the stock market crashed in 1929, hit South Carolina hard. People were looking for new leaders. With the backing of wealthy financier and fellow South Carolinian Bernard Baruch (1870–1965), Byrnes won election to the U.S. Senate in 1930 by a slim margin. Byrnes quickly moved up in the Senate to a position of great power. He campaigned hard for Franklin Roosevelt in the 1932 presidential election. Once in office, Roosevelt used Byrnes as a key Democratic Senate leader and assigned him to various important committees so Byrnes could push New Deal legislation through Congress. The New Deal was Roosevelt's program of economic and social relief and reform designed to ease the painful effects of the Depression on the nation. Like Roosevelt, Byrnes easily won reelection in 1936. He greatly desired to be Roosevelt's running mate in the 1940 presidential election but lost out when Roosevelt selected Secretary of Agriculture Henry A. Wallace (1888–1965) instead. In June 1941, President Roosevelt appointed Byrnes to a different lofty position: justice of the U.S. Supreme Court.

Byrnes would sit on the Supreme Court for only sixteen months before he became restless. He wanted to become more involved in the growing home front effort during World War II. Roosevelt responded by appointing Byrnes as director of economic stabilization. He was to control the domestic economy, especially by keeping prices of goods down, during the war. Byrnes was highly successful in this important role, so in May 1943 Roosevelt expanded Byrnes's responsibilities. The president appointed him chairman of the War Mobilization Board for coordinating all war agencies and federal departments. From his office in the White House, Byrnes was now fully in charge of the domestic economy, allowing Roosevelt to concentrate on the war effort. Some people referred to Byrnes as the "assistant president." However, in 1944, he was again passed over as Roosevelt's running mate; the Democratic Party selected U.S. senator Harry S. Truman of Missouri instead.

Cold War negotiator

In 1945, Byrnes began applying his strong negotiating skills to foreign relations. In February, he accompanied President Roosevelt to the Yalta Conference in the Soviet Union. There they met with Soviet premier **Joseph Stalin** (1879–1953; see entry) and British prime minister **Winston Churchill** (1874–1965; see entry). During the conference, Byrnes had lunch each day with Roosevelt and took detailed notes, reminiscent of his court stenographer days. Following Roosevelt's sudden death from a cerebral hemorrhage (bleeding in the brain) just two months later, Vice President Truman became president; Byrnes organized Roosevelt's funeral. Upon becoming president, Truman immediately called on Byrnes and his Yalta notes. Truman wanted to study Roosevelt's thoughts and postwar plans so he could make decisions consistent with those plans; he also wanted to follow through on private commitments Roosevelt made at Yalta.

Byrnes was a central figure in the developing rivalry between the United States and the Soviet Union, a rivalry that eventually came to be called the Cold War. He was confident that he had the necessary negotiating skills to establish a productive relationship with the Soviets. He traveled with President Truman to the next meeting of the Big Three leaders, at Potsdam, Germany, in June 1945. (The Big Three refers to the United States, Great Britain, and the Soviet Union; the Big Three also referred to those nations' leaders: Truman, Churchill, and Stalin.) For the rest of 1945, Byrnes served as the key U.S. representative at various high-level meetings, including the London Conference of Foreign Ministers in September, a December meeting in Moscow with the Soviet and British foreign ministers, and the United Nations (UN) organizational meeting.

In the December meeting in Moscow, Byrnes made an all-out attempt to establish friendly relations with the Soviets. Byrnes made several deals regarding international control of atomic energy and the postwar governments of Bulgaria, Hungary, and Japan. However, his concessions (issues he

Yalta and Potsdam

James Byrnes had perhaps his best moments in foreign affairs while attempting to forge a friendly relationship with the Soviet Union during the two 1945 summit meetings at Yalta and Potsdam. The summits involved the leaders of the United States, the Soviet Union, and Great Britain, the countries known as the Big Three. In February, Byrnes traveled with President Franklin Roosevelt to Yalta, a town on the Crimean Peninsula in the Soviet Republic of the Ukraine.

At the meeting, Soviet premier Joseph Stalin agreed to attack Japan to help the U.S. war effort in the Pacific. Roosevelt and British prime minister Winston Churchill conceded to the Soviet Union veto power in the newly developing United Nations organization. They also gave in to Stalin's demands to shift the west border of Poland westward to include parts of Germany. In return, Stalin agreed to allow free elections in Poland. The leaders also agreed to divide Germany into four postwar occupation zones, with the Soviets, the Americans, the British, and the French each controlling one zone. In addition, Churchill and Roosevelt agreed to require war reparations from Germany, another demand Stalin made for the Soviet Union. (Reparations are payments a defeated country must some-

times make for damages it caused during a war.) Despite reaching these agreements, the leaders of the three countries revealed in their negotiations a growing division between East and West over future goals.

The next meeting of the Big Three came on July 26, 1945, in Potsdam, Germany. Harry S. Truman had replaced Roosevelt after Roosevelt's sudden death in April, and **Clement R. Attlee (1883–1967; see entry)** had replaced Churchill as Britain's prime minister. Because the two Western leaders were new, Byrnes played a stronger role in orchestrating agreements. Regarding war reparations, he proposed that the United States, the Soviet Union, Britain, and France obtain reparations only from their own German occupation zones. If Stalin accepted this arrangement, the Americans, the British, and the French would formally accept the new Polish boundaries that Stalin and the Soviets wanted. Through Byrnes's negotiations, the four German occupation zones became more permanently fixed. In addition, Italy became part of the Western sphere of influence, and Bulgaria, Romania, and Hungary became part of the Eastern sphere. Through Byrnes's personal orchestration, the division of Europe had become firmly established.

agreed to) to the Soviets proved highly unpopular back in the United States. Byrnes's preference for diplomacy over military confrontation attracted increasing criticism. He was accused of being soft on communism. When Byrnes returned from

Moscow, Truman personally rebuffed him for being too eager to concede to the Soviets in order to make a deal. According to *Sly and Able: A Political Biography of James F. Byrnes,* in a letter to Byrnes, Truman said, "I'm tired of babying the Soviets." Byrnes's influence soon began to decline; his role as a skilled compromiser and negotiator during the Cold War occurred at a time when both the United States and the Soviet Union were unwilling to compromise.

Byrnes tried toughening his approach toward the Soviets through 1946. At Stuttgart, West Germany, on September 6, 1946, Byrnes announced in a major speech that it was now U.S. policy to reestablish an independent Germany, something the Soviets strongly opposed. Many saw this speech as the end of the wartime alliance between the West and the Soviet Union.

Byrnes's efforts to befriend the Soviets were ultimately unsuccessful, but his departure from Truman's cabinet was not about job performance; it had more to do with a personality

President Harry S. Truman (left) confers with Secretary of State James F. Byrnes in August 1945. *Reproduced by permission of the Corbis Corporation.*

conflict. Byrnes and Truman simply did not get along. Byrnes envied Truman for succeeding Roosevelt as president and often negotiated with foreign nations without consulting with Truman. In addition, Byrnes's position on white supremacy was in stark contrast to Truman's domestic policies. Byrnes finally resigned in January 1947. Just before leaving office, he negotiated peace treaties with the Soviet Union and Italy, Romania, Hungary, and Finland. It was a last-gasp effort at U.S.-Soviet friendship. General **George C. Marshall** (1880–1959; see entry) replaced Byrnes as secretary of state.

Governor Byrnes

Byrnes kept quiet in public on national issues for two years after leaving the State Department. By 1949, Byrnes began openly criticizing some of Truman's domestic policies. Returning to public life, Byrnes won election as governor of South Carolina in 1950, receiving 85 percent of the vote. While in office, he pressed Truman to bomb the People's Republic of China (PRC) during the Korean War (1950–53) because he had been so criticized for being soft on communism that he adopted a more warlike position on issues.

Byrnes also supported racial segregation, or separation of the races, in public schools. An opponent of the civil rights movement, which stressed equal rights for African Americans, Byrnes, like many Southerners in the early 1950s, switched his party affiliation and became a Republican. His fight against public school desegregation directly contributed to the landmark 1954 U.S. Supreme Court decision in *Brown v. Board of Education*, a court case that combined cases from several states, including South Carolina. The Court decided to ban racial segregation in public schools, but Byrnes vowed to fight implementation of the decision. He fought the adoption of segregation policies with limited success when implementation was delayed. Byrnes retired from office in 1955 and died in April 1972 in Columbia, South Carolina.

For More Information

Books

Brown, Walter J. *James F. Byrnes of South Carolina: A Remembrance.* Macon, GA: Mercer University Press, 1992.

Byrnes, James F. *All in One Lifetime*. New York: Harper, 1958.

Byrnes, James F. *Speaking Frankly*. New York: Harper, 1947. Reprint, Westport, CT: Greenwood Press, 1974.

Graebner, Norman A., ed. *An Uncertain Tradition: American Secretaries of State in the Twentieth Century*. New York: McGraw-Hill, 1961.

Messer, Robert L. *The End of an Alliance: James F. Byrnes, Roosevelt, Truman, and the Origins of the Cold War*. Chapel Hill: University of North Carolina Press, 1982.

Robertson, David. *Sly and Able: A Political Biography of James F. Byrnes*. New York: Norton, 1994.

Yergin, Daniel. *Shattered Peace: The Origins of the Cold War and the National Security State*. Boston: Houghton Mifflin, 1977.

Jimmy Carter

Born October 1, 1924
Plains, Georgia

U.S. president, governor, humanitarian, and farmer

"[One] responsibility of mine was to approve the testing of atomic explosive devices.... I wondered if [other top leaders] too thought about future generations and were also sometimes very discouraged. Why could we not control this most ominous of all threats?"

Jimmy Carter. *Courtesy of the Library of Congress.*

Inaugurated as the thirty-ninth U.S. president in January 1977, Jimmy Carter came to the White House with little experience in foreign affairs. Yet Carter's presidency coincided with an important period of the Cold War, the longstanding economic and political rivalry between the communist Soviet Union and the democratic United States. After two-and-a-half years of often rocky negotiations, Carter signed a new arms control agreement with the Soviets, SALT II. He granted formal diplomatic recognition to communist China. In response to a Soviet invasion of Afghanistan, President Carter punished the Soviets by boycotting the Olympic Games in Moscow in 1980; U.S. athletes were not allowed to participate in the Games.

Carter's brightest success in foreign policy was the peace agreement he helped negotiate between Egypt and Israel. The most difficult situation he faced as president was the American hostage crisis in Iran that began in November 1979 and did not end until the very day he left office. Carter's greatest accomplishment, overshadowing all else in his presidency, was the promotion of human rights on a global scale.

Young Jimmy

James Earl Carter Jr. was born in Plains, Georgia. His parents—James Earl Sr., or "Earl" for short, and Lillian Gordy Carter—were middle-income landowners who farmed peanuts and cotton and operated a warehouse and store. When Jimmy was four years old, they moved to their new home in a small community known as Archery, four miles from Plains along U.S. Route 280. Jimmy's father was a highly efficient farmer, a businessman, and a civic leader. At his death in 1953, he was a member of the state legislature. Jimmy's most memorable moments were the times his father took him on trips around their farmlands, all of which were within a few miles of Plains. Earl instilled the business ethic in Jimmy early in life. As a five-year-old, Jimmy pulled peanut plants, boiled the peanuts, and took them into Plains in his wagon to sell.

Jimmy's mother, known as "Miz" Lillian, was a trained nurse. She broke the color barrier in their segregated community by caring for black families as well as whites. (Segregate means to separate or set apart; segregated communities were places where there were separate hospitals, schools, and other public facilities for blacks and whites.) Miz Lillian was an avid reader and encouraged her children to read. The Carters had four children: Jimmy, the oldest, and Gloria, Ruth, and Billy.

As a boy, Carter worked with black farmhands on the land or tended his dad's store, where townspeople bought supplies. Many neighbors were black tenant farmers, that is, black farmers who did not own their land but instead worked the land for the landholders. Carter observed firsthand how careful with money the tenant farmers were, always buying the least expensive food and supplies. In his book *An Hour Before Daylight* (2001), Carter writes, "More than anyone else in my family, perhaps even including my father, I could understand the plight [difficult situation] of the black families because I lived so much among them."

Carter grew up in the 1930s during the Great Depression (1929–41), when up to 25 percent of Americans lost their jobs and many rural folk lost their farms and livelihood. Carter witnessed how his mother never turned anyone away who came to their door for food or a drink of water. These early experiences shaped Carter's attitudes, making him sensitive to the suffering of others and helping him understand the value of all human beings. This was the beginning of Carter's development as a great promoter of human rights.

By the time Carter was in high school, he knew the farming operation well. He could perform all the chores on the farm, knew the animals and the machinery, and had acquired skills in carpentry and blacksmithing. However, Carter was destined to move beyond Plains. Miz Lillian's brother, Tom Watson Gordy, had joined the navy at a young age. He traveled the world and sent letters to his nephew Jimmy about the exotic places where his ships docked. Because of his Uncle Tom's influence, Carter dreamed of attending the U.S. Naval Academy at Annapolis, Maryland, and becoming a naval officer. As Carter's high school graduation date neared, Earl Carter set about helping his son request an appointment to Annapolis through their local congressman Stephen Pace (1891–1970).

A naval officer

Jimmy graduated from Plains High School in the spring of 1941; he was class valedictorian, the student with the highest grade point average. In September, he enrolled in Georgia Southwestern College in Americus, where he took courses recommended by the Annapolis guidebook. For his second year, Jimmy moved to Georgia Tech in Atlanta to study engineering. At the completion of his second year of college, Jimmy received his appointment to Annapolis. He graduated from the U.S. Naval Academy in 1946 in the top 10 percent of his class. He returned to Plains that summer to marry Rosalynn Smith on July 7. They would have four children: John William, known as Jack; James Earl III, known as Chip; Donnel Jeffrey, known as Jeff; and Amy Lynn.

Carter began his naval career in 1946 and two years later volunteered for submarine duty. Graduating third out of a class of fifty-two in submarine training school, he received his first sub assignment on the USS *Pomfret,* then later, the USS *K-1.* In 1952, Carter served as an officer on the nuclear-powered submarine *Sea Wolf.* Carter served under navy captain Hyman G. Rickover (1900–1986), who headed the development program for the nation's first nuclear-powered submarines. Carter later said that except for his parents, no one had a greater impact on his conduct in life than Rickover, who demanded excellence and then gave as much as or more than he demanded of others. With his early success in the navy, Carter seemed on track to become an admiral, the navy's highest rank. Then a call from Plains came.

Return to Plains

Carter's father was diagnosed with terminal pancreatic cancer in 1953. This affliction would also take the lives of all of Jimmy's siblings while they were in their fifties. Carter took a week's leave to be with his dad. During their last time together, Carter realized even more fully the accomplishments of his father and how important his father had been to his rural Georgia community. Much to his wife Rosalynn's dismay, Carter soon resigned from the navy and returned to Plains to take over for his father on the family farm.

By 1960, the farm was prospering, and Carter was also immersed in civic duties. He was a member of the Sumter County Board of Education from 1955 to 1962, served on the local hospital and library boards, and taught Sunday school at the Plains Baptist Church. When the church voted on whether to admit black families, the Carter family and one other church member cast the only favorable votes. Similarly, when a chapter of the segregationist organization White Citizens' Council came to Plains, Carter was the only white male in the community who refused to join.

In 1962, Carter was elected to the Georgia state senate. He was reelected in 1964, then won the Georgia governorship in 1970. In his inaugural address, Carter attracted national attention by declaring that it was time for racial discrimination to end. Carter increased job opportunities for blacks in the state government and began to hang portraits of prominent black leaders in the state capitol. He increased the efficiency of state government by reorganizing about three hundred state agencies into approximately thirty agencies. Carter also became involved in the national political scene. In 1972, he headed the Democratic Governors' Campaign Committee and in 1974 served as chairman of the Democratic National Campaign Committee. As early as 1973, Carter had decided to make a run for the U.S. presidency in 1976.

In Georgia, no one can serve two consecutive terms as governor. So when Carter left office in January 1975, he began campaigning for the presidency nationwide. He attracted little attention, but he continued tirelessly and won the early Iowa caucus, where a group of people gather to select candidates. By the August 1976 Democratic National Convention in New York City, Carter had gained enough support to win the nomination. He chose U.S. senator Walter F. Mondale (1928–) of Minnesota as his vice presidential running mate. Carter and Mondale defeated their Republican opponents, President Gerald Ford (1913–) and his running mate, U.S. senator Robert Dole (1923–) of Kansas.

Carter's appeal stemmed from the fact that he was an outsider, not part of the Washington, D.C., political scene. In the minds of the American public, Ford was permanently tied to his predecessor, **Richard M. Nixon** (1913–1994; served 1969–74; see entry), who had resigned from the presidency in disgrace following the Watergate scandal, which involved administration officials participating in the burglary of a Democratic National Committee office and a subsequent cover-up. In one of his first acts as president, Ford pardoned Nixon, a very unpopular move among many citizens. Carter promised to take America toward different goals than Ford and Nixon had pursued. However, concerning relations with the Soviet Union, Carter hoped to continue the policy of détente (decreasing international tensions) that Nixon and Ford had established.

The White House years

Carter appointed Zbigniew Brzezinski (1928–) as his national security advisor and Cyrus Vance (1917–2002) as secretary of state. Brzezinski and Vance held opposing views on how to deal with the Soviets. Vance strongly supported diplomacy (talking out problems), whereas Brzezinski favored military responses to any Soviet activities that were carried out with the goal of expanding communism. Carter at first favored Vance's approach. In January 1977, Carter sent a warm letter to **Leonid Brezhnev** (1906–1982; see entry), general secretary of the Central Committee of the Communist Party in the Soviet Union. In the letter, Carter expressed his desire to improve relations with the Soviet Union and to end the nuclear weapons arms race. With this letter, Carter also intended to establish friendlier relations with the Soviets so the United States could focus more on leading the world in promoting human rights rather than being so consumed with the Cold War rivalry.

Carter's human rights campaign

Carter, a devout Christian, believed in promoting human rights on a global scale. The term *human rights* refers to certain rights that all people, simply by being human, deserve. Examples of human rights include economic opportunities, political freedoms, and an existence free from oppression, unlawful imprisonment, and torture. In March 1977, Carter increased funding for Radio Free Europe, Radio Liberty, and Voice of America, radio stations that beamed programs about basic human freedoms into the Soviet Union and into Eastern Europe, which was under tight communist control. **Andrey Sakharov** (1921–1989; see entry), a Soviet nuclear physicist-turned-dissident, or an individual who disagrees with the ideas of those in power, encouraged Carter to pursue his human rights campaign.

U.S. national security advisor Zbigniew Brzezinksi. *Courtesy of the Library of Congress.*

In November 1977, at the Conference on Security and Cooperation in Europe, the United States accused the Soviets and Eastern European countries of violating their citizens' human rights. Brezhnev and other Soviet leaders charged the United States with interfering in Soviet domestic affairs. In response, through the late 1970s, Brezhnev jailed hundreds of dissidents—anyone in the Soviet Union critical of communist rule. Brezhnev also increased oppression of Soviet Jews who were critical of communist rule. Soon détente was pushed aside, and U.S.-Soviet relations became frosty and hostile. Carter changed course in his foreign policy approach and favored U.S. national security advisor Brzezinski's hard-line attitude toward the Soviets.

Latin America

Carter also focused his human rights campaign on Latin American countries and South Korea. Latin America includes all countries in the Western Hemisphere south of the United States. Carter believed the Soviet Union was no longer a strong threat to Latin American countries, so he halted the U.S. policy of supporting oppressive dictatorships just because they were anticommunist. Argentina, Brazil, and Chile were countries known to suffer from human rights abuses. In an attempt to influence government leaders there, Carter blocked U.S. loans to these countries. He also halted other economic assistance and ended arms deals. Carter's policies resulted in chilled relations with Latin American countries that had previously been friendly to the United States.

Domestic policies

Carter's first action on the home scene was to pardon all those who had evaded the draft during the Vietnam War (1954–75). The draft was a process in which all eighteen-year-old U.S. men had to register to enter the military. Some illegally avoided being drafted by packing up and moving to Canada, where they stayed for many years. Carter's pardon of draft evaders was a popular move with some Americans, but it was very unpopular with many war veterans.

During his term, Carter won congressional approval of two new cabinet-level executive departments: the Department of Education and the Department of Energy. The Department of Energy would regulate energy suppliers and fund research into additional energy sources. Some of Carter's energy policy successes helped reduce the nation's dependence on foreign oil. By the time Carter left office in 1981, his energy programs had reduced U.S. dependence on foreign oil from 48 percent to 40 percent. The United States had also stored large amounts of oil and a surplus of natural gas; domestic production of oil and gas had increased substantially. By the mid-1980s, Carter's policies would lead to reduced prices for energy products. However, in the short term, during the late 1970s, the Organization of Petroleum Exporting Countries (OPEC) nearly tripled its oil prices from $13 a barrel to above $34 per barrel. Inflation (the rise in the cost of goods and services) soared to above 15 percent, and Carter's popularity plummeted. Carter worsened his public image by giving what became known as his "malaise speech," in which he expressed concern over the American people's malaise (though he never actually used that word in his speech), or lack of confidence and purpose, in the future of the United States. To the public, to the media, and to Congress, Carter seemed distant and arrogant. His chances for reelection grew smaller and smaller.

Successes in foreign affairs

While domestic economic troubles plagued his administration, Carter found success abroad—in relations with China, an arms limitation treaty with the Soviet Union, and a peace treaty that he helped negotiate between Egypt and Israel. Carter also succeeded in negotiating treaties to return control of the Panama Canal to the country of Panama, effective December 31, 1999; the United States had constructed the canal and controlled it since the early 1900s. The Panama Canal treaties were in keeping with Carter's policy of scaling back U.S. involvement in other countries.

The Carter administration continued the efforts of Presidents Nixon and Ford by strengthening U.S. ties with communist China. The countries granted each other full diplomatic relations on January 1, 1979. Communists interested in China's economic growth replaced many hard-line communists in China. The United States began importing finished consumer goods from China and exporting lumber and food products to China.

After six years of talks during the terms of three U.S. presidents (Nixon, Ford, and Carter), the Strategic Arms Limitation Treaty (SALT II) was completed. President Carter and Soviet leader Leonid Brezhnev signed SALT II on June 18, 1979. SALT II put a ceiling on the number of nuclear delivery vehicles each country could possess and on the number of ballistic missiles the two countries could have in their offensive weapons systems. It did not require the countries to reduce their stockpiles of weapons. On the night of June 18, 1979, Carter addressed a joint session of Congress. In the address, as noted in the *Public Papers of the Presidents of the Unit-*

Israeli prime minister Menachem Begin (far left), U.S. president Jimmy Carter, and Egyptian president Anwar Sadat meet in 1979 at the Camp David Accords. *Reproduced by permission of Getty Images.*

ed States: Jimmy Carter, 1979, Book I, Carter stated, "SALT II is very important, but it's more than a single arms control agreement. It is part of a long, historical process of gradually reducing the danger of nuclear war—a process that we in this room must not undermine.... And, of course, SALT II is the absolutely indispensable precondition for moving on to much deeper and more significant cuts under SALT III."

Unfortunately for U.S.-Soviet relations, the Soviet Union invaded Afghanistan in late 1979 and early 1980 to support an unpopular communist government there. U.S.-Soviet relations nose-dived. Carter refused to allow U.S. athletes to go to the 1980 Summer Olympic Games in Moscow. He also withdrew SALT II from the Senate ratification process. Nevertheless, Brezhnev and Carter and, later, President **Ronald Reagan** (1911–; served 1981–89; see entry), agreed to abide by the provisions of the treaty.

Carter's greatest foreign policy success came with the so-called Camp David Accords. Camp David is the presidential retreat outside Washington, D.C., in the hills of Maryland. Carter invited Israel's prime minister, Menachem Begin (1913–1992), and Egypt's president, Anwar Sadat (1918–1981), to Camp David to negotiate a peace treaty. Between September 4 and September 17, 1978, Carter effectively mediated between the two bitter enemies until a peace agreement was worked out. The agreement was formally signed in Washington, D.C., on March 26, 1979. Begin and Sadat received the 1978 Nobel Peace Prize for their efforts.

Iranian crisis

In 1979, the shah, or ruler, of Iran, Mohammad Reza Pahlavi (1919–1980), was forced to flee Iran when Ayatollah Ruhollah Khomeini (c. 1900–1989), the leader of the Shiites, a radical Muslim group, took control. Exiled, the shah journeyed to Panama in December 1979. Suffering from cancer, he asked for permission to enter the United States for treatment. President Carter agreed to the shah's request. Greatly angered by this action, Iranian revolutionaries stormed the U.S. embassy in Tehran, Iran's capital city, and took sixty-six Americans hostage, fourteen of whom were soon released. The Iranians demanded that the shah be returned to Iran for trial on charges of crimes against the Iranian people before the hostages would be released. All negotiations failed, and Carter ordered a military rescue in April 1980. A desert sandstorm downed several of the American rescue helicopters. One helicopter crashed into a transport plane, killing eight. Finally, on the very day Carter left office, January 20, 1981, the fifty-two hostages were released. The Republican candidate, former California governor Ronald Reagan, had easily defeated Carter in the presidential race by charging that Carter had been ineffective in his handling of the hostage crisis and was equally ineffective in reducing inflation and unemployment at home.

Second return to Georgia

Jimmy Carter returned to Plains in January 1981 and immediately began to write his memoirs, *Keeping Faith: Memoirs of a President,* first published in 1982. (An engaging author,

Books by Jimmy Carter

Why Not the Best? Nashville, TN: Broadman Press, 1975.

"I'll Never Lie to You": Jimmy Carter in His Own Words. New York: Ballantine, 1976.

A Government as Good as Its People. New York: Simon and Schuster, 1977.

Keeping Faith: Memoirs of a President. New York: Bantam, 1982.

Negotiation, the Alternative to Hostility. Macon, GA: Mercer University Press, 1984.

The Blood of Abraham: Insights into the Middle East. Boston: Houghton Mifflin, 1985.

Everything to Gain: Making the Most of the Rest of Your Life (with Rosalynn Carter). New York: Random House, 1987.

An Outdoor Journal: Adventures and Reflections. New York: Bantam Press, 1988.

Turning Point: A Candidate, a State, and a Nation Come of Age. New York: Times Books, 1992.

Talking Peace. New York: Dutton Children's Books, 1995.

Living Faith. New York: Times Books, 1996.

An Hour before Daylight: Memories of a Rural Boyhood. New York: Simon and Schuster, 2001.

Carter has written many other books in his postpresidential years; see sidebar.) In his postpresidential life, Carter became a model for future ex-presidents by maintaining a substantial involvement in worthwhile causes, particularly human rights issues. Considering Carter's accomplishments after 1980, it seems the U.S. presidency was not the pinnacle of his career, but a stepping-stone on a path to further greatness.

In October 1984, construction began on the Jimmy Carter Library. The library is located on a 35-acre campus near downtown Atlanta, Georgia. Completed in October 1986, the facility includes the presidential library, the Carter Museum, privately maintained offices for Jimmy and Rosalynn Carter and the staff of foundations supported by the Carters, and the Carter Center. The Carter Center operates in partnership with Emory University and is governed by an independent board of trustees chaired by the former president. According to the Center's Web site, its mission "is guided by a fundamental commitment to human rights and the alleviation of human suffering; it seeks to prevent and resolve conflicts, enhance freedom and democracy, and improve health."

Through the Carter Center Jimmy and Rosalynn Carter have been involved in many dispute resolution activities, especially in civil war situations in Third World countries. They have also monitored elections in countries where open and honest elections are difficult to carry out and given advice to government officials on a variety of issues. Jimmy Carter has served as an unofficial ambassador for several administrations. President **George Bush** (1924–; served 1989–93; see entry), Reagan's successor, sent Carter to Panama in 1989 to oversee presidential elections there. Then in 1990, Carter led a team that monitored presidential elections in Nicaragua. President Bill Clinton (1946–; served 1993–2001) sent Carter to North Korea in 1994 to defuse a nuclear weapons dispute. For all his efforts, Carter was awarded the Nobel Peace Prize in 2002.

For More Information

Books

Carter, Jimmy. *An Hour before Daylight: Memories of a Rural Boyhood.* New York: Simon and Schuster, 2001.

Carter, Rosalynn. *First Lady from Plains.* Boston: Houghton Mifflin, 1984.

Morris, Kenneth E. *Jimmy Carter: American Moralist.* Athens: University of Georgia Press, 1996.

Public Papers of the Presidents of the United States: Jimmy Carter, 1979, Book I. Washington, DC: U.S. Government Printing Office, 1980.

Richardson, Don, ed. *Conversations with Carter.* Boulder, CO: Lynne Rienner Publishers, 1998.

Wade, Linda R. *James Carter: Thirty-Ninth President of the United States.* Chicago: Childrens Press, 1989.

Web Sites

The Carter Center. http://www.cartercenter.org (accessed on August 24, 2003).

Jimmy Carter Library and Museum. http://www.jimmycarterlibrary.org (accessed on August 24, 2003).

Fidel Castro

Born August 13, 1926
Mayarí, Cuba

Cuban president

"If there ever was in the history of humanity an enemy who was truly universal, an enemy whose acts and moves trouble [and] threaten the entire world ... that real and really universal enemy is precisely Yankee imperialism."

Fidel Castro. *Reproduced by permission of the Corbis Corporation.*

Cuba's proximity to the United States, only 90 miles (145 kilometers) from the Florida Keys, and its hard-line pro–Soviet Union communist government led successive U.S. presidential administrations to fear the island, both as a base for subversive activities throughout the Western Hemisphere and as a platform for a Soviet attack on the United States. These fears led to the Bay of Pigs invasion, the Cuban Missile Crisis, and American efforts to isolate the Cuban government and assassinate its leader, Fidel Castro. In the early twenty-first century, Cuba still operated under communism, a governmental system in which a single political party, the Communist Party, controls nearly all aspects of society. In a communist economy, private ownership of property and businesses is banned so that goods produced and wealth accumulated can be shared equally by all.

Although the Soviet Union never entered into a formal military alliance with Castro, Castro was useful to the Soviets because his presence challenged U.S. dominance in Latin America. In this sense, Castro's Cuba was an irritant to the Americans just as West Berlin was to the Soviets. Castro regularly appeared at international meetings, where he criticized American imperialism, the process of expanding the authority of one government over other nations and groups of people, and offered aid and encouragement to national liberation movements in the Third World. (Third World refers to poor underdeveloped or economically developing nations in Africa, Asia, and Latin America. Many of these countries were seeking independence from the political control of Western European nations.

A land of opportunity

Fidel Alejandro Castro Ruz was born on his father's farm, "Las Manacas," near the town of Mayarí in the former province of Oriente. He was the third child of seven born to Lina Ruz Gonzalez and Angel Castro Argiz. Angel was a Spaniard who fought as a cavalry officer in the Spanish army during the Spanish-American War (1898). This conflict was an ongoing civil war between Spain, which controlled Cuba at that time, and rebel forces seeking independence for Cuba. The United States had an interest in ridding Cuba of its Spanish rulers, because it no longer wanted European influences in the Western Hemisphere. The United States wanted to control or influence resources and economies for its own benefit and not allow possible growth of influences from abroad. By April 1898, U.S. military forces were sent in to assist the rebels. Within only a few months, Cuba was liberated from Spanish domination.

After the war, Angel Castro stayed on in Cuba to become a relatively prosperous sugarcane grower. He was a powerful authoritarian figure who was often in a state of conflict with his young sons. At the age of thirteen, Fidel went so far as to organize a strike of the workers on his father's plantation. Fidel inherited his father's height, which contributed to his success as a superior athlete.

Fidel's mother was a very religious woman who had received little education herself. She therefore stressed the importance of education for her children. She combined warmth and affection with high expectations and a determination that they would succeed. In 1942, at the age of fifteen, Fidel attended Belen, a Jesuit, or Catholic missionary, boarding school in Havana that had close ties with Spain. The prestigious school served the nation's upper class and offered the best education and opportunity in Cuba. From the moment young Fidel arrived at the school, the faculty singled him out as a boy with exceptional talent and leadership potential.

At Belen, Castro was exposed to the writings of Cuban national hero José Martí (1853–1895). Martí was a towering figure in Cuban history, a patriot who fought for Cuba's freedom. Like Castro, Martí was the son of an officer in the Spanish army, the army that opposed the Cuban rebels who fought for independence in the late nineteenth century. Despite his father's political leanings, José Martí was dedicated to the struggle for an independent Cuba.

The fascist, or dictatorial, views of José Antonio Primo de Rivera (1903–1936) were another significant influence on Castro. De Rivera fought under Spanish leader Francisco Franco (1892–1975) in order to free Spain from strong communist and British influences. Like Castro, de Rivera came from a wealthy background, but he had given up an easy life to fight for what he believed in.

While at Belen, Castro was very active in a Jesuit organization called the "Explorers," which was similar to the Boy Scouts. They went on rigorous camping trips into rugged mountain areas, and Castro acquired a reputation for stamina and endurance, eventually becoming the leader of the troop.

Revolution

In 1945, Castro went on to study law at the University of Havana, and it was there that he became involved in politics. Castro joined the left-wing, or liberal, Cuban People's Party. In 1948, he married Mirta Diaz-Bilart, and they had a son. Castro graduated with a law degree from the University of Havana in 1950 and set up a law practice in the city.

During most of Castro's early years, Fulgencio Batista y Zaldívar (1901–1973), an oppressive dictator, a leader who uses force and terror to maintain control, ruled Cuba. Since 1933, either directly or through others who were leaders in name only, Batista had been in complete control of the island. Batista's economic policies helped establish such light industry businesses as canneries and allowed foreign companies, many from the United States, to build their businesses in Cuba. U.S. corporations dominated the sugar industry, oil production, and other key elements of the island's economy. As a result, most of Cuba's wealth was therefore only owned by a small percentage of the population, meaning most Cuban citizens lived in dire poverty. Cuba was ripe for revolution by the 1950s. Castro, the handsome, intense young lawyer, proved to be a charismatic leader for the rebel cause.

Castro started organizing a revolution to overthrow Batista. On July 26, 1953, Castro was arrested after leading an armed assault on the Moncada army barracks in Santiago de Cuba. The attack was a failure, and most of his followers were killed. Castro conducted his own defense at his trial and used the opportunity as a platform to call for free elections, land reform, profit sharing, and industrialization. These issues formed the foundation of his revolutionary movement, and they appealed to many Cubans. Both Castro and his brother, Raúl Castro (1931–), were sentenced to fifteen years in prison for insurrection, or revolt. They were released under an amnesty, or official forgiveness, program in 1955. Castro's marriage to Mirta was dissolved that year as well.

Naming a tiny group of rebels the "26th of July Movement," Castro went into exile in Mexico and began to organize an armed rebellion. The small band of guerrillas, small groups of soldiers specializing in surprise attacks, returned to Cuba on December 26, 1956, aboard an old 38-foot (12-meter) wooden boat, the *Granma*, which had been purchased from an American. Upon landing back at home in Oriente, they encountered government forces and suffered heavy losses. Castro and eleven others, including his brother Raúl and Argentinian revolutionary leader Ernesto "Che" Guevara (1928–1967), survived the encounter and escaped to the mountains of the Sierra Maestra on the southeast end of the island. There they joined allies, all part of a widespread opposition to Batista. Castro began to launch a military offensive against Batista's Cuban army in the fall of 1958. With his regime collapsing around him and Castro marching on Havana, Batista fled for the Dominican Republic in the early hours of January 1, 1959. Fidel Castro and his forces immediately took control of the capital and the country. Castro took the oath of office as premier of Cuba on February 16, 1959, and became the youngest head of state in the Western Hemisphere.

A new Cuban government

In the immediate aftermath of the overthrow of Batista's government, Castro appeared to be inclined toward a democratic government. A democratic system of government allows multiple political parties. Members of the different political parties are elected to various government offices by popular vote of the people. Castro arrived in Washington, D.C., in April 1959 to begin a goodwill tour of the United States, a staunchly democratic country. In Washington and in New York City, enthusiastic crowds greeted Castro; he was seen as a democratic reformer, not a communist. However, after Castro returned to Cuba, it quickly became evident that he was basing his regime on opposition to the Americans. In May, against the objections of the United States, Castro nationalized, or took control and ownership of, the sugarcane industry, which had been dominated by an American corporation, the United Fruit Company. He proceeded to collectivize agriculture, or place control of farmlands under group control in specific areas rather than by individual ownership. Castro also took over native- and foreign-owned industry, placing it under the government's control. Many of the wealthy, property-owning classes fled the country.

The United States was heavily invested in the Cuban economy and had virtually controlled it for decades. Being the dominant power in Cuba, America had also intervened in Cuban politics to ensure that the Cuban government would stay friendly to the United States. Castro's policy of transforming Cuba from a capitalist to a socialist society did not sit well with the United States, which had always had a capitalist economy. In a capitalist economy, property and businesses are privately owned. Production, distribution, and prices of goods are determined by competition in a market relatively free of government intervention. In contrast, a socialist economy allows the government to control all means of production and to set prices.

Castro's new economic policies made Cuba a focal point of the Cold War, an intense political and economic rivalry between the United States and the Soviet Union that lasted from 1945 to 1991. By September 1959, Castro had signed trade agreements with the Soviet Union, a communist country. He then signed agreements with the rest of Eastern Europe and China, all communist nations. Castro was openly critical of the United States and blamed American imperialism for inflicting economic backwardness on Cuba and the rest of Latin America. U.S. president **Dwight D. Eisenhower** (1890–1969; served 1953–61; see entry) responded by imposing trade restrictions on Cuba. One of the last official diplomatic acts of the Eisenhower administration was the severing of U.S.-Cuban diplomatic relations. In March 1960, Eisenhower authorized the Central Intelligence Agency (CIA) to begin training Cuban exiles, people who had fled Cuba, to participate in a possible attack on Cuba.

The Bay of Pigs

When President **John F. Kennedy** (1917–1963; served 1961–63; see entry) took office in January 1961, he inherited Eisenhower's plan to destabilize the Castro regime. The United States was in the midst of the Cold War with the communist Soviet Union, and Kennedy did not wish to appear soft on Communism. However, he did not want to put U.S. forces in danger by staging a full-fledged invasion of Cuba. Kennedy instead authorized a revised, top-secret plan to carry out a small-scale invasion. On April 17, 1961, the plan was put into action.

The original plan had been to land a large-scale operation at Trinidad, on the southern coast of Cuba. The landing was switched to a spot about 100 miles (160 kilometers) away, just south of the city of Matanzas, called the Bahía de Cochinos (Bay of Pigs). The armed force consisted of about fifteen hundred U.S.-trained Cuban exiles. The Cuban military quickly confronted this small group, and the whole operation collapsed within days. The victory was a major boost for Castro and a major embarrassment for the Kennedy administration. The invasion provoked demonstrations against the United States in Latin America and Europe and increased the tensions between the United States and Cuba. The event also encouraged Castro to seek military ties with the Soviet Union so he could protect his government against another attack.

A tug of war

Castro's success in maintaining independence from the United States earned him admiration in Latin America and throughout the Third World. Sporting a beard and dressed in army fatigues, Castro cultivated his image as a revolutionary hero and guerrilla fighter. Cuba provided military assistance to revolutionary movements in South America and later in Africa. U.S. presidential administrations sought to isolate Castro's government within the Western Hemisphere and made it known to other countries that having friendly relations with Castro would be considered an unfriendly act toward the United States.

American attempts to overthrow Castro shifted from invasion to a covert operation, dubbed Operation Mongoose. The goal of the top-secret effort, which was directed by the CIA, was to get rid of Castro—via overthrow or assassination. At least eight attempts were made on Castro's life, a fact revealed in documents released by the U.S. government. The assassination attempts involved contacts with the Mafia, or secret criminals, to hire hit men to assassinate Castro. Other attempts involved the use of poisoned cigars, poisoned pills, a poison pen, and a poison-impregnated skin diving suit. At one time, Castro himself claimed that at least twenty-four CIA-organized attempts had been made on his life.

Building tensions

Castro reacted to the U.S. hostility by openly describing himself as procommunist in 1961. He established close political and economic ties with the Soviet Union so that Cuba was aligned with the communist bloc, or group, of nations. Soviet aid enabled Castro to redistribute wealth in Cuba, introduce a free public health system, expand educational opportunities, and provide full employment. However, Castro also introduced a Soviet-style political structure; the Cuban Communist Party was the only legal political party. Press and television were heavily censored, and most businesses were owned by the state. In exchange for the aid they provided to Cuba, the Soviets hoped to use Castro's revolutionary enthusiasm to further the cause of communism on an international scale.

In 1962, Castro sent his finance minister, Che Guevara, and his foreign minister, Raúl Castro, to Moscow to negotiate for Soviet military aid. The Soviets refused to sign a formal military alliance with Cuba; instead they decided to install nuclear offensive and defensive missiles on the island. This would pro-

MISSILE EQUIPMENT
MARIEL PORT FACILITY
4 NOVEMBER 1962

LAUNCH STANDS

17 MISSILE ERECTORS

vide the Soviets with a strategic military base in the Western Hemisphere and protect Cuba from American attack.

Cuban Missile Crisis

One year after the Bay of Pigs invasion attempt, Kennedy and his advisors began an intensive debate about

Missile erectors and launch stands are visible in this aerial intelligence photograph of Mariel Port Facility in Cuba during the Cuban Missile Crisis of 1962. *Reproduced by permission of the Corbis Corporation.*

how to respond to the informal alliance between Cuba and the Soviet Union. Anxious U.S. leaders doubted that Cuban communism and the capitalist democracy of the United States could exist peacefully side by side, only 90 miles (145 kilometers) apart. As an added security measure, some 150,000 U.S. reserve troops were ordered to active duty, and U.S. reconnaissance, or spy, flights over Cuba increased. These flights revealed that the Soviet Union had started building launching pads for offensive ballistic missiles at San Cristóbal. Then intelligence reports revealed that twenty-five Soviet ships, carrying a cargo of ballistic missiles, had recently left ports on the Black Sea bound for Cuba. They were expected to reach the Caribbean within ten days. This left President Kennedy just over a week to decide his course of action. The only certain military solution would be a full-scale assault on Cuba. But such an attack could be used by the Soviets to justify a similar attack on West Berlin, the stronghold of Western influence in Eastern Europe. In short, Kennedy thought that military action at this point might well lead to World War III.

President Kennedy and his advisors decided to use a naval blockade around Cuba. Because blockades were against international law, they called the blockade a "quarantine." The purpose of the quarantine was to prevent the Soviet ships carrying the missiles from reaching Cuba; the United States wanted to give Soviet leader **Nikita Khrushchev** (1894–1971; see entry) time to reconsider his actions. Khrushchev quickly recognized that he was in an impossible situation: If he moved against West Berlin, he would face nuclear retaliation. If he completed and used the missile bases already in Cuba, his fate would be no different. If he simply left the missiles already in place in Cuba, the United States would invade Cuba and the Soviet Union would lose its communist foothold in the Western Hemisphere. If he tried to break the blockade, the result would be a direct Soviet-American military confrontation, which could quickly escalate out of control. Khrushchev therefore opted to negotiate with the United States, and ultimately the Soviets removed their missiles from Cuba. Castro was left out of the negotiations entirely.

The Cuban Missile Crisis frightened the leaders of both the Soviet Union and the United States. It led both countries to move toward easing international tensions in order to avoid a repeat of the event. In the months immediately following the crisis, the two countries established the Washington-Moscow Hot Line, and in August 1963 they signed the first Limited Test-Ban Treaty, which banned nuclear bomb testing in the atmosphere, in outer space, or underwater.

Home front

Although Cuba retained its political independence, the Cuban economy came to depend on billions of dollars in Soviet aid. Soviet support eventually began to drop off, and by 1985, when **Mikhail Gorbachev** (1931–; see entry) came into power in the Soviet Union, Castro was forced to reduce his expenditures. As the Cuban economy worsened, Castro's government increased food and gasoline rationing, or limited distribution. After a thirty-year absence, Cuba was given a seat in the United Nations Security Council on January 1, 1990. However, in Cuba, there were signs of discontent with Castro's government. Following the collapse of the Soviet Union in 1991, Cuba entered a crisis period. In need of foreign financial assistance to relieve the economic depression, Castro's regime began to promote tourism and open the country up to foreign investment. In 1991, Castro coauthored a book with South African leader Nelson Mandela (1918–). It was titled *How Far We Slaves Have Come: South Africa and Cuba in Today's World*. Castro remains a symbol of the Cuban Revolution and continues to lead Cuba in the twenty-first century.

For More Information

Books

Bourne, Peter G. *Fidel: A Biography of Fidel Castro*. New York: Dodd, Mead and Company, 1986.

Fursenko, Aleksandr, and Timothy Naftali. *"One Hell of a Gamble": Khrushchev, Castro, and Kennedy, 1958–1964*. New York: W. W. Norton, 2000.

Huchthausen, Peter A., and Alexander Hoyt. *October Fury*. Hoboken, NJ: John Wiley and Sons, 2002.

Leonard, Thomas M. *Castro and the Cuban Revolution*. Westport, CT: Greenwood Press, 1999.

Quirk, Robert E. *Fidel Castro*. New York: Norton, 1993.

Szulc, Tad. *Fidel: A Critical Portrait*. New York: Morrow, 1986.

Chiang Kai-shek

Born October 31, 1887
Qikou, Zhejiang Province, China
Died April 5, 1975
Taipei, Taiwan

President of the Republic of China

"We live in the present, we dream of the future and we learn eternal truths from the past."

Chiang Kai-shek. *Reproduced by permission of AP/Wide World Photos.*

Chiang Kai-shek was a longtime leader of China. First, he ruled Mainland China from 1927 to 1949. In 1949, Chinese communist forces defeated Chiang in a civil war. He fled to the island of Taiwan, where he established the Republic of China (ROC). He ruled over Taiwan in a dictatorial fashion into the 1970s.

Young revolutionary

Chiang Kai-shek was born in October 1887 in the village of Qikou, within the coastal Zhejiang Province, about 100 miles (160 kilometers) south of the city of Shanghai. His father, a salt merchant, died when Chiang was nine years old. Chiang's early education was in the Confucian tradition, instilling him with strong self-discipline. Confucianism is an educational system based on the teachings of the early Chinese philosopher Confucius (551–479 B.C.E.); it includes training in ethics and diplomacy. Because of his schooling in Confucianism, which teaches students to be inwardly reflective, respect authority, and not call attention to oneself, Chiang would always be quiet and passionless in his mannerisms and diplomatic relations.

Chiang gained admission to the Paoting Military Academy in 1906 and was a good enough student to be sent to a Japanese academy in 1907 for advanced study. While in Japan, Chiang met a Chinese revolutionary named Sun Yat-sen (1866–1925), who became his mentor. When student revolts broke out in China in 1911 against the Manchu dynasty, Chiang became a military commander for Sun. In 1912, Sun founded the Kuomintang, or Nationalist movement, based in Canton in southeast China. With the fall of the Manchu in 1913, the young revolutionaries continued fighting the new Chinese leader, Yüan Shih-k'ai (1859–1916). When Yüan died in 1916, the country fragmented into a number of regions ruled by local warlords, or dictatorial leaders. For the next several years, Chiang shifted back and forth between China and Japan, at times doing work for Sun. In 1921, Chiang became chief of staff of Sun's Nationalist government.

During the early 1920s, the Kuomintang were allied with Chinese communist forces and supported by the newly established communist government in the Soviet Union. Sun sent Chiang to the Soviet Union in 1923 to study Soviet military organization and obtain aid. Using the information Chiang gathered in the Soviet Union, Sun established the Whampoa Military Academy and appointed Chiang commander of the academy. The academy would train many of China's future military leaders. Chiang had returned from the Soviet Union with valuable military information, but during his stay he had formed strong anticommunist views.

Leader of the Chinese Nationals

Sun died in 1925, and after a power struggle, Chiang took command of the Kuomintang. Still holding power only in the south of the country, Chiang launched a major military expedition in July 1926 to gain control of the remainder of China. However, Chiang felt threatened by the increasing popularity of the Chinese communists. In April 1927, during his expedition, Chiang carried out a surprise bloody massacre of thousands of communists. Surviving Chinese Communist Party members, led by **Mao Zedong** (1893–1976; see entry) and **Zhou Enlai** (1898–1976; see entry), fled to the southern Jiangxi Province. With the communists temporarily beaten back, Chiang established a base for the Nationalist government in the city of Nanking. However, the warlords still controlled much of northern China.

In September 1927, during a lull in the military expedition, Chiang journeyed to Japan to marry Soong Mei-ling (1897–), an American-educated daughter of a prominent Chinese Christian family. To fulfill a condition of the December wedding, Chiang became a devout Christian. Mei-ling, who became known as Madame Chiang, would later help Chiang gain crucial support from the United States.

Leader of China

In 1928, Chiang continued his military expedition to the north. Gaining control of the northern city of Peking in June, Chiang claimed rule over all of China. He proceeded to build a strong political and military base. However, warlords still persisted in controlling some areas, the communists were expanding their control of the Jiangxi Province, and in 1931 Japan invaded Manchuria, a northeastern region of China. Even though the Japanese were clearly interested in expanding their influence, Chiang decided to focus his efforts on eliminating the communists. In 1934, Chiang's Nationalist army encircled the communist forces. However, many of the communists escaped, and in a 6,000-mile (9,654-kilometer) journey known as the Long March, they made their way to northwestern China, where they would regroup once again.

Chiang modernized China by bringing in foreign-educated intellectuals and emphasizing higher education. He began the "New Life Movement," promoting a lifestyle combining Confucian values, the Western Christian religion values of Protestantism, and strict military discipline. However, as urban development flourished, conditions in rural China declined.

From their distant location in northwest China, the communists tried to negotiate with Chiang to end the hostilities between them and join forces against the Japanese in Manchuria. However, Chiang refused to cooperate with the communists. Then, in December 1936, the Sian Incident occurred: A group of warlords kidnapped Chiang and insisted that he confront the Japanese. Seizing on the opportunity, communist leader Zhou Enlai rushed to where Chiang was

Madame Chiang Kai-shek

Soong Mei-ling, the wife of Chiang Kai-shek, played a major role in sustaining U.S. financial and military support for the Republic of China (ROC) through much of the Cold War. The Soong family was prominent in Chinese politics throughout the twentieth century. Mei-ling's father, Charlie Soong (1866–1918), became a wealthy businessman by the 1890s. All four of his children were educated in the United States.

In 1894, Charlie became a supporter of Sun Yat-sen's revolutionary movement to overthrow the oppressive Manchu dynasty in China. He financed Sun's newly formed Kuomintang, or Nationalist Party. An older sister of Mei-Ling, Soong Ch'ing-ling, married Sun in 1914, even though he was twenty-six years older than she was. After Sun's death in 1925, Ch'ing-ling actively supported the more liberal wing of the Nationalist Party as Chiang Kai-shek gained control of the larger conservative wing. When Chiang purged communists in 1927, Ch'ing-ling denounced the slaughter and left China for the Soviet Union. Later that same year, her sister Mei-ling married Chiang.

Graceful and charming, Mei-ling became better known as Madame Chiang. She introduced Chiang Kai-shek to Western culture and promoted Chiang's cause throughout the United States, building strong support for his war against the Chinese communist forces. During World War II, Madame Chiang wrote many articles, published in U.S. journals, in support of the

Madame Chiang Kai-shek. *Reproduced by permission of AP/Wide World Photos.*

China Lobby, an influential U.S. group of Chinese Nationalist supporters. After the war, her sister Ch'ing-ling returned to Chinese politics, actively opposing Chiang's war against the Chinese communist movement. When Chiang lost to the communists in 1949 and fled to Taiwan, Ch'ing-ling remained in Mainland China and became an important official in the Communist People's Republic of China (PRC) government.

In 1943, Madame Chiang became the first Chinese citizen and only the second woman in history to address a joint session of the U.S. Congress. In 1951, she received the Stalin Prize; in 1967, her name appeared on a U.S. list of the ten most admired women in the world; and in 1981, she was named honorary chairperson of the PRC.

being held. Arguing to save Chiang's life, Chou was able to reach an agreement on ending the Chinese civil war and joining forces with Chiang's army and the warlords to battle the Japanese. Their alliance, called the United Front, benefited both sides: The Chinese communists gained public respect for obtaining a peaceful end to the incident, and during the late 1930s Chiang's popularity soared in China and the United States because of his ability to hold full military power over the union of nationalists and communists.

Decline of the Nationalist government

The United Front stayed together until 1941, splitting just before the United States entered World War II (1939–45) against Japan. The United States threw its support behind Chiang's Nationalist government. However, the Chinese people were growing weary of war, and the Chinese economy was suffering; Chiang's popularity sagged. In addition, Allied leaders soon grew wary of Chiang's increasingly corrupt and inefficient government. During this period, the Chinese communists gained popularity by deciding to take a different strategy and take advantage of the growing discontent to gain greater political strength, albeit underground; however, some degree of cooperation persisted with Chiang and Zhou Enlai acting as the go-between until civil war broke out again after Japan was defeated.

After the Japanese surrendered in August 1945, ending World War II, Chiang once again focused on eliminating the Chinese communists. The United States made diplomatic efforts to help the different Chinese factions form a coalition government, or partnership, but this attempt was unsuccessful. Civil war once again broke out between the army supporting Chiang and the communist forces led by Mao Zedong. Chiang's support was weak, primarily coming from merchants, large landowners, and the military. The communists appealed to the peasants, who made up 90 percent of the Chinese population. Despite their numbers, Chiang had largely ignored them during his period in power. Seeing no advantage in further supporting Chiang, President **Harry S. Truman** (1884–1972; served 1945–53; see entry) reduced U.S. aid to Chiang's forces. Mao's forces finally captured Mainland

Chiang Kai-shek in front of Nationalist headquarters in Taipei. *Reproduced by permission of AP/Wide World Photos.*

China and formed the Communist People's Republic of China (PRC) in October 1949.

Republic of China (ROC) on Taiwan

Chiang fled with over one million refugees to the island of Taiwan, located 90 miles (145 kilometers) off the south coast of Mainland China. There, he established the Republic of China (ROC). On Taiwan, Chiang was unchallenged and gained unlimited power over the fifteen million inhabitants of Taiwan. Chiang declared martial law (military rule) and jailed dissenters. Martial law would continue into the late 1980s, and the ROC government was essentially a dictatorship. Chiang Kai-shek's son, Chiang Ching-kuo (1910–1988), gained a reputation for ruthlessness as head of the ROC secret police.

In the United States, President Truman faced renewed pressure from influential Chinese Nationalist supporters, who were greatly dismayed by the communist takeover of Mainland China. They criticized U.S. leaders for not assisting Chiang more during the struggle. Therefore, the United States renewed its support of Chiang and officially recognized the ROC as the only legitimate government of China. For years, the China Lobby, an influential U.S. group of Chinese Nationalist supporters with lots of money and political clout, continued to pressure the U.S. government to recognize ROC as the main government of China, not the PRC. The United States fought against the Communist PRC's entrance into the United Nations for thirty years.

Chiang had long harbored a desire to invade Mainland China and recapture it from the Chinese communists. The outbreak of the Korean War (1950–53) in 1950 raised his hopes of attacking the PRC from the south while PRC forces were busy to the east in Korea. However, Truman did not want to potentially draw the Soviet Union into a much wider conflict. During the 1950s, feeling threatened by Chiang, the PRC twice bombarded the ROC-controlled islands of Quemoy and Matsu, off the southern coast of China. In both cases, the United States intervened, threatening the PRC with nuclear weapons while extracting guarantees from Chiang that he would drop any ideas of invading Mainland China.

Taiwan, the island Chiang controlled under the ROC government, enjoyed strong economic growth after 1954, achieving one of the highest standards of living in Asia. It became a center of technology. However, the 1970s brought important changes for Chiang. The PRC replaced the ROC in the United Nations in 1971. With **Richard M. Nixon** (1913–1994; served 1969–74; see entry) now president, the United States backed off on its opposition and the inevitable UN switch occurred. Most countries had favored recognizing PRC over ROC to begin with, since it represented the bulk of the population and Chiang was essentially a leader in exile. In 1972, Nixon became the first U.S. president to visit the PRC. During his visit, Nixon verbally agreed with Mao and the Chinese communist leaders that Taiwan was part of Mainland China. Also during 1972, Chiang's son, Chiang Ching-kuo, assumed most leadership responsibilities in Taiwan. Chiang remained leader in title only, until his death from a heart attack in April 1975; his son succeeded him in power. In 1979, the United States wanted to open up a new market for U.S. businesses, but it could not expand relations with the PRC while still recognizing the ROC; so it dropped formal diplomatic relations with the ROC and officially recognized the PRC.

For More Information

Books

Chiang Kai-shek, Madame (Soong Mei-ling). *The Sure Victory.* Westwood, NJ: Revell, 1955.

Crozier, Brian. *The Man Who Lost China: The First Full Biography of Chiang Kai-shek.* New York: Scribners, 1976.

Furuja, Keiji. *Chiang Kai-shek: His Life and Times.* New York: St. John's University, 1981.

Seagrave, Sterling. *The Soong Dynasty.* New York: Harper and Row, 1985.

Winston Churchill

Born November 30, 1874
Oxfordshire, England
Died January 24, 1965
London, England

British prime minister

"Never give in—never, never, never, never, in nothing great or small, large or petty, never give in except to convictions of honour and good sense."

Winston Churchill.
Reproduced by permission of the Corbis Corporation.

W inston Churchill was one of the greatest political figures of the twentieth century. He led Britain from the brink of defeat to ultimate victory in World War II (1939–45). Churchill later became the first of the major Western leaders to warn of the communist threat, and he was the first to use the term "Iron Curtain" to describe the growing division or barrier between the communist East and the democratic West. Communism is a system of government in which a single political party, the Communist Party, controls almost all aspects of people's lives. In a communist economy, private ownership of property and business is prohibited so that goods produced and wealth accumulated can be shared equally by all.

Churchill's courage and independence of mind often created difficulties for him in his early career, but they served him well during the critical moments of World War II, when he demonstrated rare qualities of leadership and outstanding gifts as a public speaker. He was a soldier, writer, artist, and statesman. Britain's Queen Elizabeth II (1926–) conferred on Churchill the dignity of knighthood and invested him with the insignia of a special honor called the Order of the Garter in

1953. That year, Churchill also received the Nobel Prize in literature. In 1963, President **John F. Kennedy** (1917–1963; served 1961–63; see entry) made Churchill an honorary U.S. citizen.

A prestigious inheritance

English on his father's side, American on his mother's, Winston Leonard Spencer Churchill was born at Blenheim Palace, near Oxford, England, in 1874. He was the eldest son of Jennie Jerome and Lord Randolph Churchill (1849–1895). Young Winston was born into a long, distinguished family history. He was named Winston after the Royalist (supporter of the British monarchy) family the Churchills married into before the English Civil War in the mid-seventeenth century. He was given the name Leonard in honor of his maternal grandfather, a wealthy American financier from New York named Leonard Jerome. The name Spencer was the married name of the daughter of the first duke of Marlborough, from whom the family descended. And lastly, he received the Churchill surname. It was the original family name of the first duke of Marlborough (John Churchill [1650–1722]), a great soldier and the family patriarch.

Young Winston's talents were not apparent during his unremarkable schooldays at Harrow, an exclusive English private school. On his third attempt to gain admittance, he was accepted for army training at the Royal Military Academy at Sandhurst. He graduated from the academy in 1894. Winston entered the army as a cavalry officer. He took to soldiering, including regimental polo playing, with great enthusiasm.

Churchill made his mark as a journalist and writer, not as a soldier, though he did participate in three major military campaigns. He was a war correspondent in 1895 with the Spanish forces fighting the guerrillas, or irregular and independent fighters, in Cuba. He served as both a war correspondent and an officer in two later campaigns: In 1897, Churchill fought in India, and in 1898 he took part in the Sudan campaign in Africa. While in Sudan, he participated in the British army's last cavalry charge at the Battle of Omdurman.

In 1899, Churchill went to South Africa to report on the Boer War (1899–1902) for the London *Morning Post* and was captured within a month of his arrival. Taken to a prison camp in Pretoria, Churchill made a dramatic escape and traveled by way of Portuguese East Africa back to the fighting front in Natal. His escape made him world-famous overnight. He returned to Britain as a national hero, and in 1900 he capitalized on his popularity by running for political office and winning a seat as a Conservative member of Parliament for Oldham, a city in northwest England. He would remain a member of Parliament for sixty-four years.

Politics

In 1904, Churchill left the Conservative Party to join the Liberals. He spent a considerable amount of his time and energy working on his father's biography, which was published in 1905. In 1908, his book *My African Journey* was published. It recounted his experiences—both for work and for pleasure—while touring East Africa. That same year, Churchill married Clementine Ogilvy Hozier. Together, they had five children and, in his own words, "lived happily ever afterwards."

Churchill held many high government posts during the first three decades of the century. From 1911 to 1915, he was first lord of the admiralty, which is the political head of the Royal Navy. In 1915, when he became embroiled in a heated dispute over Britain's tactics in World War I (1914–18), he resigned from the government and joined the fighting in France as a lieutenant colonel. In 1916, Churchill returned to Parliament as minister of munitions. While holding that job, he helped develop the world's first tanks. Churchill abandoned the Liberals and rejoined the Conservative Party in the early 1920s but found he was now being personally excluded from elections by officials of all major parties because of his repeated switching of party affiliation and because of military decisions he made during World War I that did not work out. Excluded from office, Churchill spent the 1930s as a private citizen and continued his writing.

Throughout the 1930s, Churchill spoke out publicly to warn the world about the threat posed by Adolf Hitler (1889–1945), the leader of Germany's Nazi Party (known primarily for its brutal policies of racism). When Germany invaded Poland in 1939, thereby starting World War II, the moment

Writings and Honors

Winston Churchill's literary career began in 1898 with military campaign reports. His first book, *The Story of the Malakand Field Force* (1898), recounted his experiences fighting the tribesmen of the North-West Frontier in India. Churchill next wrote about his experiences in the Battle of Omdurman in *The River War* (1899).

In 1900, Churchill published his only novel, *Savrola,* and six years later he published his first major work, a biography of his father, titled *Lord Randolph Churchill.* He later wrote another famous biography, *Marlborough,* which tells of the life of his great ancestor, the first duke of Marlborough. It was published in four volumes between 1933 and 1938. In the 1930s, while he was out of public office, Churchill wrote *My Early Life* (1930), *Thoughts and Adventures* (1932), and

the first draft of *History of the English-Speaking Peoples,* a multivolume work that was published in the 1950s. During the 1930s, he also took up painting as a hobby, and he remained devoted to it for the rest of his life. A collection of his portrait sketches, *Great Contemporaries,* came out in 1937, and he published *Painting as a Pastime* in 1948.

Churchill's history of World War I appeared in four volumes under the title *The World Crisis* (1923–29). His memoirs of World War II, titled *The Second World War,* were published in six volumes between 1948 and 1954. Churchill published the four-volume *History of the English-Speaking Peoples* (1956–58) after he retired from his position as prime minister. In 1958, the Royal Academy in London devoted its galleries to a show of Churchill's paintings.

of confrontation between Britain and Hitler had finally arrived. Churchill found himself uniquely positioned as a symbol for action and national resolve because of his longstanding strong stance against Hitler's aggression, unlike Prime Minister Neville Chamberlain (1869–1940) and other contemporary leaders. This gave Chamberlain no choice but to return Churchill to the cabinet as head of the navy. Chamberlain's efforts to appease Hitler failed, as Germany continued to expand. Chamberlain soon lost his position as prime minister to Churchill, who also became minister of defense in 1940.

Alliances

After Germany defeated France, Britain's major ally in the war, Britain stood alone against the Germans for much of

British prime minister Winston Churchill inspects his troops during World War II. *Reproduced by permission of the Corbis Corporation.*

1940. Churchill had inherited a grim situation: Great Britain was under constant air attack and lay under the threat of German invasion. Churchill nevertheless stood firm, refusing Hitler's offers to join his side, and requested help from other world leaders.

Churchill's genius lay in his ability to communicate his conviction that the war could and must be won. By the autumn of 1940, he became confident that the Germans could not succeed if they attempted to invade Britain. Britain had successfully withstood the first few months of German bombing of London and its other cities and had garnered support from the United States in terms of war materials to fend off potential efforts of German forces to try to cross the English Channel in a sea invasion. From the earliest days of the war, Churchill had sought an alliance with both the United States and the Soviet Union; he knew he would need their aid in the fight against Hitler's forces. When Hitler launched his surprise attack on the Soviet Union in June 1941,

Churchill immediately pledged Britain's aid to the Soviet people. On December 7 of that year, the United States entered the war after Japan bombed Pearl Harbor, a U.S. naval base in Hawaii. By May 1942, Churchill had his formal alliance with the United States and the Soviet Union. The leaders of the Allied nations—Churchill, U.S. president Franklin D. Roosevelt (1882–1945; served 1933–45), and Soviet premier **Joseph Stalin** (1879–1953; see entry)—were thereafter referred to as the Big Three.

Summit meetings

Churchill's years as Hitler's only opposition had earned him prestige equal to that of Roosevelt and Stalin, the world's two superpower leaders. Working closely with Roosevelt and keeping on equal terms with Stalin, Churchill traveled widely throughout the war and was present at the three great Allied summit meetings. The first of these was held in Tehran, Iran's capital city; the second was in Yalta in the Soviet Crimean region; and the third took place in Potsdam, Germany.

When the Big Three met at the Tehran Conference in early December 1943, the beginnings of victory were visible. The leaders began discussing strategy for the final stages of the war and plans for the postwar world. The historic Yalta Conference was held in February 1945. The postwar division of Germany was the first and most important item on the agenda. The boundaries of the occupation zones of Germany became controversial, and the exact divisions were left to later discussions.

The second item on the agenda was the formation of the United Nations (UN), an international organization, composed of most of the nations of the world, created to preserve world peace and security. It was proposed that the UN would have a Security Council and that Britain, the United States, China, and the Soviet Union—the four permanent members of the council—would each have a veto. This meant that these nations would always have the power to block any proposed UN actions that might be detrimental to their own well-being and goals.

The third item on the agenda was German war reparations, or payments for war damages. The three leaders could only agree to refer the issue to a reparations commission. The final and most difficult subject on the Yalta agenda was the future of Poland, which was occupied by Soviet forces. This subject dominated the discussions, yet no agreement or resolution was forthcoming. Poland would become a major point of conflict between the East (the Soviet Union) and the West (the other Allies).

The Potsdam Conference took place during the British general election in July 1945. It was the first major diplomatic forum at which it became apparent that the wartime alliance might not survive into peacetime. The East-West differences came to the forefront, especially over the issue of Poland. The world had changed dramatically since the Yalta Conference five months earlier. Germany had surrendered, and the Soviet Union was preparing to enter the war against Japan. Roosevelt had died, and **Harry S. Truman** (1884–1972; served 1945–53; see entry) was the new U.S. president. The day before the conference started, the United States had successfully tested the world's first atomic bomb.

Midway through the conference, Churchill was replaced by a newly elected prime minister, **Clement R. Attlee** (1883–1967; see entry). A general election in Great Britain was being held as the meetings began. Conservative Party candidate Churchill and Labour Party candidate Attlee had both traveled to Germany and awaited the results. The Labour Party was victorious, meaning Attlee became prime minister, replacing Churchill in the Big Three. The only easy decision to come out of the conference was an agreement regarding the eventual peace conference. The leaders agreed that foreign ministers representing the members of the UN Security Council would form another council to prepare for the peace conference.

At the Potsdam Conference, the key issues that became grounds for the Cold War began to emerge. The Cold War was an intense political and economic rivalry between the United States and the Soviet Union that lasted from 1945 to 1991. At Yalta, the Big Three leaders had agreed that Germany would be divided into four occupation zones. Each of the Allied countries—Britain, France, the United States, and the Soviet Union—would occupy one zone. Berlin, Germany's capital city, was to be similarly divided. The Soviets had rejected an earlier proposal that would have left Germany as a unified and democratic nation; still hurting from the German attack on their country during the war, the Soviets wanted a weak Germany. The United States, on the other hand, believed that a unified Germany would help keep Europe politically stable and strengthen the postwar European economy. This fundamental U.S.-Soviet disagreement remained one of the central points of contention throughout the Cold War. The leaders failed to reach a compromise on several issues, and the Potsdam Conference ended in deadlock.

Transitions

Churchill was deeply affected by his loss of position in world politics. He felt frustrated because his wartime government was broken up before he had seen the war come to an end. However, it was clear that the British people had not voted against Churchill but rather against the twenty-year reign of Conservatives in Parliament. In Britain, citizens vote for parties, and the leader of the victorious party becomes the prime minister. Churchill continued to enjoy esteem as leader of the Opposition (in Britain, the "Opposition" means the political party that, at any given time, does not hold power in Parliament). He used this position as a platform for criticizing Stalin's policies in the early Cold War years.

Churchill had begun to fear that the Soviets would spread communism throughout Europe as early as the Yalta Conference. In a speech at Westminster College in Fulton, Missouri, on March 5, 1946, he warned of an "iron curtain" that was descending across the European continent—that is, the strict communist policies that were shutting democracy and free trade out of the Soviet Union. A phrasemaker all his life, Churchill had provided a memorable symbol for the world's next great conflict, the Cold War. An actual "iron curtain" came fifteen years later in the cement and barbed wire of the Berlin Wall, which acted as a physical barrier between East Berlin and West Berlin.

Reelected

Churchill was elected prime minister once again in October 1951. U.S. relations remained at the center of his foreign policy because of his long-standing friendship with the United States; he also wanted to strengthen those ties as the Cold War continued escalating. Churchill sought U.S. cooperation in nuclear weapons research but could not be helped by President Truman because Congress had passed the McMahon Act in 1946, which prohibited the sharing of nuclear weapons research with foreign powers. Undeterred, Churchill pursued an independent atomic research program. In October 1952, Britain exploded its first atomic bomb. Churchill later authorized production of a British hydrogen bomb, which he considered a deterrent to war. Following Stalin's death in March 1953, Churchill proposed trying to improve relations with the Soviet Union.

Churchill retired as prime minister on April 5, 1955, at the age of eighty. He remained a member of Parliament until 1964, at which point he chose not to seek reelection. By this time, he no longer played a significant role in shaping world affairs. Winston Churchill died on January 24, 1965, at the age of ninety. He received a hero's funeral and was buried in St. Martin's Churchyard at Bladon, Oxfordshire, near the place of his birth.

For More Information

Books

Edmonds, Robin. *The Big Three: Churchill, Roosevelt, and Stalin in Peace and War.* New York: Norton, 1991.

Gilbert, Martin. *Churchill: A Life.* London: Heinemann, 1991.

Harbutt, Fraser J. *The Iron Curtain: Churchill, America, and the Origins of the Cold War.* New York: Oxford University Press, 1986.

Jenkins, Roy. *Churchill: A Biography.* New York: Straus and Giroux, 2001.

Keegan, John. *Winston Churchill.* New York: Viking, 2002.

Lukacs, John. *Churchill: Visionary, Statesman, Historian.* New Haven, CT: Yale University Press, 2002.

Web Sites

"Winston Churchill—Biography." *Nobel e-Museum.* http://www.nobel.se/literature/laureates/1953/churchill-bio.html (accessed August 29, 2003).

Clark M. Clifford

Born December 25, 1906
Fort Scott, Kansas
Died October 10, 1998
Bethesda, Maryland

U.S. secretary of defense and counsel

C lark M. Clifford's public career spanned the years of the Cold War (1945–91). He was an influential advisor to every Democratic president from **Harry S. Truman** (1884–1972; served 1945–53; see entry) to **Jimmy Carter** (1924–; served 1977–81; see entry). As a special advisor to President Truman, Clifford assisted in the formulation of the Truman Doctrine, the U.S. policy of giving aid to forces engaged in resisting communist aggression. He was a political strategist in both foreign and domestic policy and was one of the most prominent and influential members of Truman's staff.

Clark Clifford guided the merger of the military service departments into the Department of Defense under the National Security Act of 1947. The act also established the Central Intelligence Agency (CIA) and the National Security Council. In 1968, Clifford became the secretary of defense and played a major role in persuading President **Lyndon B. Johnson** (1908–1973; served 1963–69; see entry) to de-escalate the Vietnam War (1954–75). Clifford was awarded the Presidential Medal of Freedom, the highest honor awarded to civilians in the United States, on January 20, 1969.

"I was part of the generation that I hold responsible for our country's getting into [the Vietnam] war. I should have reached the conclusion earlier that our participation in that war was a dead end."

Clark M. Clifford. *Reproduced by permission of AP/Wide World Photos.*

109

Early life

Clark McAdams Clifford was born Christmas Day, 1906. He was the son of Frank Andrew Clifford, an official for the Missouri Pacific Railroad, and Georgia McAdams Clifford. For several years in the 1930s, his mother, a professional storyteller, had her own weekly program on the CBS Radio Network. Named for his mother's brother (Clark McAdams, a newspaper editor), Clark had one older sister, Alice.

Growing up in St. Louis, Missouri, Clark graduated early from high school and spent a year working on the railroad. In 1923, he entered Washington University in St. Louis and went on to graduate from its law school. In 1928, Clark passed the state bar exam and began working as a trial attorney, later switching to corporate and labor law. While traveling in Europe in 1929, Clifford met his future wife, Margery Pepperell Kimball, whom he married in 1931. They would have three daughters.

Government service

During World War II (1939–45), Clark Clifford enlisted as an officer in the United States Naval Reserve. He was assigned to the White House in 1945 as an assistant to his friend James Vardaman, President Truman's naval aide, a presidential advisor who oversees activities of the navy. In 1946, Clifford replaced Vardaman, and nine weeks later Truman made Clifford his special counsel.

Initially, Truman relied on Clifford for advice on labor issues and speech writing. Soon, however, the president was turning to Clifford for advice on relations with the Soviet Union. The Soviet Union operated under a governmental system called communism, which was very different from the capitalist democracy of the United States. Under a communist government, a single political party, the Communist Party, controls nearly all aspects of people's lives. In a communist economy, private ownership of property and business is prohibited so that goods produced and wealth accumulated can be shared equally by all. Already holding enormous influence in his position as special counsel to the president, Clifford further distinguished himself with the drafting of the Clifford-Elsey Report in 1946. It was a top-secret report to the president; its original title was

"American Relations with the Soviet Union." Clifford coauthored the report with his assistant, George M. Elsey.

In the report, Clifford warned of Soviet expansionism, or the spread of communism into other countries, stating that the threat of Soviet aggression, described in previous reports written by others, was real. Clifford went on to state that the Soviet Union's intention was to dominate more and more countries and spread communism worldwide. He emphasized that the United States needed to develop a clear strategy and adopt containment, a policy to restrict the territorial growth of communist rule, to deal with this communist threat.

Clifford and Elsey wrote the report before there was an open break between the United States and the Soviet Union; therefore, the report rather optimistically declared that the primary objective of U.S. policy would be to convince Soviet leaders that it was in the Soviet Union's best interests to participate in a system of world cooperation. The report argued for cultural, intellectual, and economic interchange to promote the peaceful coexistence of communism and capitalism, an economic system where property and businesses are privately owned. However, it also argued that the United States needed to maintain sufficient military strength in order to restrain the Soviet Union. Clifford believed that military power was the only language that the Soviets would understand. He believed that the Western European nations and the United States needed to form an anti-Soviet alliance and be willing to back up any diplomatic efforts with military action. This idea led to the creation of the North Atlantic Treaty Organization (NATO), a peacetime alliance of the United States and eleven other nations, and a key factor in the attempt to contain communism.

Cold War strategy

The political and economic rivalry between communist and democratic countries became known as the Cold War. The two principal players were the communist Soviet Union and the democratic United States. These two countries had emerged from World War II as the world's most powerful nations, or superpowers.

The United States devised a three-pronged strategy for winning the Cold War. Clifford played a key role in developing each part of the strategy. The first part of the strategy was the

Truman Doctrine, which further spelled out the ideas in the Clifford-Elsey Report. The Truman Doctrine was a policy President Truman announced in 1947. He declared that the United States would provide aid to any forces engaged in resisting communist aggression. Greece and Turkey, two countries devastated by World War II, both faced communist expansionism; in fact, the situation in these countries is what spurred President Truman's announcement. The desperately poor Greek and Turkish people looked to the communists to provide a better life. In the past, Great Britain had aided both countries, but after the devastating effects of World War II, Britain could no longer afford to support them. American leaders felt that the United States had to step in and help rebuild the Greek and Turkish economies before the countries turned to communism.

Clifford also was involved in the creation of the second prong in the U.S. policy of containment; this part of the Cold War strategy came to be known as the Marshall Plan. The Soviet Union had emerged from World War II in a very strong military position. Its neighbors in Europe had not fared as well. The Marshall Plan was designed to help the European nations rebuild their economies and strengthen their military defenses and thereby protect themselves against attacks in the future. This plan was first introduced by Secretary of State **George C. Marshall** (1880–1959; see entry) in a speech at Harvard University on June 5, 1947.

The final prong in the overall plan was the formation of NATO in 1949. Twelve free, democratic nations, including the United States, formed this alliance and stated that an attack on one member of NATO would be considered an attack on all the members. This was an effective deterrent because the Soviets were unlikely to start any war that would involve the United States. Having been an ally of the United States during World War II, the Soviets were well aware of American military strength and knew that the United States had possession of nuclear weapons. NATO was an answer to Clifford's call for an anti-Soviet alliance, an idea he initially proposed in the Clifford-Elsey Report.

Private practice

Clifford resigned from government service in January of 1950 in order to open a private law practice. The firm of Clifford and Miller opened up across the street from the White House. The firm represented many large corporations and continued to advise government officials. **John F. Kennedy** (1917–1963; served 1961–63; see entry) used Clifford as his personal lawyer; when Kennedy was elected president in 1960, he put Clifford at the head of his transition team. Kennedy frequently enlisted Clifford's help and in 1961 appointed him to the Foreign Intelligence Advisory Board. The board was put in charge of supervising the CIA after the CIA botched a top-secret invasion of Cuba at the Bay of Pigs. Clifford became the chairman of the board in 1963. After Kennedy's assassination in November 1963, President Lyndon B. Johnson called on Clifford to reorganize the White House staff.

Secretary of defense

In 1968, President Johnson appointed Clifford as his secretary of defense. Although Clifford held this post for only a short time, it was an intense period in U.S. history. The controversial and unpopular Vietnam War was nearing its climax. When Clifford became secretary of defense, he supported U.S. involvement in Vietnam. However, the day before Clifford's Senate confirmation, North Vietnam launched the Tet Offensive, a massive attack on the U.S. and South Vietnamese armies. U.S. military leaders had been optimistic about their progress in the war, but this attack demonstrated once and for all that their optimism was unfounded. The Johnson administration was bitterly divided about what to do next in the war. Clifford now publicly called for an end to American involvement in the war. He persuaded President Johnson to order a total halt in bombing and to de-escalate U.S. involvement in the war from that point on. He encouraged Johnson to hand over military responsibilities to the South Vietnamese forces.

Return to private practice

Clifford left office in January of 1969 to return to the legal profession. His firm, then Clifford and Warnke, represented major multinational corporations. Seeing that the Vietnam conflict had shifted from the battlefield to the conference table and that the Soviet Union was showing a new willingness to discuss arms limitations, Clifford expressed hope that international tensions would abate. He briefly returned to government service in 1977 as an advisor on several missions for President Jimmy Carter.

Final days

Clifford suffered a major reversal in 1992, when he was president of First American Bankshares, a Washington, D.C., bank. A grand jury indicted, or charged, him for his role in concealing the bank's ties to the Bank of Credit and Commerce International (BCCI). BCCI was a foreign bank whose criminal activities and later collapse cost investors around the world billions of dollars. Despite Clifford's indictment, he was not required to go to trial, because he was in ill health.

In his memoirs, Clifford considered his role in helping to remove the United States from what he called the "wretched conflict in Vietnam" to be his finest moment. The day when he was indicted and fingerprinted like a common criminal he cited as the worst. Clifford died at his home in Bethesda, Maryland, at the age of ninety-one.

For More Information

Books

Clifford, Clark M. *Counsel to the President: A Memoir.* New York: Random House, 1991.

Parrish, Thomas. *The Cold War Encyclopedia.* New York: 21st Century Books, 1996.

Smith, Joseph, Simon Davis, and John W. Burbidge. *Historical Dictionary of the Cold War.* Lanham, MD: Scarecrow Press, 2000.

Web Sites

Berger, Marilyn. "Clark Clifford, Key Advisor to Four Presidents, Dies." From *New York Times,* October 11, 1998. *Mount Holyoke College International Relations Program.* http://www.mtholyoke.edu/acad/intrel/clifford.htm (accessed on August 22, 2003).

"Secretary of Defense Histories: Clark M. Clifford." *DefenseLINK.* http://www.defenselink.mil/specials/secdef_histories/bios/clifford.htm (accessed on August 21, 2003).

Deng Xiaoping

Born August 22, 1904
Guangan, Szechwan Province, China
Died February 19, 1997
Beijing, People's Republic of China

Leader of the People's Republic of China

"Seek truth from facts."

Deng Xiaoping. *Reproduced by permission of AP/Wide World Photos.*

Deng Xiaoping was the leader of the People's Republic of China (PRC) from 1977 until his death in 1997. Besides introducing major economic reforms, Deng strove to increase the PRC's economic ties with the West while keeping distant relations with the Soviet Union. Under former leader **Mao Zedong** (1893–1976; see entry), the PRC had operated in political and economic isolation; under Deng, the communist nation began to participate in international markets.

Young revolutionary

Deng Xiaoping was born in August 1904 to a wealthy landowner, Deng Xixian, in the Szechwan Province of China. In 1921, he went to Paris, France, on a work-study program. There, he met future Chinese premier **Zhou Enlai** (1898–1976; see entry), and in 1922 he joined the branch of the Chinese Communist Youth League Zhou had formed. Showing strong organizational skills, Deng was soon elected to a leadership position.

In 1925, Deng went to Moscow, where he studied at the Oriental University for two years before returning to China.

During the mid-1920s, the Chinese Communist Party had joined forces with the Chinese Nationalist army in an effort to overthrow the unpopular Manchu dynasty rulers. (Nationalism refers to the strong loyalty of a person or group to its own country.) Deng taught at the Chungshan Military Academy in 1926 and 1927 until Chinese Nationalist leader **Chiang Kai-shek** (1887–1975; see entry) abruptly purged communists from the army alliance in April 1927. At first, Deng went underground, or lived in secrecy, in Shanghai; then he joined Mao Zedong and other communists in the southern province of Jiangxi. In Jiangxi, Deng became head of the Red Army's Propaganda Bureau, which was charged with the responsibility of establishing a communist government in the province, in opposition to the Chinese Nationalist government. However, Chiang remained intent on crushing the Chinese communist movement. His forces defeated the communist Red Army in Jiangxi. The communists retreated, setting out on the Long March, a 6,000-mile (9,654-kilometer) trek from Jiangxi to northwestern China, where they hoped to establish a new base. Almost eighty-six thousand communists took part in the Long March; only nine thousand survived the grueling journey.

In 1937, the Communists and Nationalists in China once again joined forces; they were united by necessity—the Japanese had invaded China and were threatening to take over the country. With a common goal of protecting China from foreign influence, the Communists and Nationalists maintained their alliance throughout World War II (1939–45). Deng served as political officer (commissar) for the Red Army during World War II, and he remained in that position when the Chinese civil war resumed in 1946. His Second Field Army led the attack against Chiang's Nationalist government. Meanwhile, Deng moved up through the Communist Party ranks. In 1945, he joined the Central Committee, which ran the day-to-day operations of the Communist Party. The fiery Deng was only 4 feet 11 inches (1.5 meters) tall and earned the nickname "Little Cannon."

The Communists gain power

In October 1949, the Chinese Communists succeeded in overthrowing Chiang Kai-shek's Nationalist government. Communist leader Mao Zedong established the People's Republic of China (PRC) on the Chinese mainland, and the defeated Chiang led a million refugees to the island of Taiwan, located off the south coast of China, where he formed the Republic of China (ROC). The United States established formal relations with the ROC and refused to recognize the Communist PRC government.

Deng was appointed head of the Communist Party in southwest China in 1949, and the following year the Red Army finally gained full control of that region. Deng busily instituted farming reform in the region and steadily climbed in influence. However, Deng at times clashed with Mao because Deng had adopted a moderate political position in contrast to Mao's more radical revolutionary agenda. Nevertheless, in 1952 Deng was summoned to Beijing and was appointed to various senior posts in the Communist Party and in Mao's government. For example, he became the Central Committee's general secretary in 1954; he also served as minister of finance and as deputy to Premier Zhou Enlai. In 1955, Deng was appointed to the Politburo, the important policy-making body of the Communist Party. In 1956, he joined the six-member Politburo Standing Committee.

As a major policy maker, Deng focused primarily on domestic economic development. One of Deng's priorities was to reduce Soviet control of PRC's railways and industry. In 1957, Deng was part of the PRC delegation to Moscow that denounced the de-Stalinization program of Soviet leader **Nikita Khrushchev** (1894–1971; see entry). Khrushchev had regularly criticized the strict communist rule of his predecessor, **Joseph Stalin** (1879–1953; see entry); the attempt to discredit Stalin and his policies is referred to as de-Stalinization. Deng went to Moscow again in 1960. On that visit, he denounced Khrushchev's policy of peaceful coexistence with the West. Deng traveled to the Soviet Union again in 1963, hoping to improve the PRC's relations with the Soviets, but the trip only reinforced the split between the two communist countries.

In 1958, Mao introduced the Great Leap Forward, a program designed to improve the PRC economy through agricultural reforms. The program was distinctly different from Deng's emphasis on industrial reform. Mao wanted to go back to an emphasis on agriculture and peasant farming, while Deng wanted to push China more into the industrialized age. Mao's program resulted in failure and led to increased influence for

Deng. Mao stepped down as chairman of the PRC, and Deng's associate Liu Bocheng (1892–1986) replaced Mao. Mao remained chairman of the Chinese Communist Party, the more powerful position.

In 1965, Mao launched the Cultural Revolution to regain more complete control of the nation and drive Deng and Liu from power. Mao wanted to refocus the economy on peasant farming and turn it away from the capitalist trend he saw in Deng's programs. (A capitalist economic system means prices, production, and distribution of goods are determined by competition in a market relatively free of government interference.) Mao's efforts were successful, and Deng was removed from all government and party positions in 1967. From 1967 to 1973, Deng and his family were forced to live in a rural region, where he performed manual labor.

Rise to leadership

In April 1973, with help from Zhou Enlai, Deng suddenly reemerged in PRC politics and was made deputy premier. The Communist Party needed Deng's experience and ability, so he was placed back on the Central Committee later in the year; in 1974, he was back on the Politburo. As Zhou's health began to deteriorate, Deng took over most functions of the premier position for a two-year period, essentially running the government. During this time, he accompanied Mao at all meetings with foreign leaders. He also journeyed to France, becoming the highest-ranking PRC official to visit a Western European country. In April 1974, Deng went before the United Nations in New York to address a special session on Chinese foreign policy. His raised stature before the UN resulted in him returning home a hero.

The death of Zhou in January 1976 led to a power struggle. Mao's wife, Jiang Qing (1914–1991), and three other radical Chinese communists exerted a strong influence over Mao. This group, known as the Gang of Four, pushed Deng from power in April 1976. Mao died in September, leaving power to the Gang of Four. However, Hua Guofeng (c. 1920–), who at one time had been Mao's chosen successor, soon gained power and reinstated Deng in July 1977.

Chinese leader Deng
Xiaoping (center) walks
with Soviet leader Mikhail
Gorbachev and his wife,
Raisa. *Photograph by Peter
Turnley. Reproduced by
permission of the Corbis
Corporation.*

Deng would this time rise to prominence as the PRC
leader. Before proceeding with his reforms, he sought to end
the stature of Mao, which Deng believed was too big, and to
decrease the influence of Mao's past political doctrine. Deng
believed that communism should be focused on the system
and equality of all citizens (theoretically), not on the celebrity of one or a few. As part of this effort, he put the Gang of
Four on public trial in November 1980 in order to discredit
their earlier actions to control the country. Hua would remain
prime minister, but Deng wielded actual control. In January
1979, shortly after the United States established formal relations with the PRC, it was Deng who traveled to Washington,
D.C., to visit President **Jimmy Carter** (1924–; served 1977–81;
see entry).

Even though Deng held utmost power, he preferred to
exert it indirectly and not hold a top post. In 1980, a Deng associate, Zhao Ziyang (1919–), replaced Hua as prime minister.
Another associate, Hu Yaobang (1915–1989), assumed the

Tiananmen Square

While Soviet leader **Mikhail Gorbachev** (1931–; see entry) was visiting Beijing in April 1989, massive demonstrations for political reform in the People's Republic of China (PRC) broke out. Gorbachev was introducing political reform in the Soviet Union, and many in China wanted the same to occur in their nation. The demonstrators wanted greater political freedom and a more democratic government. Demonstrations occurred in Tiananmen Square, a large public area in Beijing originally built in 1651 and traditionally the place of mass gatherings. It is one of the largest public squares in the world.

Some three thousand Chinese students went on a hunger strike on May 13 and demanded Deng's resignation. The protests gained much international attention through televised broadcasts. Even some PRC army units showed support for the protesters. In response, the government declared martial law (when the law is administered by the military, rather than by civilian agencies) on May 20. On June 4, the army moved in with Deng's approval, crushing the protest. Hundreds of demonstrators were killed in Beijing, and unknown numbers of people died in other cities where similar demonstrations were occurring. The following week, protest leaders were executed in public. Deng blamed Zhao Ziyang for the demonstrations and replaced him with the more conservative Jiang Zemin. Deng also tightened controls over the Chinese people by restricting the freedom of expression, particularly in public gatherings.

Despite international protests over the Tiananmen incident, economic relations between the PRC and the West were unaffected. China was able to retain its most-favored-nation trade status despite protests from some in the U.S. Congress, and in the years that followed, trade continued to expand. However, China withdrew from international politics and became isolated once again.

Communist Party chairmanship in 1981. Deng chose to hold the top position in the Central Military Commission, through which he maintained control of the armed forces. He also held the position of deputy prime minister.

To further strengthen his power, Deng established the Central Advisory Commission in 1982 and named himself the chairman. In 1987, he retired from the Central Committee but still retained full power. Through the 1980s, Deng introduced major reforms, decentralizing various parts of the economy. This gave China's provinces greater input in their economic programs and also gave peasant farmers control over their production and profits. He emphasized each citizen's individual responsibility to make good decisions. He also introduced family planning to curb the country's rapid population growth. With fields leased to farm families, farmers gained greater control over their production and profits. By the early 1980s, farm production was showing a significant improvement.

For industries, Deng introduced incentive systems, rewarding industries for improved efficiency and production. Many industries and businesses were also freed from the control of the central government. Factory managers were given authority to set production levels and seek profits. Previously, the PRC's major economic emphasis was heavy industry, major businesses that demand a lot of capital investment or are labor intensive, such as steel manufacturing or industrial machinery. Deng shifted the emphasis to production of consumer goods, transportation, and energy production. He also formed groups of knowledgeable technicians and managers to lead industrial development. Deng took steps to increase trade and cultural relations with the West and to open PRC businesses to foreign investment. To sustain this economic development, Deng's reforms included sending Chinese students abroad to learn the newest technologies.

Despite the economic improvements, the citizens of the PRC strained under Deng's leadership, in part because he did not allow reforms in the political or social systems. Deng's army remained in control of the country. Though the quality of life was improving, the differences between rich and poor grew. Inflation and unemployment also began to rise during the 1980s. In addition, corruption in the government created further unrest in the population. These conditions led to massive protests by students demanding democratic reforms. In early 1989, one such protest led to bloodshed when the PRC army stepped in to respond (see box).

Jiang Zemin (1926–) replaced Deng as chairman of the Central Military Commission in 1989. Through the 1990s, Deng's direct involvement in the PRC government continued to decline, but he still remained the most influential person in China. The collapse of communism in the Soviet Union in late 1991 convinced Deng that the PRC needed to continue with the economic reforms he had instituted, otherwise the Chinese Communist Party might also fail. By the time Deng died in February 1997, at the age of ninety-two, the PRC had achieved increased domestic stability and economic growth. The standard of living rose, and personal freedoms increased. The Chinese Communist Party remained intact as the sole political party in the nation.

For More Information

Books

Cohen, Warren I. *America's Response to China: A History of Sino-American Relations*. 4th ed. New York: Columbia University Press, 2000.

Hsu, C. Y. *The Rise of Modern China*. 4th ed. New York: Oxford University Press, 1990.

Meisner, Maurice. *Mao's China and After: A History of the People's Republic*. New York: Free Press, 1999.

Schaller, Michael. *The United States and China: Into the Twenty-First Century*. 3rd ed. New York: Oxford University Press, 2002.

Short, Philip. *Mao: A Life*. New York: Henry Holt, 2000.

Terrill, Ross. *Mao: A Biography*. New York: Harper and Row, 1980.

Yang, Benjamin. *Deng: A Political Biography*. Armonk, NY: M. E. Sharpe, 1998.

John Foster Dulles

Born February 25, 1888
Washington, D.C.
Died May 24, 1959
Washington, D.C.

U.S. secretary of state

"Many Europeans [saw] Dulles as a fire-and-brimstone anti-Communist fanatic who would risk the nuclear annihilation of the continent in an effort to blow a hole in the Iron Curtain." — *Historian Richard H. Immerman*

John Foster Dulles.

John Foster Dulles was perceived by many as cold and combative, but he served six distinguished years as secretary of state for President **Dwight D. Eisenhower** (1890–1969; served 1953–61; see entry). He worked hard at protecting the West from communist expansion.

A privileged start

John Foster Dulles was born in February 1888 in Washington, D.C., to Elizabeth Foster and the Reverend Allen Macy Dulles, a Presbyterian minister. His family had a rich history of involvement in international diplomacy and the ministry. One grandfather, John Watson Foster (1836–1917), was secretary of state for President Benjamin Harrison (1833–1901; served 1889–93). His other grandfather, John Welsh Dulles, was a prominent missionary. He also had an uncle, Robert Lansing (1864–1928), who was secretary of state for President Woodrow Wilson (1856–1924; served 1913–21). A brother, Allen Dulles (1893–1969), would become director of the Central Intelligence Agency (CIA) from 1953 to 1961.

A sister, Eleanor Dulles (1895–1996), would serve in the U.S. State Department as an expert on Central Europe.

Dulles enjoyed a privileged upbringing in Watertown, New York, and entered Princeton University in 1904. His father had always encouraged him to become a minister. However, in 1907, young Dulles traveled with his grandfather John Foster to the Second International Peace Conference in Europe. At the meeting, they served as advisors to the Chinese government. It was a impressionable experience for the nineteen-year-old Dulles, giving him a firsthand taste of international diplomacy. He would eventually choose a career in diplomacy, not ministry.

After graduating at the top of his 1908 Princeton class, Dulles entered George Washington University in Washington, D.C., to study law. While at George Washington, he freely mingled with the city's inner circle of influential people. He left George Washington before receiving a degree and passed the bar exam in 1911. Dulles joined the New York law firm of Sullivan and Cromwell, beginning as a clerk, then working his way up to senior partner by age thirty-eight. Dulles specialized in international law, advising foreign clients and American companies that had foreign holdings. He was respected for his very sharp mind, but at times he oversimplified issues, sometimes to the frustration of others. On June 26, 1912, Dulles married Janet Pomeroy Avery. They had three children.

A search for world peace

Dulles's first diplomatic assignment came in early 1917. President Wilson sent Dulles to Central America on a special mission. Dulles was to request the cooperation of the leaders of Panama, Costa Rica, and Nicaragua in declaring war on Germany. The United States needed these countries to protect the Panama Canal from possible German attempts to gain control of the canal or sabotage it. The United States had built the canal in the early twentieth century to improve transportation between the east and west coasts of the United States. Critical to the U.S. economy, the canal and the area immediately surrounding it were under U.S. control. (This changed in 1977, when U.S. president **Jimmy Carter** [1924–; served 1977–81; see entry] signed a treaty giving Panama control of the canal beginning on December 31, 1999.)

During World War I (1914–18), Dulles served on the War Trade Board, which was in charge of negotiating trade with other nations under wartime restrictions. Sharpening his skills in international law and finance, Dulles became highly regarded by President Wilson's advisors. As a result, Dulles was sent to the peace treaty negotiations at Versailles, France, in 1919 to act as legal advisor to Bernard Baruch (1870–1965), the U.S. representative. The resulting treaty involved establishment of German war reparations, or payment for war damages, and creation of the League of Nations, an international organization designed to resolve disputes between nations.

Dulles became discouraged by the heavy demands the victorious European countries placed on Germany. He predicted that the demand for reparations would spur yet another war. (Dulles's prediction came true: Germany's bleak economic situation after the war gave rise to the extremist Nazi Party. Led by Adolf Hitler [1889–1945], the Nazis made aggressive moves to take over neighboring countries, drawing nations around the globe into World War II, which lasted from 1939 to 1945.) The U.S. Senate agreed with Dulles and refused to approve the resulting Treaty of Versailles. Dulles and Wilson, however, did support joining the League of Nations, but the Senate did not. Dulles was greatly disappointed with the U.S. decision not to join the League, which became an official entity in January 1920. However, the Versailles experience brought Dulles increased prestige and attracted new international clients to his law firm.

Though he chose a career in diplomatic relations rather than ministry, Dulles still held deep religious convictions that greatly influenced his approach to ensuring international peace. Dulles attended numerous international meetings and conferences of church leaders, primarily through his work with the Federal Council of Churches of Christ in America from 1937 to 1946. This organization represented twenty-five million Protestants and one hundred twenty thousand churches. In 1940, the council established the Commission on a Just and Durable Peace and appointed Dulles as chairman. The commission developed a pamphlet titled *Six Pillars of Peace* in 1943. The pamphlet called for the creation of worldwide organizations to establish international economic and diplomatic cooperation, promote arms control, and ensure religious and political freedoms.

Early Cold War diplomacy

By the end of World War II in 1945, Dulles was considered the top foreign affairs specialist in the Republican Party. Near the close of the war, President Franklin D. Roosevelt (1882–1945; served 1933–45) had died suddenly, and **Harry S. Truman** (1884–1972; served 1945–1953; see entry) became president. President Truman wanted to involve both Democrats and Republicans in shaping postwar U.S. foreign programs. Dulles's disappointments at Versailles after World War I made him determined to try again when postwar planning for World War II began. Truman, a Democrat, would send Dulles, a Republican, along with Secretary of State **James F. Byrnes** (1879–1972; see entry) to international meetings of top foreign policy makers. Because of the limited success of the League of Nations, Dulles was particularly interested in creating a new international organization to replace the League for the sake of securing world peace. Therefore, Dulles was also appointed as a U.S. delegate to the 1945 United Nations (UN) organizational conference in San Francisco, California.

Despite their party differences, Dulles generally supported Truman, especially as he and Truman both came to realize that the communist Soviet Union and the democratic United States were going in separate and opposing directions. The Soviets had a communist government; this meant that a single political party, the Communist Party, controlled nearly all aspects of Soviet society. Under communist economic principles, private ownership of property and businesses was prohibited so that goods produced and wealth accumulated could be shared equally by all Soviet citizens. In contrast, the United States preferred its democratic system of government consisting of several political parties whose members could be elected to various government offices by vote of the general population. The U.S. economy followed capitalist principles: prices, production, and distribution of goods were determined by competition in a market relatively free of government interference.

Dulles's prominence in the Republican Party continued. In the presidential campaigns of 1944 and 1948, Dulles served as foreign affairs advisor to Republican candidate Thomas Dewey (1902–1971), governor of New York. Dewey lost the elections but selected Dulles in 1949 to complete the term of Democratic U.S. senator Robert Wagner (1877–1953), who had resigned because of poor health. While in the Senate, Dulles strongly promoted congressional approval of the North Atlantic Treaty, which called for the creation of the North Atlantic Treaty Organization (NATO), a military defense alliance consisting of the Western European nations, the United States, and Canada. However, Dulles lost his bid to be elected to the Senate on his own in November 1950.

Dulles returned to serving as an advisor to the Democratic Truman administration. Truman sent Dulles to Japan to negotiate an important peace settlement in 1951. The U.S. military had occupied Japan since the Japanese surrender in August 1945 that ended World War II. The peace settlement restored Japan's independence as a nation and established U.S. military bases in Japan to help contain communist expansion in the Far East. Dulles sought to ease the fears of other West Pacific nations that had suffered from Japanese military expansion in the 1930s and 1940s. He introduced the Australia–New Zealand–United States (ANZUS) Treaty to ensure the future security of the western Pacific region.

The New Look

In the 1952 presidential election, Dulles acted as foreign affairs advisor to the Republican candidate, Dwight D. Eisenhower. By now, Dulles was attacking Truman's Cold War policies, which centered on containing communist expansion. (The Cold War was an intense political and economic rivalry between the democratic United States and the communist Soviet Union that lasted from 1945 to 1991. Containment was a key U.S. Cold War policy to restrict the territorial growth of communist rule.) Claiming that Truman's plan abandoned those already subjected to communist rule, Dulles called containment immoral. He proposed "rolling back" communism rather than just containing it.

Eisenhower won the election and appointed Dulles as his secretary of state. Dulles would become a worldwide symbol of the hard-line anticommunist approach. His dour and forbidding presence was enhanced by an eye tic (sudden muscle contraction) that he had developed after contracting malaria on a business trip to British Guiana earlier in his law career. Dulles spoke briskly and would repeatedly catch the

U.S. president Dwight D. Eisenhower (left) and Secretary of state John Foster Dulles greet South Vietnamese president Ngo Dinh Diem on May 8, 1957. *Reproduced by permission of AP/Wide World Photos.*

world's attention by bringing up massive nuclear retaliation as an answer to Soviet aggression. This hard-line position was called brinkmanship. The policy of brinkmanship meant that the United States was willing to push any conflict with the Soviets to the brink of nuclear war in order to deter communist expansion. The brinkmanship strategy was more formally called the "New Look." Critics of the New Look believed this policy would put the world at risk for nuclear war over relatively minor conflicts.

Eisenhower was significantly less harsh in expressing his viewpoints on foreign matters; nonetheless, he and Dulles grew closer together through the years. Despite Dulles's reputation for tough talk, the United States avoided major military conflict while Dulles was secretary of state. Dulles passed over opportunities to support Eastern European revolts against communism, such as a workers' strike against the East German communist government in 1953 and a broader rebellion in Hungary in 1956. Even though the Soviets used force in both cases to suppress the revolts and killed thousands of Hungarians in the streets of Budapest, the United States failed to take action. Eisenhower feared that intervention could lead to a bigger conflict; it was also October, a month before his reelection bid, and he did not want to risk war at that time.

In early 1954, rather than sending U.S. support for French troops under siege in Vietnam, Dulles worked out a cease-fire with the Soviets, the People's Republic of China (PRC), and the Vietnamese rebel forces. However, Dulles was criticized for not shaking the hand of PRC representative **Zhou Enlai** (1898–1976; see entry) at the negotiations—an illustration of how tiny details loom large in foreign diplomacy. The cease-fire led to the division of Vietnam into North Vietnam and South Vietnam. Dulles then began funneling substantial U.S. aid to South Vietnam, a first step toward the later U.S. role in the costly Vietnam War (1954–75).

Dulles also promoted the creation of the Southeast Asia Treaty Organization (SEATO) in September 1954 to help contain communism in the region. Dulles continued building a system of alliances around the world, adding the Baghdad Pact in 1955. The pact was a military alliance between Turkey, Iran, Iraq, and Pakistan. Using the Baghdad Pact, SEATO, ANZUS, and the treaty with Japan, Dulles had surrounded the communist world—the Soviet Union, Eastern Europe, and the PRC—with alliances of countries friendly to the United States.

Cold War hot spots

Several limited confrontations occurred during Dulles's time as secretary of state. Two confrontations came in 1954 and 1958 between the communist PRC of Mainland China and the noncommunist Republic of China (ROC), which was located off the coast of Mainland China on the island of Taiwan. In both instances, the PRC shelled, or bombed, two small islands controlled by the ROC. President Eisenhower refused to commit the U.S. military, even though Dulles thought a PRC invasion of the ROC was imminent both times. As part of his brinkmanship philosophy, Dulles issued threats of nuclear war toward the PRC, and on each occasion, the PRC stopped the shelling after a period of time. To ease tensions in the area, Dulles obtained a guarantee from ROC leaders that they would never invade the PRC.

A Tribute

During the first few months of 1959, John Foster Dulles sometimes experienced intense pain from his abdominal cancer. Nevertheless, he refused to take painkillers. He did not want to impair his judgment in any way while still serving as secretary of state. He took one last trip to Europe from January 30 to February 8 to meet with West German chancellor **Konrad Adenauer** (1876–1967; see entry). At that meeting, Dulles guaranteed Adenauer continued U.S. commitment to the security of West Germany. Confined to bed by late February, Dulles submitted his resignation, but President Dwight Eisenhower refused to accept it until mid-April. At that time, Eisenhower appointed Dulles as special advisor within the presidential administration.

When Dulles died in May, Eisenhower ordered a full military funeral. Dulles lay in state at the National Cathedral in Washington, D.C., and was buried in Arlington National Cemetery in Virginia. Despite the cold mannerisms Dulles had displayed and the belligerent speeches he made throughout the Cold War years, the funeral was attended by almost all top U.S. government officials as well as world leaders from all the NATO countries and Japan, the United Nations secretary general, and even Soviet foreign minister **Andrey Gromyko** (1909–1989; see entry). In 1950, Congress authorized the construction of a new airport to serve the Washington, D.C., area. On November 17, 1962, President **John F. Kennedy** (1917–1963; served 1961–63; see entry) dedicated the newly completed Washington Dulles International Airport, named in honor of John Foster Dulles. Former president Eisenhower was also in attendance, along with many of Dulles's friends and associates. Dulles had won a deep respect from his colleagues for his years of commitment to protecting the West from communist expansion.

Another major Cold War crisis happened in the Middle East. In October 1956, Israel, Britain, and France attacked Egypt to regain control of the British-owned Suez Canal. The Suez Canal is the main shipping lane connecting the Red Sea to the Mediterranean Sea, a critical route from the Middle East oil fields to Western Europe. A few months earlier, in July, Egyptian leader Gamal Abdel Nasser (1918–1970) had seized control of the canal; he intended to charge fees for its use. Dulles and Eisenhower were irate over the military response, believing it would push Nasser to seek support from the Soviet Union. They believed diplomacy would have been much more appropriate. In a rare instance of Cold War cooperation, the United States and the Soviet Union obtained a UN resolution for a cease-fire, and the canal was placed under UN control. Britain, France, and Israel were very upset with Dulles for not supporting their actions, and their relations with the United States became strained.

Dulles's response to the Suez Canal crisis unsettled the members of the Baghdad Pact; they were confused about what to expect from the United States. To clarify the U.S. position in the Middle East and settle their confusion, Dulles issued the Eisenhower Doctrine in January 1957. The Eisenhower Doctrine stated that, when requested, the United States would assist any Middle East nation engaged in combating armed communist aggression. This policy would lead to Dulles's only use of force as secretary of state: At the request of the Lebanese leader, he sent troops to Lebanon in the summer of 1958 to put down a rebellion thought to be supported by communists.

Yet another crisis came in November 1958, when Soviet leader **Nikita Khrushchev** (1894–1971; see entry) demanded that the Western nations pull out of West Berlin. Since the end of World War II, Berlin had been divided among the victors of the war. The Western allies (the United States, France, and Great Britain) had retained control of West Berlin; the Soviets controlled East Berlin. This arrangement had been a nagging problem for the Soviets, because the entire city of Berlin was located well within Soviet-controlled East Germany. West Berlin was a capitalist island within a communist state. In his ultimatum, Khrushchev stated that if the Western allies did not leave West Berlin, he would turn over control of access to West Berlin to Communist East Germany, forcing the West to deal with a country it did not formally recognize. However, Dulles and Eisenhower refused to withdraw, and eventually Khrushchev backed down on his demand.

While fighting Cold War crises, Dulles was also fighting a personal crisis of his own. Shortly after the Suez crisis in the fall of 1956, Dulles was diagnosed with abdominal cancer. He had an operation to remove it, but the cancer returned two years later, in late 1958. Bedridden by February 1959, he finally resigned on April 15. He died the following month in Washington, D.C.

For More Information

Books

Gerson, Louis L. *John Foster Dulles*. New York: Cooper Square Publishers, 1967.

Guhin, Michael. *John Foster Dulles: A Statesman and His Times*. New York: Columbia University Press, 1972.

Hoopes, Townsend. *The Devil and John Foster Dulles*. Boston: Little, Brown, 1973.

Immerman, Richard H. *John Foster Dulles: Piety, Pragmatism, and Power in U.S. Foreign Policy*. Wilmington, DE: Scholarly Resources, 1999.

Marks, Frederick W., III. *Power and Peace: The Diplomacy of John Foster Dulles*. Westport, CT: Praeger, 1993.

Pruessen, Ronald W. *John Foster Dulles: The Road to Power*. New York: Free Press, 1982.

Web Site

Dwight D. Eisenhower Library. http://www.eisenhower.utexas.edu (accessed on August 28, 2003).

Dwight D. Eisenhower

Born October 14, 1890
Denison, Texas
Died March 28, 1969
Washington, D.C.

U.S. president and army general

"Though force can protect in emergency, only justice, fairness, consideration and cooperation can finally lead men to the dawn of eternal peace."

Dwight D. Eisenhower.
Courtesy of the Library of Congress.

Though highly respected for his key military role in guiding the U.S. armed forces to victory in Europe in World War II (1939–45), as president Dwight D. Eisenhower also skillfully guided the nation through eight years of the Cold War (1945–91), from 1953 to 1961. After reaching a truce in the Korean War (1950–53) during the early months of his first term in office, he succeeded in not sending U.S. troops into combat for the next seven and one-half years of his presidency. In his farewell speech as president in 1961 as the Cold War continued, the fabled war hero warned the nation of giving too much power and influence to the military services and the war industries that support them.

A pacifist background

Dwight David Eisenhower was born in Denison, Texas, on October 14, 1890; he was the third of seven sons born to David J. Eisenhower and Ida Stover. When Dwight was a year old, the family moved to Abilene, Kansas, where ancestral Eisenhowers had earlier lived as part of a Mennonite community. (Mennonites are members of various Protestant groups noted for their opposition to war.) Having failed financially as a shopkeeper, Dwight's father worked at a creamery. Dwight was raised in an atmosphere of hard work and strong religious tradition. The family would read from the Bible together every night.

Eisenhower had well-rounded skills. He was athletic, bright, an above-average student, and ambitious. After graduating from Abilene High School in 1909, he worked for two years at the creamery to help pay for an older brother's college education. In 1911, Eisenhower, known as "Ike," received a scholarship to the U.S. Military Academy at West Point, New York. While at West Point, Eisenhower became a football star in his first years, but then he suffered a serious knee injury that forced him to quit sports. In 1915, he graduated and was commissioned second lieutenant in the infantry at Fort Sam Houston in Texas. There, he met Marie "Mamie" Doud, daughter of a wealthy Denver, Colorado, meat packer. They married in 1916 and would have two sons, one of whom died in infancy of scarlet fever.

During World War I (1914–18), Eisenhower was in charge of tank training camps in the United States and was about to go overseas when the war ended. Following the war, he served in several assignments and, encouraged by one of his commanders, decided to become a student of military science. In the 1920s, he attended the Army Command and General Staff School in Fort Leavenworth, Kansas, graduating first in his class, and the Army War College in Washington, D.C.

World War II supreme commander

In 1933, Eisenhower became an aide to the flamboyant General **Douglas MacArthur** (1880–1964; see entry). He accompanied MacArthur to the Philippines for several years to build up the Filipino armed forces. After the outbreak of war in Europe in September 1939, Eisenhower returned to Washington, D.C. He was promoted to full colonel in March 1941 and given an army command position. Gaining a strong reputation among his superiors in the army, he was promoted to brigadier general in September 1941. On December 12, 1941, five days after the Japanese surprise attack on U.S. military installations at Pearl Harbor, Hawaii, he was summoned to the War Department in Washington, D.C. President Franklin D. Roosevelt (1882–1945; served 1933–45) put Eisenhower in charge of the army War Plans Division. Eisenhower energetically tackled the daunting task of developing a strategy for the Allied response to Germany. He promoted the "Europe first" strategy, that is, combating the Germans first, then dealing with the Japanese in the Pacific.

Eisenhower was promoted to major general in March 1942 so he could implement his "Europe first" strategy. In May, he was placed in command of U.S. forces in Great Britain. The strategy was to first defeat the German forces occupying North Africa and then invade Europe. By July, Eisenhower was promoted again, to lieutenant general, and took command of the joint U.S.-British forces gathered for the invasion of North Africa. In February 1943, Eisenhower became a four-star general. By May 1943, Eisenhower had forced the surrender of enemy forces in Tunisia. He then led amphibious (water) invasions in July 1943, landing first in Sicily and then in Italy in September.

The time had finally come to retake Western Europe from the Germans. In December 1943, President Roosevelt made Eisenhower supreme commander of the Allied forces. Eisenhower was to lead a massive European invasion, crossing the English Channel and landing on the shores of France at Normandy. On this mission, Eisenhower would demonstrate his exceptional ability to plan complex strategies and to keep the commanders under him working together toward a common objective. In June 1944, Eisenhower launched the Normandy invasion, the largest amphibious attack in history. He orchestrated the campaign of U.S. and British forces that slowly fought their way through Western Europe toward Germany. By December 1944, after liberating France from German occupation and pressing toward Germany's border, Eisenhower was promoted to a five-star general. At that time, the German army mounted a major counteroffensive. The resulting Battle of the Bulge was the largest single battle in U.S. Army history. By the end of March 1945, the Allied forces had again gained the upper hand and were pushing into Germany.

During the final war months in Germany, Eisenhower made controversial decisions regarding the advance of Soviet

troops from the east; these decisions played a role in shaping the Cold War. Eisenhower decided to leave the capture of Berlin to the Soviet troops while he focused his forces elsewhere. He believed this would foster good relations with the Soviets and encourage postwar cooperation. His decision was also motivated by a desire to avoid some difficult fighting for his own troops. Many of Eisenhower's commanders were highly critical of his decision. They thought that the U.S. and British forces should push hard to Berlin. Instead, the Soviets took Berlin in April while Eisenhower's troops swept through southern Germany and Czechoslovakia. On May 7, Germany surrendered to the Allies. It was a crowning moment in Eisenhower's military career.

U.S. general Dwight D. Eisenhower speaks to paratroopers during World War II. *Reproduced by permission of AP/Wide World Photos.*

Postwar life

Following the German surrender, Eisenhower briefly returned to the United States, where he received a hero's wel-

U.S. general Dwight D. Eisenhower sits in his jeep in 1944 during World War II.
Reproduced by permission of AP/Wide World Photos.

come complete with a ticker tape parade in New York City. Eisenhower also gave what amounted to a victory speech before an exuberant joint session of Congress. Roosevelt appointed Eisenhower head of the German zone occupied by the United States. (Immediately upon Germany's surrender, an Allied plan divided Germany into four zones. Each zone was occupied by troops from one of the Big Four countries of Britain, the United States, France, and the Soviet Union. Within a few years, the democratic U.S., British, and French zones became one, referred to as West Germany; the Soviet zone became known as East Germany.) Back in Germany, Eisenhower tried to carry out postwar Allied policies in cooperation with Soviet leader **Joseph Stalin** (1879–1953; see entry). However, this turned out to be a frustrating job, because Stalin ignored key policies as well as promises the Soviets had made, including the promise to allow free elections in Eastern Europe.

In November 1945, Eisenhower returned to Washington, D.C., to replace General **George C. Marshall** (1880–1959;

see entry) as army chief of staff. Eisenhower served in that position for two years. During that period, U.S. forces were downsized from their high wartime levels, and U.S. relations with the Soviet Union continued to deteriorate. In February 1948, Eisenhower, considered the most popular World War II general, retired from the army.

Struggling financially upon his retirement, Eisenhower wrote his memoirs of World War II, titled *Crusade in Europe.* Published in 1948, the book became an instant best-seller and made Eisenhower a wealthy man. Also in 1948, Eisenhower was named president of Columbia University, where he would stay for the next two years. During this postwar period, both the Republican and Democratic parties tried to recruit him to be their candidate for president. As revealed in diaries uncovered in 2003, President **Harry S. Truman** (1884–1972; served 1945–53; see entry), a Democrat, even offered to run in the 1948 election as the vice presidential candidate if Eisenhower ran for president. However, Eisenhower declined to run.

As Cold War tensions continued to build, Western Europe increasingly felt the threat of Soviet expansion. In response to this potential threat, the United States and Western Europe established a new military alliance called the North Atlantic Treaty Organization (NATO). In 1950, President Truman reinstated Eisenhower as supreme commander of the Allied forces in Europe, with the job of organizing NATO forces to contain possible communist aggression. Eisenhower was hugely popular in Europe, so Truman hoped Eisenhower's presence would give some degree of comfort to the region, which was still recovering from the war.

White House years

In 1952, Republican leaders were finally able to convince Eisenhower to be their candidate for president in the fall election. Eisenhower's running mate, **Richard M. Nixon** (1913–1994; see entry), was a young California congressman with a strong anticommunist record. Eisenhower and Nixon took a hard-line anticommunist position in their campaign, claiming that Truman was responsible for the communist takeover of China in 1949 and the failure to secure victory in the ongoing, increasingly unpopular Korean War. At one point during the campaign, Eisenhower made the bold proposal to liberate Eastern Europe from communism.

Eisenhower easily defeated the Democratic candidate, Illinois governor Adlai E. Stevenson (1900–1965). The new president's first priority was to end the stalemate in Korea. After difficult negotiations, a cease-fire was signed in July 1953. Not another soldier was killed in combat throughout the remainder of Eisenhower's presidency. Another one of Eisenhower's goals was to balance the federal budget, which required reductions in military spending. To help achieve this goal, Eisenhower decided to emphasize the role of nuclear weapons as a deterrent to Soviet aggression rather than maintaining a large traditional force and costly conventional weapons.

In the years immediately following the end of World War II, fear of the Soviets and communism began to run high in the United States. Before Eisenhower became president, U.S. senator **Joseph R. McCarthy** (1908–1957; see entry) of Wisconsin had begun a witch-hunt for alleged communist sympathizers in the United States. McCarthy had gone so far as to accuse President Truman of harboring communists in his administration. McCarthy persisted with similar claims when Eisenhower took office. At first, Eisenhower avoided confrontation with McCarthy; however, when the senator began attacking the U.S. Army with similar communist accusations, the president responded decisively. Working behind the scenes, Eisenhower put an end to McCarthy's radical anticommunist campaign by arranging public hearings that exposed the lack of supporting evidence for McCarthy's charges against the army.

Though some Republicans wanted him to take the offensive, Eisenhower chose not to confront communism in Korea and Eastern Europe. He selected a moderate course to combat communist expansion without committing armed forces. In April 1953, shortly after the death of Stalin, the Soviet leader, Eisenhower made several attempts to ease relations between the United States and the Soviet Union. He sought to restrict the arms race and offered an "open skies" plan, which would have allowed each of the two superpowers to do overflight inspections of the other to alleviate fears of surprise attacks. Eisenhower also proposed that nations around the world pool their atomic research information and materials, putting all of it under the control of the United Nations; this was referred to as the "Atoms for Peace" program. New Soviet leader **Nikita Khrushchev** (1894–1971; see entry) and other top Soviet officials were not receptive to Eisenhower's ideas.

Eisenhower took more aggressive action against revolutionaries in Third World countries, poor underdeveloped or economically developing nations in Africa, Asia, and Latin America. Believing that the revolutions in these countries were communist-inspired, Eisenhower authorized the Central Intelligence Agency (CIA) to intervene with covert, or secret, operations. In 1953, the CIA overthrew the elected government of Iran, which was thought to be procommunist, and in 1954 the same thing occurred in Guatemala.

However, in 1954, when the French appealed for assistance in Vietnam, a country where communism had already taken hold, Eisenhower chose not to respond. He did not think that the American public would support commitment of U.S. troops in Asia so soon after the Korean War. The British also refused to assist France in the conflict. The French were ultimately defeated, and an agreement was reached to divide Vietnam. North Vietnam would be communist-controlled, and South Vietnam would have a pro-Western government.

Eisenhower had participated in the conference that decided Vietnam's fate, but he refused to sign the agreement that surrendered northern Vietnam to the communists. Instead, he increased U.S. support to South Vietnam. In September 1954, Eisenhower created the Southeast Asia Treaty Organization (SEATO), a military alliance composed of the United States, France, Great Britain, Australia, New Zealand, the Philippines, Thailand, and Pakistan. The purpose of SEATO was to contain further communist expansion in the region. Eisenhower also signed a 1954 treaty with the noncommunist Republic of China (ROC), located on the island of Taiwan. The treaty offered the ROC protection from communist Mainland China and included a guarantee from ROC leaders that they would make no attempt to invade the mainland.

Unexpectedly, Eisenhower suffered a heart attack in September 1955, but he was able to fully recover and resume his presidential duties in a short time. He ran for reelection in 1956 and again handily won—again over the Democratic loser in the 1952 election, Adlai Stevenson. The economy was booming, and the United States was not at war in any region of the world. However, just before the U.S. presidential election, the Soviet Union invaded Hungary to put down an uprising against the communist government. Eisenhower again refused to militarily confront the Soviets. At the same time, Egypt had seized the Suez Canal, which connects the Red Sea with the Mediterranean Sea. The canal had been under British and French control. With Israel's cooperation, the British and French launched a surprise attack on Egypt to regain control of the canal, but they failed to advise Eisenhower of their plan beforehand.

The United States and the Soviet Union were both unhappy about the attack on Egypt, because any crisis in the oil-rich Middle East was a potential threat to their economies. In a rare instance of Cold War cooperation, the two superpowers worked together to obtain a United Nations resolution condemning the attack. Britain and France were humiliated, but the Arab nations were impressed that Eisenhower would go against longtime European friends to protect an Arab nation. However, they were also somewhat confused: First, the United States had failed to respond to Soviet aggression in Hungary; now it seemed that America was actually siding with the Soviets. To reaffirm the United States' anticommunist policy, the president announced the Eisenhower Doctrine. The doctrine stated that the United States would offer assistance to any Middle East government threatened by communist expansion. After the Hungary and Suez crises, the general public held Eisenhower in even greater esteem.

The next Cold War crisis for Eisenhower came in October 1957, when the Soviets successfully launched the first man-made satellite into orbit. (A satellite is a constructed object that orbits, in this case, the Earth.) The American public was stunned. They assumed that the Soviets had overtaken the United States in technological achievements. Through spy plane information, Eisenhower knew that was not the case, but he could not reveal this information, because the spy planes were flown in violation of international law. Under intense pressure, Congress formed committees to determine how the United States could catch up with the Soviets' technology. Much more funding was committed to science and the military. The National Aeronautics and Space Administration (NASA) was formed in July 1958 to guide future space research.

"I Like Ike"

The most popular presidential campaign slogan for Dwight D. Eisenhower was simply "I Like Ike." Eisenhower was an unusually popular American leader, first as an army general and then as president. During his eight years as president, his average monthly approval rating was a remarkable 64 percent. He was intelligent and exuded warmth and sincerity with a wide friendly grin. He showed a strong love for life and people. He was described as quick to anger and quicker to forgive.

At a time when the U.S. middle class was rapidly growing, he exhibited middle-class interests, including golf, bridge, and American Western literature. For years after his presidency, he was judged more on what did not happen during his presidency than on what did. But what he *did* achieve was a cease-fire agreement in the unpopular Korean War only six months after taking office. He then successfully avoided military conflict for the remainder of his two terms, despite the escalating rivalry with the Soviet Union.

On the domestic front, the United States enjoyed a period of economic growth and prosperity during his presidency. Eisenhower added to his popularity during his last two years in office by making many public appearances worldwide; while touring in motorcades, Ike would stand up

An automobile sticker reads "I Like Ike" during the 1952 presidential election. *Reproduced by permission of the Corbis Corporation.*

in an open car despite his advancing age, waving to cheering crowds and showing his broad grin. He also enhanced his image through televised news conferences, a new media phenomenon at that time.

Interestingly, while Americans derived great comfort from the very personable "Ike" Eisenhower, the Soviets considered Eisenhower a threatening figure. In their minds, the fact that the American public had elected a military general as president meant the United States was preparing to go to war.

The next threat of communist expansion came closer to the shores of the United States. On New Year's Day 1959, revolutionary **Fidel Castro** (1926–; see entry) captured Havana, the capital of Cuba, and overthrew the U.S.-supported government there. Before long, Eisenhower suspected that Castro was procommunist. Eisenhower put the CIA in charge of a top-secret plan to invade Cuba. The CIA would train a group of Cuban exiles (people who had fled Cuba) living in Florida and then provide some air support while the exiles carried out the invasion. The landing point for the small invading force was to be at the Bay of Pigs on the southern coast of Cuba. As it turned out, Eisenhower never launched this invasion. That task would fall to his successor, President **John F. Kennedy** (1917–1963; served 1961–63; see entry). The invasion would prove a major failure.

The new Eisenhower

During his last year in office, President Eisenhower seemed to take on a new persona. He used a new four-engine jet, *Air Force One,* to travel the world lobbying for peace. He traveled over three hundred thousand miles and visited twenty-seven countries. Large crowds greeted him at every stop. Eisenhower invited Soviet leader Khrushchev to visit the United States in September 1959 and then proposed a summit meeting in May 1960 in Paris to discuss a nuclear test-ban treaty. Optimism was high, and Eisenhower hoped to finish his presidency on a grand note. However, on May 1, the Soviets shot down a U.S. spy plane over the Soviet Union and captured the pilot. Khrushchev, angry that the United States was spying during a period when the superpowers were working on the easing of relations, asked for an apology. Eisenhower angrily resisted giving in to a Khrushchev demand and refused to apologize. Khrushchev refused to participate in the May summit.

After a memorable farewell address, in which he urged Americans to be responsible with their economic, military, and technological power, Eisenhower retired to a farm near Gettysburg, Pennsylvania. He was reinstated as a general in the army, though he only served in an advisory capacity. In his retirement, Eisenhower wrote a two-volume set of political memoirs titled *The White House Years* (1963–65). He also did oil paintings and watercolors and played golf. He died in Walter Reed Hospital in Washington, D.C., in March 1969, shortly after his former vice president, Richard Nixon, entered the

White House as president. Eisenhower was buried in a small chapel next to his boyhood home in Abilene, Kansas.

For More Information

Books

Ambrose, Stephen F. *Eisenhower.* 2 vols. New York: Simon and Schuster, 1983–84.

Brands, H. W., Jr. *Cold Warriors: Eisenhower's Generation and American Foreign Policy.* New York: Columbia University Press, 1988.

Brendon, Piers. *Ike: His Life and Times.* New York: Harper and Row, 1986.

Burk, Robert F. *Dwight D. Eisenhower: Hero and Politician.* Boston: Twayne Publishers, 1986.

Divine, Robert A. *Eisenhower and the Cold War.* New York: Oxford University Press, 1981.

Eisenhower, Dwight D. *Crusade in Europe.* Garden City, NY: Doubleday, 1948. Reprint, Baltimore, MD: Johns Hopkins University Press, 1997.

Eisenhower, Dwight D. *The White House Years.* 2 vols. Garden City, NY: Doubleday, 1963–65.

Pach, Chester J., Jr., and Elmo Richardson. *The Presidency of Dwight D. Eisenhower.* Lawrence: University Press of Kansas, 1991.

Web Site

The Dwight D. Eisenhower Library and Museum. http://www.eisenhower.utexas.edu (accessed on September 3, 2003).

Mikhail Gorbachev

Born March 2, 1931
Privolnoye, Stavropol province, Russia

General secretary and
president of Soviet Union

"An end has been put to the Cold War, the arms race and the insane militarization of our country, which crippled our economy, distorted our thinking and undermined our morals," Gorbachev said. "The threat of a world war is no more."

Mikhail Gorbachev.
Reproduced by permission of the Corbis Corporation.

Mikhail Gorbachev spoke the following words in a televised address to the Soviet people on December 25, 1991, when he resigned as president of the Soviet Union, "Fate had decided that, when I became head of state, it was already obvious that there was something wrong in this country. We had plenty of everything: land, oil, gas and other natural resources, and God has also endowed us with intellect and talent—yet we lived much worse than people in other industrialized countries and the gap was constantly widening."

Gorbachev rose within the Communist Party the only way possible, by holding to the strict party line. But once he reached its highest office, he began to reform the system with an intensity and boldness that amazed all around him. Two words will be forever linked to his reform of the Soviet Union's political and economic line of command: *perestroika,* meaning restructuring, and *glasnost,* meaning openness, as opposed to secrecy and cover-up.

Growing up under Stalin's rule

Mikhail Sergeyevich Gorbachev was born March 2, 1931, in the village of Privolnoye to Sergei Andr and Maria Panteleyevna. Privolnoye, where peasant families worked the land, was located in southern Russia in the Stavropol province. The Stavropol province was a multiethnic society where young Mikhail, as he recalled in his *Memoirs,* learned "tolerance and consideration and respect toward others."

The hardship of Gorbachev's early childhood and teen years left permanent impressions, marking his character and view of the world around him. Before he entered school, Gorbachev lived mainly with his maternal grandfather, Pantelei Yefimovich Gopkalo, and grandmother, Vasilisa Lukyanoona. A highly respected village member, Gopkalo had joined the Communist Party in 1928 and became chairman of a collective farm in the area. The few books in his hut were those by Karl Marx (1818–1893), Friedrich Engels (1820–1895), V. I. Lenin (1870–1924), and **Joseph Stalin** (1879–1953; see entry), all early influences on the communist system. Gorbachev's grandmother was deeply religious and kept a religious icon (picture) along with pictures of Lenin and Stalin in a corner of the room.

The first of several occurrences that Gorbachev would remember the rest of his life happened at his grandparents' home during the Stalin-driven purge of 1937 and 1938. The purge, when thousands were arrested and many murdered for little or no cause, reached into the peasants' village. Gopkalo was arrested in 1937 and taken away in the middle of the night on made-up charges that he was a member of an organization opposed to Stalin. He was deemed an "enemy of the people," and neighbors avoided the house. Gorbachev's young friends ignored him, for those who continued to associate with the family of an "enemy" could also be arrested. Gopkalo was released from prison in December 1938. Gorbachev remembers sitting around the fire with family as a seven-year-old listening to his grandfather recall his arrest and torture to attempt to make him "confess."

Although he had been too young to remember, Gorbachev also was told how his paternal grandfather, Andrei Moiseyevich Gorbachev, met a similar fate under the brutal Stalin rule. There was a terrible famine in 1932 and 1933 in the

Stavropol area. Authorities arrested Gorbachev's grandfather in the spring of 1934 for not planting enough, even though there was no seed available. Three-year-old Mikhail's father Sergei was Andrei's eldest son. Gorbachev's father took over all farming duties, providing not only for his wife and son but for his mother Stepanida and two sisters. Grandfather Andrei was released from a work camp in 1935, returned to the village, and soon managed a collective pig farm that won awards for the region.

World War II

By 1938, with both grandfathers back home, Gorbachev recalled that life, although at a poverty level by any standards, returned to normal. It had even improved. Gorbachev occasionally got to see a silent movie and delighted in ice cream that was brought to the village. Families took Sundays off, picnicking, playing, and visiting. Then on one Sunday morning on June 22, 1941, terrifying news reached the village and the Gorbachevs and Gopkalos. The Germans had invaded Soviet territory, and the Soviets were suddenly drawn into World War II (1939–45). By August, men in the village headed to the war. Ten-year-old Gorbachev took over farm duties to provide for him and his mother. In *Memoirs,* Gorbachev observed, "Our way of life had changed completely. And we, wartime children, skipped from childhood directly into adulthood." Over the next three years, Gorbachev watched refugees pass by, saw tired, worn Red Army soldiers in disarray, stumbled on a site with friends in the springtime where remains of soldiers killed in battle were left unburied, and endured German occupation of his village for four-and-a-half months in late 1943.

Happier moments also occurred during the war years, thanks to Gorbachev's paternal grandfather, who looked after the growing boy. However, in August 1944, the family received word that Gorbachev's father had been killed, only to learn soon after that he was actually alive and would return to them. Gorbachev never forgot the hardships of the time.

A life back to normal

In 1944, Gorbachev was able to return to school. His learning depended on teachers and his own resourcefulness.

Middle School and High School Experiences

Unlike previous Soviet leaders, Mikhail Gorbachev had fully grown up in the well-established Soviet communist system. His school experiences in the early twentieth century differ markedly from what U.S. schoolchildren experienced in the early twenty-first century. In his book *Memoirs*, Gorbachev describes his school experiences:

> The school of that time, its teachers and its pupils, defies unemotional description. As a matter of fact, it was not even a school. Aside from being housed in various village buildings built for completely different purposes, it possessed only a handful of textbooks, a few maps and visual aids and some chalk, an item not obtained without some effort. That was virtually all we had. The rest was up to the teachers and pupils. We made our ink ourselves. The school had to bring in firewood, and therefore it kept horses and a car. Our teachers, too, had a hard life during the war, what with the cold, the hunger, the anguish. But to do them justice: even then they tried (and one can only

> guess how hard it must have been) to do their job conscientiously, exerting every effort imaginable. Our village school had eight grades. For the ninth and tenth grades we had to attend the district secondary school some twenty kilometres away. With the other children from my village I rented a room in a flat at the district centre and once a week had to return to the village to get some food. Nobody supervised my studies. My parents considered me responsible enough to work on my own.

> I studied zealously. My interest emanated [came] from my inquisitive mind and the desire to get to the bottom of things. I enjoyed physics and mathematics. History fascinated me, while literature made me oblivious to anything else.

> In those years everybody was keen to participate in amateur theatre, and loved athletics, although there were virtually no facilities for these activities. Once our drama group went on a tour of the district villages giving paid performances. The money we collected was used to buy thirty-five pairs of shoes for children who had nothing to wear to school.

Few books or supplies were available. In summer, he worked up to twenty hours a day with his father, who had started operating a combine harvester on the farm. The two had long conversations about life, duty, family, work, and country.

Young Gorbachev had a bright, quick mind and noted how hard the peasant families worked yet could never improve their impoverished life. Every household had to deliver much of what they produced to the government. Yet in 1947, when Gorbachev was seventeen, he and his father produced a very large amount of grain with their combine and were rewarded. His father received the Order of Lenin award, and young Gorbachev received the Order of the Red Banner of

Labor. Gorbachev's honor at seventeen remained his most prized award over all those he received as an adult.

Continuing education and party participation

Gorbachev finished secondary school in 1950 with a silver medal, the award for second best student in the graduating class. About the same time, he became a "candidate" member of the Communist Party. His Red Banner award, work record, party status, and "worker peasant" background helped him to be accepted into Moscow State University law school. Gorbachev quickly developed an interest in politics and became active in the Komsomol, the Young Communist League. In 1952, he became the Komsomol leader for the entire law school and also was admitted as a full member to the Communist Party. Although he proclaimed the Stalin propaganda, Gorbachev's personal decency was evident to his fellow students.

Gorbachev had arrived in Moscow in 1950 at the height, at least to date, of the Cold War (1945–91). The Cold War was a prolonged conflict for world dominance between the democratic, capitalist United States and the communist Soviet Union. The weapons of conflict were commonly words of propaganda and threats. Both the Soviets and the United States possessed the atomic bomb and were busily developing the more powerful hydrogen bomb, or H-bomb. The Korean War (1950–53) had broken out. Communism and U.S. capitalism were presented by his professors as totally incompatible systems, one of which would eventually win over the other. (Communism is a system in which the government or state controls production and there is no private ownership of property, whereas in capitalism there is corporate or private ownership of goods, where competition and a free market are emphasized.)

As a law student, Gorbachev was a disciplined hard worker. He read the works of many authors and particularly liked a two-year course on the history of political ideas. In the midst of Gorbachev's university years, Stalin died in 1953. He had doubts about Stalin's approach to leadership which held that anyone against his ideas was a criminal. Yet Gorbachev kept those views to himself. Stalin was replaced by **Nikita**

Khrushchev (1894–1971; see entry), and soon Gorbachev heard the words "peaceful coexistence" with the United States. This turn-about in philosophy impressed Gorbachev. Classmates recall he enjoyed attending various lectures and art exhibitions and was always ready to discuss his latest intellectual experience. However, it was Raisa Maximovna Titorenko who greatly expanded Gorbachev's interests. Gorbachev met Titorenko, his future wife, at the university.

Raisa

Raisa Titorenko was born in the Siberian town of Rubtsovsk. All through school, she was an outstanding student, graduating with the gold medal, first in her class. Not only intelligent, Raisa was quite a beauty. At the university, she studied philosophy and, like Gorbachev, loved to soak in all the cultural experiences available in Moscow. They were soon inseparable and married on September 25, 1953. After graduation in June 1955, the young couple went back to Stavropol, where Gorbachev became an organizer for the Komsomol. Much as Khrushchev had done, Gorbachev returned to his home to begin a rapid climb through party ranks. Their only child, Irina, was born in 1956.

The capital of the Stavropol province was the city of Stavropol, with a population of 130,000. Here, Gorbachev established relationships with other young Komsomol members including **Eduard Shevardnadze** (1928–; see entry), whom one day Gorbachev would appoint as Soviet foreign minister. Between 1956 and 1958, Gorbachev was first secretary (chief officer) of the city of Stavropol's Komsomol.

By 1961, Gorbachev was first secretary for the Komsomol of the larger Stavropol province. In 1962, he jumped from Komsomol to the party and also enrolled in the Stavropol Agricultural Institute's department of agricultural economy. Gorbachev realized that agricultural successes in his area might translate into a job in Moscow.

During this time, Raisa Gorbachev also continued her work on a doctoral dissertation. The topic was changes in peasant life on the collective farms of the Stavropol area. She received her candidate of science degree in philosophy, the equivalent of a Ph.D. in the United States. She authored a book based on her dissertation and taught at the same institute where her husband was working on his second degree.

Rising through the party

Gorbachev continued his rise in the party ranks. He became first secretary of the party for the city of Stavropol, then first secretary of Stavropol province. The first secretary of a province held the power of the region firmly in his hands. Gorbachev managed all the party affairs for the area. Most members of the Communist Party Central Committee were first regional secretaries, to which post Gorbachev was elected in 1971. The Central Committee was the main administrative body of the Communist Party. Their votes elected the general secretary of the Communist Party, who held the highest position of power in the Soviet Union.

During the early and mid-1970s, Gorbachev was able to travel to countries in both Western and Eastern Europe, considerably broadening his view of European politics. He also caught the attention of Yuri Andropov (1914–1984), chairman of the KGB, the Soviet secret police, which was also the most powerful Soviet intelligence agency. Andropov often vacationed in Stavropol. He was highly impressed with Gorbachev and became a mentor to him. Then on November 27, 1978, much to Gorbachev's surprise, General Secretary **Leonid Brezhnev** (1906–1982; see entry) appointed him secretary of the Central Committee in charge of agriculture, no doubt based on Andropov's recommendation. Gorbachev and his wife moved from Stavropol, where they had lived for twenty-three years, to Moscow. By October 1980, Gorbachev had been promoted to full member of the Politburo. The Politburo was a group of select people in the Central Committee that directed policy.

The party experienced a rapid succession of leaders between 1983 and 1985. Brezhnev died in 1983, and Andropov became general secretary. However, Andropov died in 1984 and was replaced by another aged and ill hard-line communist, Konstantin Chernenko (1911–1985). Chernenko died in 1985. The vigorous fifty-four-year-old Mikhail Gorbachev became the new general secretary of the Communist Party on March 11, 1985. **Andrey Gromyko** (1909–1989; see entry), veteran Soviet foreign minister and a leader in the Politburo, enthusiastically nominated Gorbachev for the position. In Gromyko's nomination speech, he characterized Gorbachev by saying, "This man has a nice smile, but he has teeth of iron." At last, Gorbachev was in position to bring reform.

A changing nation

Gorbachev had long exhibited a can-do attitude. He was a man of action and wasted no time setting a tone in the country to expect change. One immediate outward example of the change was seen with Raisa. Unlike any general secretary's wife before, she accompanied her husband on travels around the Soviet Union and to foreign countries. She became a partner and ally in her husband's initiatives. She also took up the cause of conservation and promotion of the Russian cultural heritage. Gorbachev began an antialcohol campaign that proved very unpopular. At first, he held a tight line but was forced to abandon the campaign a few years later. Nevertheless, he had indicated to the people of the Soviet Union that he would be a leader for change.

The nuclear reactor disaster of Chernobyl occurred on April 26, 1986. Still under the old communist system of not disclosing internal problems to the outside world, Gorbachev did not publicly respond to the disaster quickly. He first spoke on television about the disaster on May 14. However, that was the last time Gorbachev would use secrecy and cover-up. Almost immediately, he instituted the official government policy of *glasnost,* or openness, and *perestroika,* or restructuring. Gorbachev saw that for the Soviet Union to survive in the late twentieth century world marketplace of ideas and goods, it would have to completely reform its cumbersome political and economic chain of command. Glasnost showed the horrors the Soviets had lived under through the decades and the corruption of the huge government system.

Gorbachev set into motion the most radical domestic reforms of the Soviet political system since it was first established in 1917. Most reforms were started in 1989 and 1990. Gorbachev moved the center of political power away from the Communist Party and into a government structure. The party was no longer manager of the country. He decided the Soviets needed an executive presidency much like the French and American presidencies. So he introduced to the Constitution the word "president," taking the place of the position of chairman of the Presidium of the Supreme Soviet, also known as the head of state. Supreme Soviet was the Communist Party's legislature. Under the presidency, he established two executive councils, the Presidential Council, like the U.S. president's cabinet, and the Council of the Federation, which brought together the top representatives of the Soviet republics. The Presidential Council took over most duties of the Politburo.

On the legislative side of government, he introduced competitive elections to the Soviet Congress of the People's Deputies that comprised 2,250 positions. In 1988, Gorbachev got approval for the first multicandidate elections since the 1920s. However, 750 places were reserved for organizations such as the Communist Party (100 seats). In turn, Congress elected from its members a Supreme Soviet—a two-part body made of the Soviet of the Union and the Soviet of Nationalities. These were similar to genuine Western-style debating bodies and parliaments. In 1988, Gorbachev got rid of many of the old party faithfuls and replaced them with those whose ideas were like his.

Cold War ends

Gorbachev also undertook a radical restructuring of the economy. He took the party out of detailed management of the economy by slashing the Central Committee from twenty departments to nine. The essence of Gorbachev's economic restructuring was decentralization, giving more control to localities. Although he pushed the economy toward a real marketplace competition, he had to walk a fine line between moving too fast and too slow. Commercial banks and trading associations were not yet well organized. Gorbachev laid out plans to drastically increase production of consumer goods and services between 1985 and 2000.

To ease the difficult economic transition, Gorbachev knew the Soviet Union needed to halt its all-out Cold War arms race with the United States. In July 1985, he replaced Gromyko with Shevardnadze as foreign minister to help in easing Cold War tensions with the United States.

The relaxing of tensions between the two superpowers would allow Gorbachev to devote energy and resources to domestic issues. The Soviet Union had no economic means to continue matching the relentless American missile buildup. U.S.-Soviet arms control talks had stalled in 1983 due to stubborn nonproductive Cold War hard-line diplomacy between Andropov and U.S. president **Ronald Reagan** (1911–; served 1981–89; see entry). Reagan was the most intensely anti-Soviet American president to date. Gorbachev was determined to show a new look of flexibility in negotiations and to eventually win over Reagan. When Gorbachev came into office, he inherited a U.S.-Soviet impasse over Reagan's proposed "Star Wars" program, an elaborate system to defend the United States from missile attacks. The Soviets had demanded Star Wars and all research toward it be canceled. Gorbachev considered this an unnecessarily tough stance. In October 1986, Gorbachev met with Reagan in Reykjavik, Iceland. There, he proposed a grand compromise, the eventual elimination of intermediate-range nuclear forces (INF) in exchange for withdrawal and destruction of U.S. missiles deployed in Europe in 1983 and aimed at the Soviet Union. Furthermore, he proposed to make deep cuts in offensive missiles, if Star Wars was confined to laboratory research only.

Although the talks fell apart, the precedent of better cooperation was set, and Gorbachev began altering his position on Star Wars more and more. In December 1986, Gorbachev in a brilliant political move released Nobel Peace Prize–winning physicist **Andrey Sakharov** (1921–1989; see entry) from exile in Gorky. This won worldwide approval. Sakharov had fallen out of favor with the Soviets because of his outspokenness and went into exile in early 1980. He had long advocated control of nuclear weapons, and now Gorbachev spoke of a need only for a sufficient defensive position and "mutual security" for the Soviets and America. Gorbachev was laying the groundwork for the end of the Cold War. His new thinking was tremendously intriguing for western strategists.

By 1987, some Western European polls showed Gorbachev as more popular than Reagan. In December 1987, Gorbachev visited Reagan in Washington, D.C., for another summit. Gorbachev quickly became a local and national television media celebrity. Delighted to visit America, he exhibit-

U.S. president Ronald Reagan (left) and his wife Nancy walk with Soviet leader Mikhail Gorbachev and his wife Raisa at a Washington, D.C., function in 1987. *Reproduced by permission of the Corbis Corporation.*

ed enthusiasm and goodwill and even stopped his motorcade to get out and shake hands with Washingtonians on the street. Clearly, Gorbachev was a new kind of Soviet leader.

In January 1988, Gorbachev announced plans to withdraw Soviet troops from the decade-long costly war in Afghanistan that further showed a dramatic change in Soviet thinking. The next two years saw an impressive amount of interaction between Gorbachev and U.S. leaders. In response, Reagan went to Moscow in May for yet another U.S.-Soviet summit. Then Gorbachev returned to the United States the following winter. On December 7, 1988, Gorbachev made his famous speech to the United Nations in New York City in which he called for an end to the Cold War. By the end of 1989, Gorbachev had allowed the people of Eastern European states to remove communist dictatorships and regain independence. He watched the toppling of the Berlin Wall, which had kept people from fleeing from communist East Germany to noncommunist West Berlin since 1961, and later saw the reunification of East and West Germany. In 1990, the Nobel Peace Prize was awarded to Gorbachev. In March 1990, the Congress of People's Deputies elected Gorbachev as president of the Soviet Union. He met with the new U.S. president, **George Bush** (1924–; served 1989–93; see entry) in Washington in June 1990.

The fall of Gorbachev

All of the initiatives made Gorbachev extremely popular in the West, but in the Soviet Union major problems existed. The combination of raised economic expectations coupled with continuing shortages of basic goods and growing unemployment caused Gorbachev's popularity at home to drop significantly. Also, many old-time party hard-liners were aghast watching their former satellite countries break away. The old-line conservatives wanted the reforms to slow or even stop. Liberals wanted much faster progress in reform. Gorbachev briefly turned to some of the hard-liners for support. But on August 18, 1991, while on a vacation in the Crimea (a peninsula reaching into the Black Sea), a coup was attempted. Gorbachev and his wife were held at their villa for several days. The coup collapsed thanks to resistance by the people of Moscow led by Russian president Boris Yeltsin (1931–). Gorbachev returned to Moscow but never gained back any real authority. Yeltsin would essentially become the most influential Soviet leader. In a last effort to distance himself from the Communist Party, Gorbachev resigned from the party on August 24, 1991. However, power formally shifted to Russian president Yeltsin on November 7, 1991. He banned the Communist Party in Russia.

Gorbachev resigned as Soviet president on December 25, 1991. The Soviet Union ended its existence on December 31, 1991. Gorbachev kept a residence in Moscow and bought a villa in Finland. He made a run for election as Russian president in 1996 against Yeltsin but garnered less than 1 percent of the vote. In 1999, Raisa Gorbachev died of leukemia, a blood disease. Gorbachev founded several organizations including the International Organization for Soviet Socioeconomic and Political Studies (Gorbachev Foundation), based in Moscow, and Green Cross International, headquartered in Geneva. He also lectures extensively abroad.

For More Information

Books

Doder, Dusko, and Louise Branson. *Gorbachev: Heretic in the Kremlin.* New York: Viking, 1990.

Gorbachev, Mikhail. *Memoirs.* New York: Doubleday, 1995.

Gorbachev, Mikhail. *Perestroika: New Thinking for Our Country and the World.* New York: Harper & Row, 1987.

Gorbachev, Mikhail. *A Time For Peace.* New York: Richardson & Steirman, 1985.

Gorbachev, Mikhail, and Zdenek Mlynar. *Conversations with Gorbachev.* New York: Columbia University Press, 2002.

Gorbachev, Raisa. *I Hope.* New York: HarperCollins Publishers, 1991.

McCauley, Martin. *Gorbachev.* New York: Longman, 1998.

Morrison, Donald, ed. *Mikhail S. Gorbachev: An Intimate Biography.* New York: Time Books, 1988.

Web Sites

President Mikhail Sergeyevich Gorbachev. http://www.mikhailgorbachev.org (accessed on September 3, 2003).

Andrey Gromyko

Born July 18, 1909
Starye Gromyki, Belorussia (now Belarus)
Died July 2, 1989
Moscow, Russia

Soviet foreign minister and president

For over forty years, Andrey Gromyko was a skilled representative and spokesman for the Soviet Union while serving in a number of positions under various Soviet leaders. He maintained a persistent loyalty to official Soviet perspectives in its prolonged Cold War rivalry with the United States. To many in the West, his was the most familiar face of the communist-ruled superpower.

Making use of the new communist system

Andrey Andreyevich Gromyko was born to Russian peasant farmers in the Belorussian village of Old Gromyki. Residents of that region would traditionally adopt the name of their village, so most inhabitants had the same last name: Gromyko. The Bolshevik Revolution occurred in 1917, when Gromyko was only eight years old. The Bolsheviks, mostly Russian peasants and workers rising in revolt against the Russian ruling class, professed the communist ideology of Vladimir I. Lenin (1870–1924), who established the Communist Party in Russia. Communism is a governmental system in

"Even after the defeat of American mercenaries at the Bay of Pigs, [the U.S. government] had not changed its course on Cuba ... a loud propaganda campaign about the 'Soviet threat' in the region was launched."

Andrey Gromyko.
Reproduced by permission of the United Nations.

159

which the Communist Party controls nearly all aspects of citizens' lives. In a communist economy, private ownership of property is banned, and accumulated wealth is, in theory, shared equally by all. The Bolsheviks prevailed over the ruling classes and established communist rule throughout the country. The new communist system gave rural peasant youths new educational opportunities, and the intellectually gifted Gromyko would later take full advantage of them. In the meantime, to help support his family, fourteen-year-old Gromyko began working with his father, Andrey Matveyevich, at various jobs, including timber-cutting in the forests surrounding his village.

After completing his secondary education, Gromyko attended the Economics Institute in the city of Minsk and studied agricultural economics. In 1931, at age twenty-two, he joined the Communist Party. He married Lydia Dmitrievna Grinevich that same year; they would have two children. Continuing in the Soviet educational system, Gromyko completed a graduate program in economics and English in 1936 at the Minsk Agricultural Technical School. Moving to Moscow's Institute of Economics of the Soviet Academy of Sciences, Gromyko completed a doctoral dissertation on U.S. agricultural mechanization. He remained at the institute until 1939 as a senior researcher and lecturer specializing in the American economy. In later years, he would publish three Russian-language books on U.S. economics. Gromyko also worked as a staff member on an economics journal through the late 1930s.

From 1936 to 1938, while Gromyko was completing his higher education, Soviet premier **Joseph Stalin** (1879–1953; see entry) carried out massive purges of Communist Party leaders as well as ordinary party members; this period of purging is referred to as the Great Terror. Millions of Stalin's opponents—and even some of his supporters—were executed or exiled. Young party members of Gromyko's generation suddenly saw great opportunities open up in the Soviet government; after all, those who had been purged needed to be replaced. As a result, in 1939, Gromyko was recruited into the Soviet Diplomatic Service. Apparently making a quick and highly favorable impression, Gromyko was sent to work in the Soviet embassy in Washington, D.C. He became a favorite of Soviet foreign minister **Vyacheslav Molotov** (1890–1986; see entry), and by 1943 Gromyko, only thirty-three years old at the time, was appointed Soviet ambassador to the United States. By then, he had become fluent in English.

During the mid-1940s, Gromyko became a prominent presence at meetings with world leaders. With his solemn facial expressions, Gromyko personified the long-term chilly relations between the United States and the Soviet Union. Gromyko was nicknamed "Old Stone Face," "Grim Grom," and "Mr. Nyet." (*Nyet* means "no" in Russian.)

A rapid rise to foreign minister

In 1943, Gromyko traveled to Tehran, Iran, to attend the first meeting of Allied leaders during World War II (1939–45). The Allied leaders were Great Britain's **Winston Churchill** (1874–1965; see entry), the United States' Franklin D. Roosevelt (1882–1945; served 1932–45), and the Soviet Union's Stalin. The meeting focused on plans for postwar Europe. Gromyko then led the Soviet delegation at the 1944 Dumbarton Oaks conference in Washington, D.C.; at this meeting, world leaders discussed proposals for the creation of the United Nations (UN), an international organization created to resolve disputes among nations. Gromyko traveled to San Francisco in April 1945 to write the UN charter. He assisted Stalin and Molotov at two other important meetings in 1945, the first at the Crimean resort of Yalta and the second in Potsdam, Germany. Negotiating with Allied wartime leaders from the United States and Great Britain, Gromyko managed to keep Poland under Soviet control and keep Germany a divided nation, two important goals for the Soviet government. In return, the Soviets agreed to help the United States in its continuing war with Japan.

In 1946, Gromyko was named Soviet representative to the newly formed UN Security Council. Because of Gromyko's earlier involvement in writing the UN charter, the Soviets received veto power over any proposals they found disagreeable; proposals posed by the United States and other Western countries were the most frequent offenders. Gromyko used his veto power freely while serving in the UN, casting twenty-six vetoes to prevent adoption of resolutions. He also dramatically stormed out of one Security Council session in protest over discussions of attempted Soviet expansion into Iran.

Structure of the Communist Party

Andrey Gromyko served as a top leader in the Soviet government for decades; he also held various positions of influence in the Soviet Communist Party. Communism is a system of government in which national leaders are selected by a single political party, the Communist Party, which controls almost all aspects of society. No other political parties are allowed. Therefore, the Soviet Communist Party held more power than the government of the Soviet Union. The Party provided political and social guidance and handled foreign relations, while the government existed for administrative purposes for public works and social services. The head of the Communist Party is the most powerful person in a Communist nation.

The structure of the Communist Party was very different from that of U.S. political parties. Party leadership was divid-

ed into several bodies: the Central Committee, the Secretariat of the Central Committee, the Politburo, and the Council of Ministers. The Central Committee was the administrative body of the Communist Party; it consisted of about one hundred of the party's leading figures. The general secretary (also called the first secretary between 1953 and 1966) was head of the Central Committee and top officer of the Communist Party. The Secretariat of the Central Committee consisted of about eleven members; this group of leaders ran the day-to-day activities of the Central Committee, such as keeping the numerous Party positions filled around the Soviet Union, making sure local Party officials were properly carrying out policy, and resolving Party disputes. The Central Committee's executive body was the Politburo (known as the Presidium between 1953 and 1966). It

In 1949, Gromyko was promoted to deputy foreign minister under Molotov, a rather rapid rise since entering the diplomatic field just ten years earlier. His work in the foreign minister's office was briefly interrupted in 1952 and 1953 because Molotov had fallen out of favor with Stalin. During this time, Gromyko was Soviet ambassador to Britain. However, immediately after Stalin's sudden death in 1953, Gromyko returned to Moscow to work as assistant foreign minister under Molotov once again. Making a break from past Stalin policies, new Soviet leader **Nikita Khrushchev** (1894–1971; see entry) replaced Molotov with Gromyko as foreign minister in 1957. Gromyko served in that post for the next twenty-eight years. Gromyko was moving up rapidly in the Soviet Communist Party as well. In 1952, he had become a candidate member in was a small body that directed party policy. The Politburo had no chairman, operating on the communist principle that all the members were equal. Therefore, the general secretary held top power in the country. Another body, the Council of Ministers, was in charge of economic issues.

The Soviet national government was separate from the Communist Party structure but totally subordinate to it. The legislative body of the Soviet government was the Supreme Soviet. The head of state and head of the Supreme Soviet was the premier. The person holding the position of premier was essentially a figurehead and served as the chief administrative officer of the Soviet government. The Presidium of the Supreme Soviet, composed of forty-two members, was in charge of passing Soviet legislation.

In actuality, the division of functions and responsibilities between the Central Committee, the Politburo, the Council of Ministers, and the Supreme Soviet was not distinct. The system was greatly dependent on individual personalities and how much support they could gain from others of influence. Therefore, no set path for selecting leaders existed. Anyone who had ambitions to lead the Communist Party needed to gather a personal following. Such a leader could come from any of the ruling bodies of the party. There were no set terms of office, so a leader was vulnerable to personal rivalries, conflicts over policy, and the rise of influential people. The system was ripe for and always suffered from corruption and secret deals.

the Central Committee of the Communist Party. He gained full membership in the Central Committee in 1956.

Man of influence

By 1957, Gromyko was well known worldwide for his extensive knowledge of international affairs; he was also highly respected for his negotiating skills. His fellow Soviets trusted him as their sole representative on major diplomatic missions and as their chief foreign policy advisor.

During his career as foreign diplomat and foreign minister, Gromyko would meet with every U.S. president from Franklin D. Roosevelt to **Ronald Reagan** (1911–; served

1981–89; see entry). Gromyko accompanied many different Soviet leaders, from Joseph Stalin (1879–1953) to **Leonid Brezhnev** (1906–1982; see entry), on foreign visits. Gromyko was very intelligent and able to adapt his philosophies to the particular Soviet leader he was serving. He was the person Khrushchev sent to Washington, D.C., to meet with President **John F. Kennedy** (1917–1963; served 1961–63; see entry) during the Cuban Missile Crisis.

Gromyko's role as foreign minister would change over time. Khrushchev's flamboyant personal style kept the much more reserved Gromyko in the background for his first seven years in the post. When Brezhnev replaced Khrushchev as Soviet leader in October 1964, Brezhnev kept Gromyko as foreign minister. Under Brezhnev, Gromyko's influence and power grew significantly, and he regained his previous visibility in world affairs. Gromyko even met with Pope Paul VI (1897–1978) in 1966 while visiting Rome, Italy. Gromyko was one of the few Soviet officials to meet with a pope during the Cold War. His visit to the leader of one of the major world religions was notable because a key aspect of communism was the belief in no God and the discouragement of religious practices.

When meeting with world leaders, Gromyko made efforts to keep relations open and honest, but he was nevertheless staunchly dedicated to preserving Soviet communist rule. In 1968, when Czechoslovakia began to reform communist policies and introduce greater freedoms, Gromyko urged Brezhnev to respond with force. Gromyko also charted an aggressive course in Third World, or underdeveloped, countries. During the 1970s, he supported an overthrow of the Angolan government in Africa and encouraged Soviet leaders to provide aid to a procommunist government in Ethiopia. He also pushed for the Soviet invasion of Afghanistan in 1979 to support a pro-Soviet government there. The invasion led to a prolonged and costly war.

Much of Gromyko's career was spent negotiating arms control agreements. He played a key role in negotiating the Strategic Arms Limitation Treaty (SALT I) with U.S. president **Richard M. Nixon** (1913–1994; served 1969–74; see entry) in the early 1970s, including final negotiations. SALT I was the first treaty to set limits on some nuclear weapons and eliminate antiballistic missile (ABM) systems. Gromyko

proved a quick learner in the technical aspects of ballistic missiles and nuclear weapons. Impressing the negotiators from other nations, Gromyko often negotiated without the immediate need of technical advisors.

As Gromyko's influence in foreign affairs increased, so did his standing in the Soviet Communist Party. In 1973, Gromyko became a member of the Communist Party's policy-making committee, the Politburo. Through his Politburo position and foreign ministry post, Gromyko was a key force in the Soviet Union's efforts to ease tensions with the West; this new policy of promoting better relations was known as détente. Gromyko wanted the Soviet Union to have access to new advanced technologies of the West. In order to gain such access, Gromyko helped negotiate various agreements with Western nations to improve relations. His efforts led to agreements with West Germany addressing central European relations and to the Helsinki Accords of 1975, which made the postwar political boundaries in Eastern Europe permanent, a

Soviet foreign minister Andrey Gromyko (left) shakes hands with U.S. president Richard Nixon at a SALT I signing ceremony in October 1972. *Reproduced by permission of the Corbis Corporation.*

key to maintaining gains in Soviet influence in the region. In November 1974, Gromyko and Brezhnev met with U.S. president Gerald Ford (1913–; served 1974–77) in Vladivostok to begin discussions on another nuclear arms treaty, SALT II. SALT II was eventually signed on June 18, 1979, in Vienna, Austria, by President **Jimmy Carter** (1924–; served 1977–81; see entry) and Brezhnev. Gromyko and U.S. secretary of state Cyrus Vance (1917–2002) had been the main negotiators.

Gromyko's influence within the Soviet Union expanded further in 1983 when he became first deputy chairman of the Council of Ministers. The Council of Ministers controlled Soviet economic and cultural life. Brezhnev became increasingly feeble during his last years of power, and his immediate successors, Yuri Andropov (1914–1984) and Konstantin Chernenko (1911–1985), both suffered from ill health during their short terms in office. As a result, Gromyko was the person who actually ran Soviet foreign affairs in the early 1980s. For example, in 1982, he spoke before the United Nations in opposition to U.S. deployment of new nuclear missiles in Europe. It was clear to those in attendance that Gromyko was speaking from a position of great authority. During this period, Soviet foreign policy became much more aggressive. In 1981, Gromyko supported the Polish government in crushing strikers who were protesting increased food prices. He also took a tough stance against President Reagan, who was threatening a renewed arms race. Gromyko later met with U.S. secretary of state George Shultz (1920–) in Geneva, Switzerland, in early 1985 to discuss arms control.

By 1985, Gromyko was the senior member of the Politburo and had great influence in the Soviet Communist Party. After the death of Chernenko, Gromyko proposed that **Mikhail Gorbachev** (1931–; see entry) be the next general secretary. Gorbachev did in fact become the new head of the Communist Party; he was the first of a new generation of Soviet leaders. Stressing much-needed economic reform, Gorbachev appointed **Eduard Shevardnadze** (1928–; see entry) to replace the old-guard Gromyko as foreign minister in June 1985, ending Gromyko's twenty-eight years in that position. However, out of respect for Gromyko and gratitude for his personal support, Gorbachev made him chairman of the Supreme Soviet, a position of prestige rather than power. Gorbachev shook up Soviet leadership again in 1988. Gromyko fell victim to this change and resigned from his Politburo position. By April 1989, he was removed from the Central Committee as well.

Gromyko died of a stroke only a few months after leaving the Central Committee. He had been one of the last remaining members of the old-time hard-line Communist Party generation; indeed, despite Gromyko's long service to the Soviet Union, only one Politburo member attended his funeral. Just before his death, Gromyko published memoirs he had been compiling since 1979. However, for historians, the memoirs revealed few new insights about Gromyko's decades in the Soviet foreign ministry department. Instead Gromyko's writings reflected the traditional, rigid, hard-line communist interpretation of the Cold War.

For More Information

Books

Edmonds, Robin. *Soviet Foreign Policy: The Brezhnev Years.* New York: Oxford University Press, 1983.

Gromyko, Andrei Andreyevich. *Memoirs.* New York: Doubleday, 1990.

Kelley, Donald R. *Soviet Politics in the Brezhnev Era.* New York: Praeger, 1980.

Linden, Carl A. *Khrushchev and the Soviet Leadership, 1957–1964.* Baltimore, MD: Johns Hopkins University Press, 1966.

Tatu, Michel. *Power in the Kremlin: From Khrushchev to Kosygin.* New York: Viking, 1969.

W. Averell Harriman

Born November 15, 1891
New York, New York
Died July 26, 1986
Yorktown Heights, New York

**U.S. secretary of commerce,
statesman, industrialist**

"Conferences at the top level are always courteous. Name-calling is left to the foreign ministers."

W. Averell Harriman.
Courtesy of the Library of Congress.

W. Averell Harriman played a key role in many important political events of the twentieth century, including events during the Cold War. Born to privilege, Harriman believed passionately in public service; he believed in his ability—and obligation—to make the world better. He exercised his influence in major negotiations of the 1940s, 1950s, and 1960s.

Harriman is often considered the architect of the Cold War policy of containment, the strategy of keeping communist influence within the borders of existent communist nations. Communism is a political and economic system in which the Communist Party controls nearly all aspects of citizens' lives and private ownership of property is banned. It is not compatible with American political and economic values. Harriman had a strong, long-term relationship with the Soviet Union, but he came to believe that communism, the Soviet form of government, was a threat to the United States and to democracies around the world. Harriman advised U.S. presidents accordingly; he also negotiated with dictators. Putting his beliefs into action, he helped craft the Cold War.

"To whom much is given, much is expected"

William Averell Harriman was born on November 15, 1891, the son of wealthy railroad baron E. H. Harriman, who built and owned the Union Pacific and Southern Pacific railways. He imparted his ideals of hard work and obligation to his children. Harriman's father cautioned his children that possessing wealth creates a personal obligation to give back something meaningful to the nation and world. The Harriman children took this to heart, believing in their obligation to contribute to the world around them.

Harriman, who went by his middle name, Averell, was not a talkative child, but he was candid and thoughtful. Throughout his life he was often described as methodical. In 1899, his father was instructed by doctors to take time off to relax. So E. H. Harriman organized a ship of scientists to travel along the Alaskan coast, studying the animals and plants. The ship ventured as far as Siberia in eastern Russia. Young Averell went along on this journey, the first of his many trips to Russia.

Harriman attended Groton, a strict New England boarding school modeled after an English public school. He was not an excellent student, but he was well respected by his classmates. Just as Harriman was entering Yale University, his father died. Harriman's mother received the family fortune, and Harriman was set to assume a key role in the family's railroad business. By his senior year at Yale, he had been elected to the board of directors of the Union Pacific Railroad, appearing at his first board meeting with a textbook in hand.

At the beginning of World War I (1914–18), Harriman was a new husband and father and was playing an increasingly influential role in the family business. Harriman determined that the best way he could serve the country during the war was by building much-needed ships. So he built a shipyard, and after the war he increased production and expanded the business into a shipping empire. At the same time, he founded an investment-banking firm to fund marine securities (stocks and bonds).

Early negotiator with the Soviets

The Harriman family had traditionally voted Republican, but Averell Harriman was drawn to the Democrats. The

Republican Party generally advocated isolationism, a policy of national isolation that would have the United States withdraw from the rest of the world in order to avoid war and economic entanglements. However, Harriman began to see isolationism as a disastrous foreign policy. In addition, Harriman felt the influence of his sister, Mary Harriman, who had developed a close relationship with Eleanor Roosevelt (1884–1962). Harriman's sister had announced that she was supporting Eleanor's husband, Franklin D. Roosevelt (1882–1945; served 1933–45), in his bid for the presidency in 1932. Harriman joined his sister in supporting Roosevelt, and Roosevelt won the election. Thus began Harriman's lifelong relationship with Democratic administrations.

In the late 1930s, as World War II (1939–45) loomed over Europe, President Roosevelt appointed Harriman to a unique position, the Lend-Lease administrator in England. The Lend-Lease program was established to provide England, which by now was broke, with supplies to fight the war against Germany, in exchange for leases to military bases throughout the remaining British empire around the world. Roosevelt directed Harriman while in London to determine everything that the United States could do to aid Britain, short of going to war. It was a position perfectly suited to Harriman, and he served effectively in the post, using his best facilitating and negotiating skills. Later, as the United States was beginning to form an alliance with the Soviet Union, Harriman approached Soviet leader **Joseph Stalin** (1879–1953; see entry) about what equipment would help the Soviets. What the Soviet Union really wanted was for the United States to fight Germany from Western Europe, drawing some German forces away from the battle with Soviet troops in the east. Stalin was initially less than gracious regarding the U.S. offer of equipment and weapons, but the United States soon became a major supplier to the Soviet Union.

In 1943, Roosevelt appointed Harriman to the position of ambassador to the Soviet Union. Though Harriman was initially optimistic that the United States and the Soviet Union could have a good relationship after the war, he came to believe that this was not possible. Harriman began to fear that the Soviet Union would try to dominate Europe after the war. From his post in the Soviet Union, he sent memos communicating these thoughts to President Roosevelt. However,

Roosevelt was not open to hearing Harriman's predictions about the possible disintegration of the Western alliance. He did not want to play hardball with Stalin at this early time; he wanted to give prospects of a postwar alliance every chance to succeed.

One of the first clear signs that the Western alliance would not survive the war was the Soviet invasion of Poland in 1944. Initially invaded by Germany in 1939, Poland was then liberated by Soviet troops. The United States demanded that Poland be allowed to hold free and fair elections to form a new government. However, it quickly became clear that this was not the Soviet Union's intention. The Soviet Union claimed that Poland was crucial to its security. Stalin wanted a sphere, or ring, of friendly countries (communist or, at least, strong socialist) surrounding him.

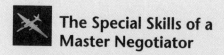

The Special Skills of a Master Negotiator

Averell Harriman was a skilled negotiator who worked closely with the world leaders of his day, including British prime minister **Winston Churchill** (1874–1965; see entry), Soviet leader Joseph Stalin, Soviet foreign minister **Vyacheslav Molotov** (1890–1986; see entry), Soviet leader **Nikita Khrushchev** (1894–1971; see entry), and Soviet leader Yuri Andropov. Harriman's negotiating skills were exceptional; so, apparently, was his skill at reading upside down. Near the time of his death, Harriman revealed a favorite negotiating strategy: "I always read everything on the desks of people I went to see in Moscow, London, Paris … I found it quite useful."

The Cold War begins

After the Soviets invaded Poland, Harriman began to believe that the United States must be increasingly firm with the Soviet Union. Harriman thought that the Soviets' goal of building a sphere of friendly states in Eastern Europe was an excuse for continuing communist expansion; he thought it was up to the United States to prevent such expansion. Furthermore, Harriman believed that the best protection for the United States was not the development of new weapons, but the establishment of democracies all around the world.

When President Roosevelt died suddenly in April 1945, **Harry S. Truman** (1884–1972; served 1945–53; see entry) took over as president. Truman was much more responsive to Harriman's concerns about the Soviets. Harriman recommended an increasingly hard-line approach in dealing with the Soviet Union; Truman agreed. For example, Harriman encouraged Truman to terminate the Lend-Lease program. As World War II ended and the Soviet Union began to expand its control over much of Eastern Europe, Truman announced what became known as the Truman Doctrine. The Truman Doctrine promised that the United States would provide aid to any nation in the world where free peoples were threatened by the spread of communism, especially in areas where poverty was threatening to undermine capitalist institutions. With that warning to the Soviets, the Cold War essentially began.

In 1946, President Truman appointed Harriman as the secretary of commerce. At the time, there was considerable debate regarding what to do about the postwar devastation of the European economies. The Soviet Union wanted to take Germany's industrial equipment and raw materials to rebuild the Soviet economy. However, Harriman believed that a rebuilt Germany would be an important buffer against potential Soviet communist expansion. As secretary of commerce, Harriman helped pass the Marshall Plan, a U.S. financial aid program designed to help rebuild postwar Europe. The plan would strengthen all the Western European countries and undermine any Soviet attempt to dominate the continent.

The Soviet Union continued to press for expansion. It refused to withdraw from the parts of Iran it had occupied during the war. It also pressured Turkey, demanding access to the shipping straits between the Black Sea and the Mediterranean Sea. Many of President Truman's advisors became increasingly concerned. Along with others in the U.S. government, Harriman believed that the first objective of communism was to extend itself to other parts of the world. This belief gave rise to the policy of containment, the attempt to resist Soviet aggression and thereby stop the further spread of communist influence. Harriman became a chief proponent of the idea that the United States must stop communism from infiltrating other countries.

As secretary of commerce, Harriman claimed that the Soviet Union had declared ideological warfare on the Western world. He believed the United States needed to maintain a strong military, especially a large and impressive air force, in order to keep communism away. At the same time, Harriman was not concerned about the anticommunist hysteria that began to sweep the country at the end of the 1940s, which he felt was unproductive and unnecessary.

Governor Harriman

When Republican **Dwight D. Eisenhower** (1890–1969; served 1953–61; see entry) took office as president in 1953, Truman and his advisors, including Harriman, all left office. Harriman's influence on international events decreased. From this point on, his influence would seesaw as Democrats gained and lost power. He was influential under Democrats Roosevelt and Truman and later under Democratic presidents **John F. Kennedy** (1917–1963; served 1961–63; see entry) and **Lyndon B. Johnson** (1908–1973; served 1963–69; see entry). Harriman lost influence during the Republican administrations of Eisenhower and **Richard M. Nixon** (1913–1994; served 1969–74; see entry).

During the 1950s, Harriman ran for the Democratic presidential nomination twice, in 1952 and 1956, losing both times to Adlai E. Stevenson (1900–1965). In 1954, Harriman ran for governor of New York and won, serving just four years before he lost his reelection race in 1958 to Republican Nelson A. Rockefeller (1908–1979). Harriman's career in elected office was not long, but people often called him "Governor" even after his term was over.

The Vietnam War

In the 1960s, the new Democratic administrations called Harriman back to public service. In 1963, at more than seventy years of age, he became undersecretary for political affairs under President Kennedy. Harriman headed the U.S. team that negotiated the 1963 Limited Test-Ban Treaty with the Soviet Union. The treaty banned aboveground testing of nuclear weapons.

Harriman originally attempted to negotiate for a total ban on the testing of nuclear weapons. However, the Soviets had some practical concerns about such an arrangement: Aboveground testing could be easily monitored, but there was no way to monitor underground testing unless there were observers present in the facilities. The Soviet Union did not want Western observers in its nuclear weapons facilities. Therefore, the two countries could only agree on a limited ban on nuclear testing.

Undersecretary of State W. Averell Harriman (left) confers with President John F. Kennedy in July 1963. *Reproduced by permission of the Corbis Corporation.*

Vietnam was one of the hot spots in the Cold War. After the Vietnamese defeated the French at Dien Bien Phu in 1954, Harriman favored U.S. military intervention in the region, because communist-controlled North Vietnam was trying to take over noncommunist South Vietnam. However, as Harriman aged, his position changed. By the time Lyndon Johnson became president, Harriman was a voice of moderation in discussions about the war, arguing for negotiation and an end to the bombing of North Vietnam. President Johnson appointed Harriman as chief of the U.S. delegation to the Paris peace talks with the North Vietnamese in 1968.

When President Nixon took office in 1969, Harriman infuriated Nixon by calling for a fixed timetable for U.S. withdrawal from Vietnam. He also recommended putting increased pressure on the South Vietnamese to assume greater responsibility in conducting the war. Americans who were protesting U.S. involvement in the Vietnam War (1954–75) were pleased by Harriman's viewpoint, even though Harriman was not aligned with the peace movement and did not support the protesters' efforts.

Last years

Harriman continued trying to improve U.S.-Soviet relations until the end of his life. He visited Soviet leader Yuri Andropov (1914–1984) in 1983 as a private citizen. Convinced that the Soviet Union wanted peace, Harriman encouraged the administration of President **Ronald Reagan** (1911–; served 1981–89; see entry) to return to a policy of peaceful coexistence. Over the years, Harriman also authored several books, including *Peace with Russia* (1959), *America and Russia in a Changing World* (1971), and *Special Envoy to Churchill and Stalin, 1941–1946* (1975). William Averell Harriman died in 1986 at the age of ninety-four.

For More Information

Books

Abramson, Rudy. *Spanning the Century: The Life of W. Averell Harriman, 1891–1986.* New York: William Morrow and Co., 1992.

Cooper, Chester L. *The Lost Crusade: America in Vietnam.* New York: Dodd, Mead, and Co., 1970.

Harriman, W. Averell, and Elie Abel. *Special Envoy to Churchill and Stalin, 1941–1946.* New York: Random House, 1975.

Isaacson, Walter, and Evan Thomas. *The Wise Men: Six Friends and the World They Made.* New York: Simon and Schuster, 1986.

Ho Chi Minh

**Born May 19, 1890
Nghe An Province, Vietnam
Died September 3, 1969
Hanoi, North Vietnam**

**President of the Democratic
Republic of Vietnam**

"Nothing is more precious than independence and freedom."

Ho Chi Minh.

Ho Chi Minh was a leading figure in the international communist movement and the principal force behind the Vietnamese struggle against French colonial rule. Founder of the Vietnamese Communist Party and its chief strategist, Ho became president of the Democratic Republic of Vietnam. Today, he remains the symbol of national pride in Vietnam. One of the most influential political figures of the twentieth century, Ho Chi Minh had magnetic appeal as well as practical leadership skills.

At a time when most of his Vietnamese colleagues were trained only in China or the Soviet Union, Ho Chi Minh traveled extensively and developed a broad world view. Ho spoke and wrote a number of languages, including English, French, Chinese, and Russian, as well as his native Vietnamese.

Colonial child

Ho Chi Minh's birth name was Nguyen Sinh Cung. The youngest of three children, he was born in 1890 in a rural hamlet in central Vietnam. Along with Cambodia, Laos, and several other countries, Vietnam forms a peninsula called Indochina, which extends from the southeastern border of China into the South China Sea. Rich in natural resources, especially rubber and rice, Cambodia, Laos, and Vietnam became French colonies in the nineteenth century before Ho Chi Minh was born. His mother was Hoang Thi Loan; his father, Nguyen Sinh Sac, was a teacher and a Confucian scholar who opposed France's presence in Vietnam. (Confucian scholars study the teachings of the Chinese philosopher Confucius, who was born in 551 B.C.E.) In keeping with Vietnamese tradition, Sinh Cung's parents gave him a new name when he reached adolescence. The new name was to reflect the parents' aspirations for their child and was recorded at the village registry. Sinh Cung's father assigned him the name Nguyen That Thanh, meaning "he who will succeed." In 1907, young Nguyen was enrolled at the National Academy, a prestigious school for students wishing to become administrative officials.

Sinh Sac had moved his family to the city of Hue in 1895. Later, Sinh Sac and his family moved to the town of Kim Lien, where he was an associate of the well-known scholar and revolutionary patriot Phan Boi Chau (1867–1940), who often visited their home. Ho Chi Minh's revolutionary outlook may have been inspired by these sessions with Phan Boi Chau and then intensified by his later experiences in France.

Leaving home

In 1911, Nguyen That Thanh sailed from Saigon to France, working aboard the French passenger liner *Admiral LaTouche-Treville*. In order to pursue his political interests without placing his family back in Vietnam in danger, he traveled under the assumed name Nguyen Van Ba. Nguyen saw vast areas of the world, including Latin America and the United States, before he arrived in Paris. At that time, Paris had become the worldwide center for anticolonial groups to debate the issue of colonialism. Colonialism is the policy or practice of controlling a dependent country or people—for example, a Western European nation controlling an underdeveloped and economically dependent nation in Asia or Africa. The French colonized Indochina (Laos, Cambodia, and Vietnam) primarily for its rice and rubber resources. Their rule of the economy drained the countries of their wealth since profits went to farm and plantation owners in France, not the Indochinese. Vietnam wanted to gain control of its economy and raise the country's standard of living.

In Paris, using the name Nguyen Ai Quoc, or "Nguyen the Patriot," Nguyen engaged in radical activities and was one of the founding members of the French Communist Party. Communism is a system of government in which a single political party, the Communist Party, controls nearly all aspects of people's lives. In a communist economy, private ownership of property and business is prohibited so that goods produced and wealth accumulated can be shared equally by all. In 1919, as Nguyen Ai Quoc, he presented a petition to democratic leaders at the Versailles Peace Conference. In

A young Ho Chi Minh.
Reproduced by permission of Getty Images.

this petition, titled "The Demands of the Annamite [Vietnamese] People," he outlined French colonial abuses in Vietnam: plantation owners ruling the local workers harshly, taking profits out of the country, and keeping a tight control on society to quell any rebellions. The French had established the colony through force in the first place in the 1850s and 1860s and maintained it with force. Nguyen also proposed that Vietnam would be governed by Vietnamese and would control its own economy. Not many nations wanted to challenge France because of long ties, but Nguyen's petition served as an important call to action among the Vietnamese.

Like many Asian leaders of that era, he had not had a happy experience with capitalism. Capitalism is an economic system where property and businesses are privately owned. Prices, production, and distribution of goods are determined by competition in a market relatively free of government intervention. Nguyen had personally observed the brutalities perpetuated by Western colonialism, and those experiences had led him to embrace the concept of a future global federation of communist societies, an idea proposed by the Russian communist leader Vladimir Lenin (1870–1924).

The following years of Nguyen's life were spent in the Soviet Union, China, and Indochina. In China, he learned guerrilla warfare, or irregular and independent attacks, from **Mao Zedong** (1893–1976; see entry), the future leader of the Communist People's Republic of China. After founding the Indochinese Communist Party (ICP) among Vietnamese exiles in Canton, China, Nguyen was arrested by the British for adopting radical politics and threatening the colonial countries, and spent two years in prison. After his release, he returned to the Soviet Union and spent several years recovering from several illnesses.

The Vietminh

In 1940, as part of their military expansion throughout Asia, Japanese troops swept into Indochina to gain control of natural resources for their own industries. Nguyen resumed contact with Indochinese Communist Party leaders and announced the formation of the League for the Independence of Vietnam, popularly known as the Vietminh. The Vietminh's purpose was to fight French rule and the Japanese occupation. In 1942, Nguyen was arrested in China by Chinese leader **Chiang Kai-shek** (1887–1975; see entry) who despised communists and was fending off Mao within China. Nguyen was falsely charged with being a spy, which Chiang believed would tarnish his reputation back home in Vietnam and undercut his power. After spending thirteen months in jail, Nguyen returned to Vietnam in 1944, where he continued his resistance.

From the Vietminh, Nguyen derived his final and most famous alias, Ho Chi Minh. The name means "enlightener" or "bringer of light." When the Japanese surrendered in 1945 at the end of World War II (1939–45), the Vietminh seized power in Vietnam and proclaimed the Democratic Republic of Vietnam (DRV); the DRV's capital city was Hanoi. After approximately thirty years as a revolutionary, Ho Chi Minh was about to become the first president of the new communist republic.

A changing world

After the bloody battles of World War II, the world found itself engaged in a different kind of conflict—the so-called Cold War. The Cold War was an intense political and economic rivalry between the world's two superpowers—the United States and the Soviet Union—that lasted from 1945 to 1991. The Cold War rivalry would eventually lead to the collapse of colonialism. Both sides advocated the liberation of their former colonies in order to win those colonies over and make them allies in the Cold War struggle for domination.

As a relatively small player in the global Cold War drama, France did not stand to gain much by liberating its colonies. Therefore, the French were unwilling to grant independence to their colonial subjects in Indochina, and in late 1946 war broke out in Vietnam. For eight years, Vietminh guerrillas fought French troops in the mountains and rice paddies of Vietnam. The Vietminh finally defeated the French at Dien Bien Phu in 1954; they then established North Vietnam as an independent country. However, South Vietnam remained out of Ho's grasp. The terms of the peace agreement would keep Vietnam a divided country. After his victory over the French, Ho returned to Hanoi. He devoted his efforts to constructing a communist society in North Vietnam but did not give up on his vision of a unified Vietnam under his leadership.

A simple man

Ho appeared rather humble in his threadbare bush jacket and frayed rubber sandals. When surrounded by luxury, he often seemed uncomfortable; he preferred to live in a stilt house built in the style used by citizens who lived in the mountains. He once vetoed a proposal to construct a small museum that was meant to commemorate his life. Ho argued that the funds could be better used to build a school. The

Western powers sometimes suspected that Ho cultivated this image of simplicity to more easily gain popularity. Ho did openly enjoy the adulation that he received from his compatriots, but in the final analysis there is little doubt that Ho Chi Minh actually preferred to live in simple, unpretentious surroundings. He sought to portray himself as a loyal adherent of the communist teachings of German political philosopher Karl Marx (1818–1883). However, Ho also made an effort to soften communism's strict policies in order to ease the lives of Vietnam's citizens.

The U.S. viewpoint

The United States was concerned about the situation in Indochina for a combination of reasons. Indochina had raw materials that the world needed, especially tin and tungsten; therefore, the United States wanted to continue free trade with Indochina. U.S. leaders saw Ho Chi Minh's communist victory over the French as a potential threat to free trade, because the new communist economy of Vietnam would be closed to all capitalist nations. The Americans feared that other nations in Indochina would fall to communism and that trade with the entire region would cease. There was a real concern among all the Western capitalist nations that the existence of a communist government in one country would cause neighboring countries to fall to communism. This idea was referred to as the "domino theory." In the view of the Western world, countries falling in succession to communist influence would be the beginning of the end for free trade.

Even within the United States, people feared the infiltration of communist influence, both in the U.S. government and in broader American society. Communism itself was the enemy, and top U.S. leaders, including President **Dwight D. Eisenhower** (1890–1969; served 1953–61; see entry), sincerely believed in the domino theory; they thought that any communist victory was a threat to U.S. democracy and capitalism. Ironically, Ho Chi Minh had an honest respect for the United States. He incorporated many of its ideals in his Vietnamese Declaration of Independence. One of Ho's slogans was "Nothing is more precious than independence and freedom." (This slogan is still seen on billboards in Vietnam.) Despite his admiration for the United States, Ho knew that the U.S. government would not grant legitimacy to his communist government in Hanoi. In fact, by the late 1950s and early 1960s, the United States would send a considerable number of military advisors to South Vietnam to help resist any communist advances orchestrated by Ho.

A hot war

In foreign policy, Ho adopted a practical attitude and moved slowly in order to adjust his communist goals to the conditions of the world at the moment. The Vietnam War (1954–75) involved U.S. efforts to protect noncommunist South Vietnam from being taken over by Ho's communist-ruled North Vietnam. U.S. aid to South Vietnam began as early as January 1955. Steadily, U.S. military support escalated until hundreds of thousands of U.S. troops were in Vietnam by 1967. As American casualties mounted, U.S. president **Lyndon B. Johnson** (1908–1973; served 1963–69; see entry) was increasingly anxious to arrange peace negotiations with North Vietnam. However, Ho made it clear to Johnson that North Vietnam would never negotiate. Even as the war physically destroyed his country, Ho remained committed to Vietnam's independence. Millions of Vietnamese fought and died to attain the same goal. Ho saw communism as a means to reach independence.

During the war, Ho was frequently ill or in China for medical treatment. He died of heart failure in 1969 at the age of seventy-nine. He did not live to see the unification of Vietnam that occurred six years later when North Vietnam and South Vietnam joined together to form the Socialist Republic of Vietnam (SRV). But the final communist triumph—the capture of Saigon, South Vietnam's capital city, in 1975—was the result of Ho Chi Minh's lifelong revolutionary efforts. After the fall of Saigon, Ho's colleagues renamed the city Ho Chi Minh City in his honor.

Last will and testament

Upon Ho's death, an official statement from Moscow lauded the Vietnamese leader as an important communist leader and friend of the Soviet Union. The reaction from Western capitals was more muted. Some U.S. news media that had protested U.S. involvement in the Vietnam War memorialized Ho as a worthy adversary and a defender of the weak and oppressed. Even those who opposed Ho's regime respected Ho himself as someone who had dedicated his life to the independence and unification of his country. Ho's critics, on the other hand, refused to overlook his long record as a follower of **Joseph Stalin** (1879–1953; see entry), the brutal communist dictator of the Soviet Union. This group felt that Ho's decades of service to the communist world revolution had done irreparable damage to the cause of democracy.

Ho Chi Minh's last will and testament contained his wish to be cremated; it also indicated that he wanted his ashes deposited at three unnamed locations in the northern, central, and southern sections of Vietnam. Ho intended this to be a symbolic act that would express his devotion to the cause of national reunification. However, Communist Party leaders ignored Ho's request for a simple funeral ceremony and cremation. They decided to erect a mausoleum (a building where bodies are entombed aboveground) to display his embalmed body for future generations.

 The Tet Offensive

Tet is the Vietnamese New Year, which is celebrated at the turning of the lunar year (the appearance of the first new moon after January 20). During the Vietnam War, it was customary for both sides to observe a truce during the Tet celebrations. However, in 1968, Vietcong guerrilla fighters (rebel forces within South Vietnam who supported Ho's Communist forces) violated the temporary truce and surged into more than one hundred towns and cities, including Saigon, South Vietnam's capital city and the center of operations for U.S. and South Vietnamese forces. This surprise attack, known as the Tet Offensive, was the final turning point in the Vietnam War. When communist forces seized the U.S. embassy in Saigon, the American public's opinion about the war shifted; it no longer seemed that the United States was winning—or could ever win—the war. Only a few months later, President Lyndon B. Johnson cut back on U.S. bombing of North Vietnam, and eventually the United States withdrew from the war in defeat.

For More Information

Books

Duiker, William J. *Ho Chi Minh: A Life.* New York: Hyperion, 2000.

Embree, Aislie T., ed. *Encyclopedia of Asian History.* New York: Charles Scribner's Sons, 1988.

Levinson, David, and Karen Christensen, eds. *Encyclopedia of Modern Asia.* New York: Charles Scribner's Sons, 2002.

Nixon, Richard. *No More Vietnams.* New York: Arbor House, 1985.

Time/CBS. *People of the Century.* New York: Simon and Schuster, 1999.

Web Sites

"Domino Theory Principle, Dwight D. Eisenhower, 1954." *Public Papers of President Dwight D. Eisenhower.* http://coursesa.matrix.msu.edu/~hst306/documents/domino.html (accessed September 4, 2003).

J. Edgar Hoover

Born January 1, 1895
Washington, D.C.
Died May 2, 1972
Washington, D.C.

Director of the
Federal Bureau of Investigation

J. Edgar Hoover joined the Bureau of Investigation (later called the Federal Bureau of Investigation) in 1917 and became its director in 1924. He would remain in that position for the next forty-eight years until his death in 1972, serving under both Democratic and Republican presidents. In the late 1920s and early 1930s, Hoover transformed the organization from a scandal-ridden agency into an elite corps of highly regimented special agents. The American public was hungry for a return to law and order. Its confidence in law enforcement was badly shaken by the lawlessness of the Prohibition Era (1920–33), a period when liquor was illegal and organized crime grew wealthy by supplying Americans with various forms of alcohol. Then, just as Prohibition ended, outlaws began sweeping across America's Midwest, robbing banks and terrifying citizens. Hoover's agency ended the crime wave and restored public confidence in law enforcement.

During the later 1930s, President Franklin D. Roosevelt (1882–1945; served 1933–45), along with many Americans, increasingly feared that the fascism taking hold in Germany and Italy and the communism of the Soviet Union could gain a

"Truth-telling, I have found, is the key to responsible citizenship. The thousands of criminals I have seen in 40 years of law enforcement have had one thing in common: Every single one was a liar."

J. Edgar Hoover. *Courtesy of the Library of Congress.*

185

foothold in the United States. Fascism is a political movement or regime characterized by dictatorship, militarism, and racism. Communism is a political and economic system in which the Communist Party controls almost all aspects of citizens' lives and private ownership of property is banned. U.S. leaders wanted American businesses to be able to compete and profit on a global scale. Therefore, neither fascism nor communism was compatible with America's democratic or capitalist values.

Roosevelt relied on Hoover to oversee the national security of the United States. Following World War II (1939–45), the democratic United States and the communist Soviet Union fought each other with words and threats. During this so-called Cold War (1945–91), Hoover and his agency staunchly guarded against the spread of communism to American soil. Preaching law and order, Hoover assumed the role of protector of America's democratic values. The legality of the FBI's activities, particularly undercover surveillance, or spying, was sometimes questioned. However, Hoover himself was esteemed for single-handedly establishing an internationally respected law enforcement agency.

Early life

John Edgar Hoover was the last of four children born to Dickerson Naylor Hoover and Annie Scheitlin Hoover; he arrived on New Year's Day in 1895 in Washington, D.C. The Hoover home was located on Capitol Hill, within blocks of the Library of Congress. Those who lived in the neighborhood, which was known as Seward Square, were predominantly white, middle-class Protestants who held government jobs. Hoover's father was a printer with the U.S. Coast and Geodetic Survey.

Hoover was a frail child, so his mother paid careful attention to him. She was his moral guide and disciplinarian. Hoover remained very close to his mother, living with her in the house where he was born for forty-three years until her death in 1938.

Efficient and effective

Hoover was very bright and graduated at the top of his class from the prestigious Central High School in 1913.

After high school, Hoover worked as a file clerk at the Library of Congress and attended night classes at National University Law School, which later became part of George Washington University. He received his law degree in 1916 and a graduate degree in law in 1917. That same year, the United States entered World War I (1914–18). The Alien Enemy Bureau in the Department of Justice hired twenty-two-year-old Hoover to process newly arriving German and Austro-Hungarian immigrants; his job was to determine whether any of them might pose a threat to America.

Besides the world war, another event held America's attention in 1917: A revolution in Russia brought the communists to power. This heightened U.S. government leaders' fears that communist influence might also be growing in the United States. To alleviate these fears, the U.S. attorney general, A. Mitchell Palmer (1872–1936), put Hoover in charge of the Justice Department's General Intelligence Division (GID). The GID's job was to track down, arrest, and deport alien radicals, citizens of other countries living in the United States who advocated extreme change. Hoover also became assistant to the attorney general in November 1918. In that position, Hoover planned and directed raids (known as the Palmer Raids) on foreign radicals in three U.S. cities in November 1919 and January 1920. The raids resulted in mass arrests and the deportation of some well-known anarchists. (Deportation is the act of sending illegal aliens out of the country. Anarchists are people who reject governmental authority.) Hoover's investigations for the GID made him the nation's premier expert in communist activities on the home front. The antiradical campaign ordered by Attorney General Palmer ended amid charges from the Justice Department that the civil liberties, or freedom from governmental interference, of those arrested had been disregarded. Nevertheless, through each assignment he undertook, Hoover had gained a reputation for being extremely efficient and effective.

Director of the Bureau of Investigation

In 1921, the attorney general placed the GID within the Bureau of Investigation (BOI) and appointed Hoover as the assistant director of BOI. Congress charged the agency with investigating federal crimes such as bank robberies, kidnapping, and car thefts. On May 10, 1924, at the age of twenty-nine, Hoover was appointed director of the BOI. The BOI was full of scandal and corruption. As director, Hoover worked diligently to improve the image and effectiveness of the organization. He raised the standards for agents and fired many whom he considered unqualified. He replaced them with an elite group of men who were mostly young, white, and college-educated. Hoover demanded total conformity and a strict moral code among his agents.

Hoover also brought scientific law enforcement techniques to the agency. He established a fingerprint identification department, modern investigation laboratories, and a system for maintaining comprehensive crime statistics. As a result, the BOI gained more importance and responsibility. Still, neither Hoover nor the BOI was well known outside government circles. Furthermore, the law placed severe limitations on the types of activities BOI agents could carry out. Agents could not make arrests or even carry guns. Often they found themselves assigned to trailing prostitutes or petty criminals. However, the role and activities of the BOI would change dramatically in the mid-1930s.

"G-Men"

The economic hard times of the Great Depression (1929–41) spawned the rise of notorious outlaws in the Midwest in 1933 and 1934. Driving fast cars and carrying machine guns, they robbed isolated banks and service stations at will, leaving a bloody trail behind. Among the outlaws were Bonnie and Clyde, "Ma" Barker (1871–1935), "Machine Gun" Kelly (1895–1954), "Pretty Boy" Floyd (1901–1934), John Dillinger (1903–1934), and "Baby Face" Nelson (1908–1934). Seeking to raise the public's awareness of the BOI, Hoover targeted these high-profile criminals for maximum publicity benefit. BOI agents, who had only recently been authorized to carry weapons and make arrests, gunned down five of these outlaws in 1934: Bonnie and Clyde in May, Dillinger in July, Floyd in October, and Nelson in November. They shot and killed "Ma" Barker in 1935.

The BOI agents, including Hoover, became national heroes and received considerable media attention. The box office hit *G-Men* was released in 1935 (The term *G-men* was thought to stand for "government men.") Popular actor James Cagney (1899–1986) played a character who was patterned after Hoover. That same year, the BOI was renamed the Federal Bureau of Investigation (FBI), and its "G-men" became known as FBI agents. The FBI's successes and related publicity restored the public's confidence in law enforcement. To maintain his heroic image, Hoover would sometimes personally lead raids with the news media on hand. For example, a classic case of Hoover heroics occurred in 1937 when a top New York City criminal surrendered personally to Hoover. Reporters and photographers captured the entire event. To Americans, Hoover and his agents became larger-than-life heroes.

Despite his success against the Midwest outlaws and individual criminals, Hoover chose not to battle organized crime. By illegally supplying alcohol to Americans during Prohibition, organized crime had become incredibly wealthy and powerful. Hoover did not want to risk a poor showing in a battle against organized crime; this would have damaged the new positive image of the FBI. Instead, Hoover preferred to hunt down lawless individuals, who were much easier targets. Throughout his career, Hoover denied the existence of organized crime in the United States. This denial contributed to the rapid growth of organized crime, which continued to grow and prosper through the mid-twentieth century. The FBI did not earnestly enter the battle against organized crime until after Hoover's death.

Threats during World War II

In the 1930s, tensions in Europe rose as Adolf Hitler (1889–1945), leader of the Nazi Party, became the dictator of Germany. Fascism had taken hold in Germany and in Italy as well. Along with communism in the Soviet Union, fascism was seen as a threat to America's democratic principles. In the late 1930s and throughout World War II, President Roosevelt assigned the FBI to secretly monitor the activities of any communists or fascists in the United States. Hoover rose in prominence as the head of U.S. domestic counterintelligence (stopping enemies from spying or gathering secret information) and countersabotage (preventing enemy destruction of U.S. facilities). He compiled information on the daily habits and

FBI director J. Edgar Hoover stands directly behind U.S. president Franklin D. Roosevelt (seated) as he signs a bill. Also standing with Hoover are (from left to right) Attorney General Homer S. Cummings, U.S. senator Henry F. Ashurst of Arizona, and Assistant Attorney General Joseph B. Keenan. *Reproduced by permission of AP/Wide World Photos.*

organizational memberships of numerous people, searching for those who might turn into enemies of democracy. He kept lists of the names of "questionable" individuals. In 1942, FBI agents captured would-be criminals from Germany who had landed in a submarine on Long Island. Their capture received extensive coverage in the media; because of such coverage, the public believed that the FBI was on top of threats to the United States.

Protecting America in the Cold War

At the end of World War II, the Cold War began. The Cold War was a prolonged battle for world dominance between the democratic, capitalist United States and the communist Soviet Union. Threats and propaganda were the chief weapons used in the conflict. The campaign against communism dominated Hoover's life, and in the late 1940s uncovering communist infiltration of the U.S. federal government was

How to Fight Communism

As director of the Federal Bureau of Investigation (FBI) for almost thirty Cold War years, J. Edgar Hoover was charged with gathering information on possible communist influences within the United States, including people who were spying for communist countries. In 1947, Hoover wrote an article titled "How to Fight Communism," which was published in *Newsweek* magazine's June 9 issue. The article contains a list of "Ten 'Don'ts' by Mr. Hoover." A few of the "don'ts" included:

> Don't let Communists in your organization or Labor union out-work, out-vote or out-number you.

> Don't be hoodwinked by Communist propaganda that says one thing but means destruction of the American Way of Life. Expose it with the truth.

> Don't give aid and comfort to the Communist cause by joining front organizations [groups that hide the identity of the actual cause], contributing to their campaign chests or by championing their cause in any way, shape or form.

Political cartoon about the FBI, entitled "Sees all—Knows all." *Cartoon by Fred Graf. Courtesy of the National Archives and Records Administration.*

> Don't let Communists infiltrate into our schools, churches and [molders] of public opinion, the press, radio and screen.

a high priority. Hoover's FBI investigated the backgrounds of numerous government employees. The Republican Party in particular supported these investigations and revived the House Un-American Activities Committee (HUAC) in Congress. The HUAC was a congressional group established to investigate and root out any communist influences within the United States. Intent on exposing communists in such organizations as labor unions, Hoover eagerly supplied HUAC with information. Scoring yet another high-visibility case, Hoover and his FBI agents uncovered information on a spy ring that had funneled secret information from the Manhattan Project, the United States' secret atomic bomb project, to the Soviets.

"Atomic spy" Klaus Fuchs (1911–1988) was exposed. Arrests in the case led to the conviction and execution of Julius Rosenberg (1918–1953) and Ethel Rosenberg (1915–1953), a husband and wife who were members of the spy ring.

To educate the public about the domestic threat of communism, Hoover authored a widely read book called *Masters of Deceit* (1958). The book sold 250,000 copies in hardback and 2 million in paperback (through twenty-nine printings, ending in 1970). Loving the spotlight and publicity, Hoover also worked with the national media on the production of radio and television programs and Hollywood movies. These productions included *The FBI Story* (1959), starring Jimmy Stewart (1908–1997), and a popular television series, *The FBI,* which ran from 1965 to 1974.

Impressed with Hoover's success in combating all manner of criminal activities, President **John F. Kennedy** (1917–1963; served 1961–63; see entry) asked Hoover to investigate the Ku Klux Klan, an antiblack hate group in the United States. However, Hoover had his own ideas of whom to target next. More and more groups caught his attention as potential threats to traditional middle-American values. For example, Hoover targeted black American organizations such as the militant Black Panthers, as well as people protesting U.S. involvement in the Vietnam War (1954–75). Hoover also waged a smear campaign, in which one attempts to tarnish another's reputation, against civil rights leader Dr. Martin Luther King Jr. (1929–1968). Claiming that King had communist ties, Hoover tried to destroy King's credibility and career. Hoover continued his warnings about communists through the 1960s, but by then the American Communist Party had ceased to have any real influence in the United States. To many Americans, Hoover's warnings began to seem irrational and misplaced; Hoover no longer projected the calm, cool image of America's chief law enforcer.

Methods questioned

In his forty-eighth year as director of the FBI (fifty-five years total working in the bureau), Hoover died in his sleep in Washington, D.C., his hometown. His body lay in state in the Capitol's Rotunda; one of only several dozen Americans who have received this honor. Throughout his career as head of the FBI, Hoover had worked hard to maintain a clean public reputation. However, casting a shadow of suspicion over his activities, Hoover ordered his personal secretary to destroy all his personal files upon his death. His tactics of surveillance, wiretapping (secretly listening to telephone conversations), and keeping detailed files on innocent citizens he deemed suspicious violated the civil liberties of many Americans.

After his death, Hoover became the subject of a Senate investigative committee in 1975 and 1976. The Select Committee to Study Governmental Operations with Respect to Intelligence Activities determined that Hoover had greatly abused his governmental authority and had violated the First Amendment rights of free speech and free assembly (freedom to meet with others) by harassing those he considered a threat. Yet Hoover's positive contributions could not be overlooked. He organized and led an effective, elite federal law enforcement agency through nearly half a century of U.S. history.

For More Information

Books

Nash, Jay R. *A Critical Study of the Life and Times of J. Edgar Hoover and His FBI*. Chicago: Nelson-Hall, 1972.

Powers, Richard Gid. *Secrecy and Power: The Life of J. Edgar Hoover*. New York: Free Press, 1987.

Sullivan, William C. *The Bureau: My Thirty Years in Hoover's FBI*. New York: Norton, 1979.

Summers, Anthony. *Official and Confidential: The Secret Life of J. Edgar Hoover*. New York: G. P. Putnam's Sons, 1993.

Theoharis, Athan G., and John S. Cox. *The Boss: J. Edgar Hoover and the Great American Inquisition*. Philadelphia: Temple University Press, 1988.

Web Site

"FBI History." *Federal Bureau of Investigation*. http://www.fbi.gov/fbihistory. htm (accessed on September 5, 2003).

Lyndon B. Johnson

Born August 27, 1908
Gillespie County, Texas
Died January 22, 1973
San Antonio, Texas

U.S. president, vice president, senator

"If one morning I walked on top of the water across the Potomac River, the headline that afternoon would read 'President Can't Swim.'"

Lyndon B. Johnson.
Photograph by Arnold Newman. Reproduced by permission of AP/Wide World Photos.

Lyndon B. Johnson suddenly became president during one of the darkest times in U.S. history—following the assassination of the popular **John F. Kennedy** (1917–1963; served 1961–63; see entry). Johnson proceeded to fight hard for the passage of the Civil Rights Act in 1964, but is best remembered for serving during the tumultuous period of the Vietnam War (1954–75). In his 1986 book *Big Daddy from the Pedernales: Lyndon Baines Johnson,* historian Paul K. Conkin said Johnson "was confused and almost helpless." The personal toll on the president "was almost overwhelming. He had aged ten years in only two and was now visibly an old man, shaken, ineffective, almost beleaguered in a White House surrounded daily by angry protesters."

During Johnson's presidency, the Cold War (1945–91) grew increasingly violent in Vietnam. The Vietnam experience caused major social upheaval in the United States and would end public support for U.S. efforts to contain communism in faraway places.

Rapid rise from humble beginnings

Lyndon Baines Johnson was born August 27, 1908, in a three-room house in the hills of southwest Texas near the town of Stonewall. He was the oldest of five children born to Sam Ealy Johnson Jr., a businessman and a member of the Texas legislature, and Rebekah Baines, a schoolteacher. One grandfather, Joseph Baines, was also a state legislator. Johnson grew up listening to lively political discussions at home.

Because of poor investments, the Johnson family struggled financially. Johnson often wore homemade clothing as a young boy, and he felt greatly embarrassed about it. Because of these early experiences, he would always have sympathy for ordinary people, particularly those who were struggling financially. Johnson graduated from high school in 1924. After working at odd jobs for three years, he entered Southwest Texas State Teachers College at San Marcos. To help pay for his studies, Johnson took a teaching job during the 1928–29 school year in a predominantly Mexican American school in Cotulla. He was profoundly impressed by the extreme poverty of the area. During Johnson's presidency, easing poverty would be one of his top priorities.

Johnson graduated in 1930 and briefly taught debate and public speaking at a Houston high school. Also in 1930, he took part in the successful congressional campaign for Democrat Richard Kleberg (1887–1955). Leaving his teaching job in early 1931, Johnson accompanied Kleberg to Washington, D.C., as a legislative assistant. Johnson found the Washington political scene captivating and worked tirelessly. Youthful and energetic, he soon caught the attention of Texas congressman Sam Rayburn (1882–1961), who became his mentor.

In 1934, Johnson met Claudia Alta Taylor (1912–), better known as "Lady Bird," of San Antonio, Texas. Within twenty-four hours, he proposed marriage to her. They would have two daughters, Lynda Bird and Luci. Lady Bird proved a shrewd judge of people and would be an invaluable stabilizing factor for the often feisty Johnson throughout his political career. In 1935, Johnson was appointed director of the National Youth Administration (NYA) in Texas, where he served for two years. The NYA was a federal agency created in 1935 to provide job training and education to unemployed youths during the Great Depression (1929–41), the worst financial crisis in American history. Johnson proved an exceptionally able administrator.

A life in Congress

Encouraged by Rayburn and others, Johnson decided to enter politics himself and ran successfully for the U.S. House of Representatives in 1936. Returning to Washington, D.C., he would serve in the House for twelve years. When the United States entered World War II (1939–45) in December 1941, Johnson became the first member of Congress to enter the armed services in active duty. With the rank of lieutenant commander, he served in the navy for six months in the Pacific. Johnson flew in one combat mission in a patrol bomber over New Guinea and came under attack by Japanese fighters. He was awarded the Silver Star, which he proudly wore the rest of his political career. After Johnson's six months of service, President Franklin D. Roosevelt (1882–1945; served 1933–45) called all congressmen back to fill their political roles. Johnson happily returned. It was also at this time that the Johnsons spent Lady Bird's inheritance to purchase a radio and television station in Austin, Texas. This investment would become very profitable for them, gaining in worth by several million dollars.

In 1948, Johnson ran for the U.S. Senate. Amidst charges of ballot-stuffing and after legal battles to determine the victor in the Democratic primary, Johnson won by only eighty-seven votes out of almost one million cast. He went on to handily win the fall election in the heavily Democratic state of Texas. Johnson would serve in the Senate for twelve years. He was a shrewd legislator capable of swinging deals to pass legislation. Known for being both tactful and ruthless, he would psychologically strong-arm his fellow legislators, giving them what came to be known as the "Johnson treatment." He became minority leader of the Senate in 1953, and when the Democrats became the majority party in the Senate in 1955, he became the youngest majority leader in U.S. history at age forty-six. A severe heart attack in 1955 did little to impede his career or effectiveness. In 1957, Johnson guided the Civil Rights Act of 1957 through Congress, the first since the 1870s.

The presidency

In 1960, Johnson hoped to gain the Democratic presidential nomination. However, U.S. senator John F. Kennedy of Massachusetts won the party's nomination instead. In a surprise move, Kennedy offered the vice presidential running mate position to the man he had just defeated—Johnson. In another surprise, Johnson in essence settled for second place—and accepted. Kennedy, a Roman Catholic from the East Coast, was greatly aided by Johnson's Protestant Texas background; it gave the campaign some balance. Having Johnson as a running mate probably made the difference in Kennedy's narrow victory over the Republican candidate, Vice President **Richard M. Nixon** (1913–1994; see entry).

Johnson's time as vice president, from 1961 to 1963, was very unsatisfying. For the six years prior to becoming vice president, he was used to being in a position of power as Senate majority leader. But Kennedy largely ignored Johnson's ability to work with Congress. With his Texas country upbringing, Johnson felt inferior to the polished, educated New Englanders who controlled the White House. In contrast to Kennedy's easy, witty style, Johnson had a tendency to appear stiff and speak too loudly in front of television cameras. He suffered a degree of deafness that he never publicly acknowledged. Johnson was clearly outside the inner circle.

This all changed on the afternoon of November 22, 1963. While traveling with Johnson on a political tour in Texas, President Kennedy was assassinated as he rode through the streets of Dallas. Johnson took the oath of office on *Air Force One,* the presidential plane, minutes after leaving the Dallas airport. The transition in power needed to be rapid and smooth to show the world, particularly the Soviet Union, that the United States remained prepared for any confrontation.

Immediately focusing on domestic issues, Johnson pressed a major legislative agenda that Kennedy had been unsuccessful in passing. Passage of the Civil Rights Act in 1964 was Johnson's greatest achievement. The act banned racial segregation, or separation of the races, in public places such as schools and in the workplace. Johnson then declared a war on poverty. He established a number of federal programs that greatly expanded the U.S. government's responsibility to assist the poor. These programs included Job Corps for training the unemployed; Volunteers in Service to America (VISTA), a domestic volunteer organization to help impoverished areas; and Head Start, a preschool program for children living in poverty. In 1965, another major piece of civil rights legislation, the Voting Rights Act, prohibited federal, state, and local governments from using racial discrimination to restrict voting rights. The Johnson administration also established health care programs, including Medicare for the elderly and Medicaid for the poor. Other programs and legislation ensured federal funding for education, low-income housing, urban renewal, transportation improvements, and environmental conservation. Johnson called his domestic program the Great Society.

The Vietnam War

Johnson's attention was soon drawn away from his domestic agenda to Cold War foreign policy—namely, containing communism around the world. Vietnam in particular dominated Johnson's presidency. The situation in Vietnam was a longstanding, complicated problem. Former presidents Kennedy and **Dwight D. Eisenhower** (1890–1969; served 1953–61; see entry) had made commitments to defend the government of South Vietnam against the communist forces of North Vietnam and the Vietcong, guerrilla forces within South Vietnam who supported the communist cause. (Communist-supported revolutionaries had earlier revolted against French colonial rule until a 1954 peace settlement was reached in Geneva, Switzerland. The settlement partitioned Vietnam into North Vietnam, controlled by the communists, and South Vietnam, supported by the United States.) U.S. officials feared that if South Vietnam fell to communism, other countries in the region would follow; this idea was called the domino theory. U.S. assistance to South Vietnam began in January 1955, and by 1960 there were seven hundred U.S. military advisors in the country.

In May 1961, Johnson personally visited South Vietnam as U.S. vice president. He became convinced that full U.S. backing was the right thing to do. At the time of Kennedy's death in November 1963, there were sixteen thousand military advisors in Vietnam. By early 1964, Johnson and his aides were secretly planning an increased military ef-

fort in Vietnam. However, they needed to build congressional support to finance the military buildup.

In August 1964, two U.S. destroyers off the coast of North Vietnam were allegedly attacked by North Vietnamese gunboats in the Gulf of Tonkin. This was the evidence Johnson needed to persuade Congress to support his military plan; the alleged attack could be presented as a threat to American interests. With congressional support, Johnson ordered U.S. planes to bomb North Vietnamese naval ports in retaliation. Though Johnson promised on national television that there would be no further escalation in the war, Congress passed the Gulf of Tonkin Resolution two days later, giving the president broad powers to conduct a war in Vietnam and surrounding countries.

Ironically, during the presidential campaign of 1964 against Republican candidate Barry Goldwater (1909–1998), Johnson accused Goldwater of being a reckless warmonger who would readily resort to nuclear weapons in combating

U.S. president Lyndon B. Johnson (far right) confers with (from left to right) Secretary of State Dean Rusk, Secretary of Defense Robert McNamara, and CIA director John McCone following McNamara's five-day tour of Vietnam in March 1964. *Reproduced by permission of the Corbis Corporation.*

A-4 Skyhawk bomber jets sit on the USS *Kitty Hawk* aircraft carrier in the Gulf of Tonkin in 1967. *Courtesy of the National Archives and Records Administration.*

communism. Representing himself as the peace candidate, Johnson pledged not to commit U.S. ground troops to Vietnam. He resisted any military buildup through the fall of 1964. With the U.S. economy flourishing, Johnson won a record landslide victory, receiving over 61 percent of the popular vote.

In February 1965, only three months after the election victory, Johnson ordered massive bombing raids on North

Vietnamese industrial and military sites in response to the death of eight U.S. soldiers at a U.S. military base in South Vietnam. He also sent 3,500 marines to protect the air base; they were the first U.S. combat troops to be sent to Vietnam. In July, Johnson sent another 50,000 troops to begin the ground war in South Vietnam. By the end of 1965, 200,000 U.S. troops were in South Vietnam. Johnson steadily increased their number to 536,000 in 1968. The steady escalation failed to bring North Vietnam to the negotiating table; instead, North Vietnam met each U.S. escalation with an escalation of its own. Johnson refrained from invading North Vietnam because Chinese troops were stationed there. He did not want to bring communist China, a powerful rival, into the conflict.

Growing social unrest in America

U.S. casualties in Vietnam climbed at an alarming rate, amounting to five hundred a week by late 1967. Public support for the war began to crumble. Student antiwar demonstrations grew on college campuses in 1965. By 1967, the antiwar movement spread into other segments of society. In October 1967, a mass demonstration against the war was held in Washington, D.C. Eventually, in 1968, Congress began opposing further escalation of the war. Making grim matters worse, the financial costs of waging war were high: In 1967, the United States spent $25 billion on the conflict in Vietnam. Protesters confronted Johnson everywhere he traveled, and he eventually became isolated in the White House. Critics claimed that the United States was wrongfully involved in a Vietnamese civil war. However, Johnson and his closest advisors, such as Secretary of State Dean Rusk (1909–1994), remained convinced that they were in the right, fighting a broad global communist movement.

Johnson's cherished Great Society programs were a major casualty of the war; with billions of dollars being spent in South Vietnam, funding for domestic programs was scarce. Johnson began reducing funding for his antipoverty program in 1965. From 1964 to 1967, Johnson had spent over $6 billion in his war on poverty, with only limited successes to show. Inner-city black Americans were frustrated by the lack of improvement in their neighborhoods, and soon blacks rioted in one city after another across the nation—New York

Dean Rusk

Secretary of State Dean Rusk was a key advisor to President Lyndon Johnson, guiding the president's decisions on the Vietnam War and other Cold War issues. Rusk was an ardent anticommunist and consistently took a hard-line approach in using U.S. military might. Like Johnson, he became a target for antiwar protesters in the United States.

Born in rural Georgia in 1909, Rusk was a Rhodes scholar and attended St. John's College in Oxford, England. Rusk began his career as a college professor, teaching political science at Mills College in Oakland, California, from 1934 to 1940. During World War II, he served as deputy chief of staff in Far Eastern matters. After the war, he joined the State Department as an East Asian expert. President **Harry S. Truman** (1884–1972; served 1945–53; see entry) appointed Rusk as assistant secretary of state for Far Eastern affairs in March 1950, just before the outbreak of the Korean War (1950–53). Rusk played an important role in guiding U.S. strategy in the war. He also argued for the first U.S. support to South Vietnam in the mid-1950s.

In 1961, President John F. Kennedy named Rusk as his secretary of state. Under Kennedy, Rusk would play a fairly restricted role in foreign policy development. Howev-

Dean Rusk. *Courtesy of the Library of Congress.*

er, when Johnson assumed the presidency in November 1963 after Kennedy's assassination, Rusk's influence increased. From 1964 to 1968, he defended heavy U.S. military involvement in Vietnam. He also argued against formal U.S. recognition of communist China. His characteristic cool and restrained manner proved an inviting target for war protesters. Nevertheless, Rusk vigorously defended U.S. war policy and continued to do so even after major setbacks in 1968. Rusk retired from government service in 1969 and resumed his teaching career. After his final retirement, he published his memoirs, titled *As I Saw It* (1990). He died in 1994.

City in 1964; Los Angeles, California, in 1965; Cleveland, Ohio, in 1966; Newark, New Jersey, and Detroit, Michigan, in 1967; and Washington, D.C., in 1968. A backlash of rioting by white Americans followed, and it seemed that the United States was on the brink of a race war.

Cold War conflicts around the world

As the war raged in Vietnam, other Cold War conflicts erupted in Latin America, the Middle East, and Korea. In April 1965, Johnson sent thirty thousand U.S. troops to the Dominican Republic to protect the ruling military dictatorship from communist-supported revolutionaries. The international community criticized this U.S. action; even Britain, America's closest ally, complained that the United States was interfering in the internal affairs of the smaller country. Another Cold War confrontation came in the Middle East in June 1967, when Israel launched a surprise attack on Egypt, Jordan, and Syria. In this conflict, known as the Six-Day War, the Soviets accused Israel of ignoring United Nations resolutions for a cease-fire. Johnson moved the U.S. Sixth Fleet closer to the Syrian coast to respond to any potential Soviet military involvement. The Soviets made no further moves.

Another incident brought Korea, the center of a Cold War conflict in the early 1950s, back to the forefront. On January 23, 1968, North Korea seized the USS *Pueblo,* an intelligence-gathering ship. Eight men were captured and imprisoned. Johnson sent a nuclear-powered aircraft carrier to the area. However, North Korea would hold the crew for eleven months until the United States finally apologized for spying. The apology was retracted immediately after the release of the U.S. prisoners.

The end of a presidency

One week after North Korea seized the *Pueblo,* communist North Vietnamese and Vietcong forces unleashed the Tet Offensive, a massive attack that occurred during the national celebrations of Tet, the Vietnamese lunar New Year. Numerous South Vietnamese cities were temporarily overrun. Intense fighting spread through South Vietnam's capital city, Saigon, and into the U.S. embassy building. Though the communist forces were soon beaten back, they had accomplished a major psychological victory. The Vietnam War no longer seemed winnable to the United States.

After reassessing the U.S. war commitment, Johnson decided to change course. In a televised speech to the nation on March 31, 1968, he announced major reductions in the bombing of North Vietnam and a renewed offer to North Vietnam to begin peace talks. He also stunned the nation by announcing that he would neither seek nor accept the Democratic nomination to run for reelection that fall. Three days later, the North Vietnamese agreed to begin peace talks in May. During 1968, the United States and the Soviet Union agreed to begin strategic arms limitation talks; the talks would lead to the 1972 treaty known as SALT I. Negotiations were scheduled to begin in late September in Leningrad. However, in August, Soviet-led forces invaded Czechoslovakia, crushing a popular movement to introduce democratic reforms in Czechoslovakia's communist government. Johnson pulled out of the arms control talks to protest the heavy-handed actions of the Soviets.

The American home front was turbulent in 1968. In April, civil rights leader Martin Luther King Jr. (1929–1968) was assassinated in Memphis, Tennessee; in June, U.S. senator Robert Kennedy (1925–1968) of New York, the late president's brother and the front-runner in the race for the Democratic presidential nomination, was assassinated in Los Angeles. Lyndon Johnson was so embattled as president that he did not even attend the Democratic National Convention that summer in Chicago, where antiwar protesters clashed violently with local police. In the presidential election that fall, the Republican candidate, former vice president Richard Nixon, representing himself as the peace candidate, narrowly defeated the Democratic candidate, incumbent (current) vice president Hubert Humphrey (1911–1978). However, the Vietnam War would continue for another seven years and become the most unpopular war in U.S. history. Besides the major loss of life, Vietnam left a legacy of spiraling inflation, which would undermine the U.S. economy through the 1970s.

Johnson retired to his Texas ranch in January 1969. There, he wrote his memoirs and worked on plans for his presidential library at the University of Texas in Austin. The library was dedicated in May 1971. Johnson died of a heart attack on his ranch in January 1973, only days before a peace agreement was reached in the war. Johnson believed he was a victim of history and poor advice. His dream of helping the underprivileged had been crushed by Cold War world events seemingly out of his control. His presidency represents a tragic period in U.S. history.

For More Information

Books

Berman, Larry. *Lyndon Johnson's War: The Road to Stalemate in Vietnam.* New York: Norton, 1989.

Conkin, Paul K. *Big Daddy from the Pedernales: Lyndon Baines Johnson.* Boston: Twayne Publishers, 1986.

Gardner, Lloyd C. *Pay Any Price: Lyndon Johnson and the Wars for Vietnam.* Chicago: I. R. Dee, 1995.

Goodwin, Doris Kearns. *Lyndon Johnson and the American Dream.* New York: Harper and Row, 1976.

Herring, George C. *America's Longest War: The United States and Vietnam, 1950–1975.* 2nd ed. New York: Knopf, 1988.

Hunt, Michael H. *Lyndon Johnson's War: America's Cold War Crusade in Vietnam, 1945–1968.* New York: Hill and Wang, 1996.

Johnson, Lyndon B. *The Vantage Point: Perspectives of the Presidency, 1963–1969.* New York: Holt, Rinehart and Winston, 1971.

Kutler, Stanley I., ed. *Encyclopedia of the Vietnam War.* New York: Charles Scribner's Sons, 1996.

Unger, Irwin, and Debi Unger. *LBJ: A Life.* New York: Wiley, 1999.

Web Sites

Lyndon B. Johnson Library and Museum. http://www.lbjlib.utexas.edu (accessed on September 5, 2003).

Vietnam Online. http://www.pbs.org/wgbh/amex/vietnam (accessed on September 5, 2003).

Where to Learn More

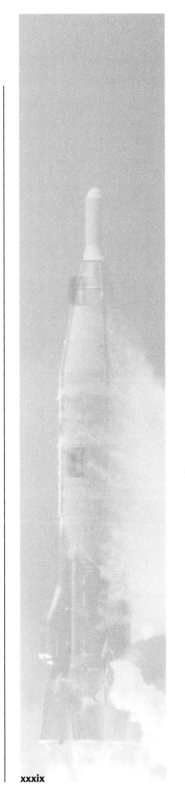

Books

Barson, Michael, and Steven Heller. *Red Scared! The Commie Menace in Propaganda and Popular Culture.* San Francisco: Chronicle Books, 2001.

Brubaker, Paul E. *The Cuban Missile Crisis in American History.* Berkeley Heights, NJ: Enslow, 2001.

Ciment, James. *The Young People's History of the United States.* New York: Barnes and Noble Books, 1998.

Collier, Christopher. *The United States in the Cold War.* New York: Benchmark Books/Marshall Cavendish, 2002.

FitzGerald, Frances. *Way Out There in the Blue: Reagan, Star Wars, and the End of the Cold War.* New York: Simon & Schuster, 2000.

Gaddis, John L. *We Now Know: Rethinking Cold War History.* New York: Oxford University Press, 1997.

Gates, Robert M. *From the Shadows: The Ultimate Insider's Story of Five Presidents and How They Won the Cold War.* New York: Simon & Schuster Trade Paperback, 1997.

Glynn, Patrick. *Closing Pandora's Box: Arms Races, Arms Control, and the History of the Cold War.* New York: Basic Books, 1992.

Grant, R. G. *The Berlin Wall.* Austin, TX: Raintree Steck-Vaughn, 1999.

Herring, George C. *America's Longest War: The United States and Vietnam, 1950–1975.* 2nd ed. New York: Knopf, 1988.

Huchthausen, Peter A., and Alexander Hoyt. *October Fury.* Hoboken, NJ: Wiley, 2002.

Isaacs, Jeremy, and Taylor Downing. *Cold War: An Illustrated History, 1945–1991.* Boston: Little, Brown, 1998.

Jacobs, William Jay. *Search for Peace: The Story of the United Nations.* New York: Atheneum, 1996.

Keep, John L. H. *A History of the Soviet Union, 1945–1991: Last of the Empires.* New York: Oxford University Press, 1995.

Kelly, Nigel. *Fall of the Berlin Wall: The Cold War Ends.* Chicago: Heineman Library, 2001.

Kort, Michael G. *The Cold War.* Brookfield, CT: Millbrook Press, 1994.

LaFeber, Walter. *America, Russia, and the Cold War, 1945–1996.* 8th ed. New York: McGraw-Hill, 1997.

Parrish, Thomas. *Berlin in the Balance, 1945–1949: The Blockade, the Airlift, the First Major Battle of the Cold War.* Reading, MA: Addison-Wesley, 1998.

Parrish, Thomas. *The Cold War Encyclopedia.* New York: Henry Holt, 1996.

Pietrusza, David. *The End of the Cold War.* San Diego, CA: Lucent, 1995.

Sherrow, Victoria. *Joseph McCarthy and the Cold War.* Woodbridge, CT: Blackbirch Press, 1999.

Sibley, Katherine A. S. *The Cold War.* Westport, CT: Greenwood Press, 1998.

Smith, Joseph. *The Cold War, 1945–1991.* 2nd ed. Malden, MA: Blackwell, 1998.

Stein, Conrad. *The Korean War: "The Forgotten War."* Springfield, NJ: Enslow, 1994.

Walker, Martin. *The Cold War: A History (Owl Book).* New York: Henry Holt, 1995.

Magazines

Hoover, J. Edgar. "How to Fight Communism." *Newsweek,* June 9, 1947.

Levine, Isaac Don. "Our First Line of Defense." *Plain Talk,* September 1949.

"X" (George F. Kennan). "The Sources of Soviet Conduct." *Foreign Affairs,* July 1947.

Novels

Brunner, Edward. *Cold War Poetry.* Urbana: University of Illinois Press, 2000.

Clancy, Tom. *The Hunt for Red October.* New York: Berkley Publishing Group, 1985.

Clancy, Tom. *Red Storm Rising.* New York: Berkley Publishing Group, 1987.

Clancy, Tom, and Martin Greenberg. *Tom Clancy's Power Plays: Cold War.* New York: Berkley Publishing Group, 2001.

George, Peter. *Dr. Strangelove, or How I Learned to Stop Worrying and Love the Bomb.* New York: Bantam Books, 1964.

Le Carre, John. *Spy Who Came in from the Cold.* New York: Coward, McCann & Geoghegan, 1978.

Littell, Robert. *The Company: A Novel of the CIA.* New York: Overlook Press, 2002.

Web Sites

The Atomic Archive. http://www.atomicarchive.com (accessed on September 26, 2003).

CNN Interactive: The Cold War Experience. http://www.CNN.com/SPECIALS/cold.war (accessed on September 26, 2003).

"Cold War History: 1949–1989." *U.S. Air Force Museum.* http://www.wpafb.af.mil/museum/history/coldwar/cw.htm (accessed on September 26, 2003).

The Dwight D. Eisenhower Library and Museum. http://www.eisenhower.utexas.edu (accessed on September 26, 2003).

George Bush Presidential Library and Museum. http://bushlibrary.tamu.edu (accessed on September 26, 2003).

Gerald R. Ford Library and Museum. http://www.ford.utexas.edu (accessed on September 26, 2003).

International Spy Museum. http://spymuseum.org (accessed on September 26, 2003).

John F. Kennedy Library and Museum. http://www.cs.umb.edu/jfklibrary/index.htm (accessed on September 26, 2003).

Lyndon B. Johnson Library and Museum. http://www.lbjlib.utexas.edu (accessed on September 26, 2003).

The Manhattan Project Heritage Preservation Association, Inc. http://www.childrenofthemanhattanproject.org (accessed on September 26, 2003).

National Atomic Museum. http://www.atomicmuseum.com (accessed on September 26, 2003).

National Security Agency. http://www.nsa.gov (accessed on September 26, 2003).

President Mikhail Sergeyevich Gorbachev. http://www.mikhailgorbachev.org (accessed on September 26, 2003).

The Richard Nixon Library and Birthplace. http://www.nixonfoundation.org (accessed on September 26, 2003).

Ronald Reagan Presidential Library. http://www.reagan.utexas.edu (accessed on September 26, 2003).

"Secrets, Lies, and Atomic Spies." *Nova Online.* http://www.pbs.org/wgbh/nova/venona (accessed on September 26, 2003).

Truman Presidential Museum & Library. http://www.trumanlibrary.org (accessed on September 26, 2003).

U.S. Central Intelligence Agency (CIA). http://www.cia.gov (accessed on September 26, 2003).

Woodrow Wilson International Center for Scholars. *The Cold War International History Project.* http://wwics.si.edu/index.cfm?fuseaction=topics.home&topic_id=1409 (accessed on September 26, 2003).

Index

objectivism and, *2:* 382
property and, *1:* 3, 42, 86, 111,
   150, 178; *2:* 211, 237,
   251–52, 313, 385, 404
Rand, Ayn, and, *2:* 385
Soviet Union and, *2:* 280–82
Stalin, Joseph, and, *2:* 210–11,
   351
United States of America and,
   1: 86, 127
West Germany and, *2:* 268
Carter Center, *1:* 80
Carter, Jimmy, *1:* 70 (ill.), **70–81,**
   78 (ill.); *2:* 391 (ill.)
Afghanistan and, *1:* 50, 70, 78;
   2: 393
African Americans and, *1:* 71,
   73
as author, *1:* 79–80
Brezhnev, Leonid, and, *1:* 49,
   50, 74–75
Brzezinski, Zbigniew, and, *1:*
   74, 75
Bush, George, and, *1:* 55, 81
Camp David Accords and, *1:*
   70, 78–79; *2:* 263
China and, *1:* 39, 70, 77, 120
Clifford, Clark M., and, *1:* 109,
   114
Clinton, Bill, and, *1:* 81
Conference on Security and
   Cooperation in Europe and,
   1: 75
Democratic Party and, *1:* 73
Deng Xiaoping and, *1:* 120
détente and, *1:* 74–75
dictatorship and, *1:* 76
discrimination and, *1:* 73
early life of, *1:* 71–72
economy and, *1:* 76–77; *2:* 391
election of, *1:* 55, 74; *2:* 390,
   391–92
elections monitored by, *1:*
   80–81
energy policy and, *1:* 76–77
as farmer, *1:* 72, 73
as governor, *1:* 73–74
Great Depression and, *1:* 71–72
Helsinki Accords and, *2:* 265
honors for, *1:* 81
human rights and, *1:* 70,
   71–72, 75–76, 80–81
Iran hostage crisis and, *1:* 70,
   79; *2:* 391

Kissinger, Henry, and, *2:* 266
Latin America and, *1:* 76
"malaise speech" of, *1:* 77
as naval officer, *1:* 72–73
Nicaragua and, *1:* 81
North Korea and, *1:* 81; *2:* 248
nuclear weapons and, *1:* 49, 70,
   74–75, 77–78, 81, 166; *2:*
   248, 392
Olympics and, *1:* 70, 78
Pahlavi, Mohammed Reza, and,
   1: 79
Panama and, *1:* 77, 81, 125
presidency of, *1:* 73–79
Reagan, Ronald, and, *2:* 391–92
Rickover, Hyman G., and, *1:*
   72–73
Sakharov, Andrey, and, *1:* 75
segregation and, *1:* 73
Soviet Union and, *1:* 50, 70,
   74–75, 77–78; *2:* 393
Strategic Arms Limitation Talks
   and, *1:* 49, 70, 77–78, 166; *2:*
   392
Vance, Cyrus, and, *1:* 74
Vietnam War and, *1:* 76
Carter, Lillian Gordy, *1:* 71
Carter, Rosalynn Smith, *1:* 72, 73,
   80–81
Castro Argiz, Angel, *1:* 83
Castro, Fidel, *1:* 82 (ill.), **82–91**
Allende, Salvador, and, *1:* 20,
   22
as author, *1:* 91
Bay of Pigs and, *1:* 87; *2:* 341
Central Intelligence Agency
   and, *1:* 87, 88
China and, *1:* 86
communism and, *1:* 86, 88; *2:*
   223
Cuban Missile Crisis and, *1:*
   88–89, 90
De Rivera, José Antonio Primo,
   and, *1:* 84
democracy and, *1:* 86
early life of, *1:* 83–84
Eastern Bloc and, *1:* 86
economy and, *1:* 86–87, 88, 91
Eisenhower, Dwight D., and, *1:*
   87; *2:* 223
Gorbachev, Mikhail, and, *1:* 91
imperialism and, *1:* 82–83, 87
Khrushchev, Nikita, and, *2:* 223
Martí, José, and, *1:* 84

military and, *2:* 213

North Atlantic Treaty Organization and, *1:* 4, 31, 58, 111, 113; *2:* 271, 327, 434, 437

nuclear weapons and, *2:* 272–73

politics and, *2:* 213

Reagan, Ronald, and, *2:* 395, 395–97

Southeast Asia Treaty Organization and, *1:* 130, 141

Stalin, Joseph, and, *2:* 433–34

Truman Doctrine and, *1:* 3–4, 29–30, 38, 112, 172

Truman, Harry S., and, *1:* 3–4, 29–30, 38, 128, 172; *2:* 458–59

Contras, *1:* 56; *2:* 398

Conventional Forces in Europe (CFE) treaty, *2:* 274

Council of Ministers
in Communist Party, *1:* 162, 163

Gromyko, Andrey, and, *1:* 166

Khrushchev, Nikita, and, *2:* 240

Kosygin, Aleksey, and, *2:* 277, 279, 280, 282

Council on Foreign Relations, *2:* 256

"Crimes of Stalin" speech, *2:* 236, 291, 436

Crusade in Europe, 1: 139

CSCE. *See* Conference on Security and Cooperation in Europe (CSCE)

Cuba. *See also* Cuban Missile Crisis

26th of July Movement and, *1:* 85

agriculture in, *1:* 86

Bay of Pigs and, *1:* 87, 113, 144; *2:* 223, 340–41

blockade of, *1:* 90; *2:* 227, 238

Central Intelligence Agency and, *1:* 87, 88, 113, 144; *2:* 223

China and, *1:* 86

communism in, *1:* 82, 88

Communist Party in, *1:* 86

Cuban Missile Crisis and, *1:* 88–91

Cuban People's Party in, *1:* 84–85

democracy in, *1:* 86

dictatorship and, *1:* 84–85

Eastern Bloc and, *1:* 86

economy of, *1:* 84–85, 86–87, 88, 91

Eisenhower, Dwight D., and, *1:* 87, 143–44; *2:* 223

Gorbachev, Mikhail, and, *1:* 91

Kennedy, John F., and, *1:* 87, 88

nationalization in, *1:* 86

nuclear weapons and, *1:* 88–91

revolution in, *1:* 84–85, 143–44

Soviet Union and, *1:* 82, 86, 87, 88–91; *2:* 223, 226–27

Spain and, *1:* 83

United Nations and, *1:* 91

Cuban Missile Crisis, *1:* 89 (ill.)

Acheson, Dean G., and, *1:* 7

blockade and, *1:* 90; *2:* 227, 238

Castro, Fidel, and, *1:* 88–89, 90

Kennedy, John F., and, *1:* 7, 89–91; *2:* 218, 226–28, 238, 308

Kennedy, Robert F., and, *2:* 227

Khrushchev, Nikita, and, *1:* 90–91; *2:* 226–27, 227–28, 230, 238

Kosygin, Aleksey, and, *2:* 277

Macmillan, Harold, and, *2:* 308

nuclear war and, *2:* 227, 238, 394

nuclear weapons and, *1:* 88–91

reconnaissance and, *1:* 90; *2:* 227

Cuban People's Party, *1:* 84–85

Cultural Revolution, *1:* 119; *2:* 246, 318–20, 471–72

Cummings, Homer S., *1:* 190 (ill.)

Czechoslovakia
Brezhnev, Leonid, and, *1:* 43, 47; *2:* 282

freedom in, *1:* 47

Gromyko, Andrey, and, *1:* 164

Soviet Union and, *1:* 43, 47, 164, 204; *2:* 216, 281, 282, 449

Sovietization of, *1:* 43

Stalin, Joseph, and, *2:* 435

Yugoslavia and, *2:* 449

D

Dag Hammarskjold Honorary Medal, *2:* 343

communism and, *1:* 140–41, 181

containment and, *1:* 141, 142

Cuba and, *1:* 87, 143–44; *2:* 223

death of, *1:* 144–45

Dulles, John Foster, and, *1:* 128–30, 131

early life of, *1:* 134–35

East Germany and, *1:* 130

Eisenhower Doctrine and, *1:* 142

election of, *1:* 128, 139–40, 141–42, 143; *2:* 302, 334, 356, 389, 461

espionage and, *1:* 144; *2:* 308

Germany and, *1:* 138

Guatemala and, *1:* 141

Hungary and, *1:* 130, 142

imperialism and, *1:* 87, 141, 144; *2:* 223

Iran and, *1:* 141

Kennan, George F., and, *2:* 215

Khrushchev, Nikita, and, *1:* 141, 144; *2:* 230, 237, 238, 308

Korean War and, *1:* 134, 140, 143

MacArthur, Douglas, and, *1:* 135

Macmillan, Harold, and, *2:* 305, 307, 308

McCarthy, Joseph R., and, *1:* 140; *2:* 334

military and, *1:* 134, 135–39

missiles and, *2:* 307

Nixon, Richard M., and, *1:* 139–40; *2:* 356, 358

North Atlantic Treaty Organization and, *1:* 139

nuclear weapons and, *1:* 140, 144; *2:* 215

"Open Skies" plan of, *1:* 140–41

Oppenheimer, J. Robert, and, *2:* 376

peace and, *1:* 134

popularity of, *1:* 143

presidency of, *1:* 139–44

Reagan, Ronald, and, *2:* 389

Republic of China and, *1:* 141

retirement of, *1:* 144

Roosevelt, Franklin D., and, *1:* 136

Southeast Asia Treaty Organization and, *1:* 141

Soviet Union and, *1:* 137, 138, 140–41, 142, 143

space race and, *1:* 142

Stalin, Joseph, and, *1:* 138

Suez War and, *1:* 131–32, 142; *2:* 306

Taiwan and, *1:* 130

television and, *1:* 143

Third World and, *1:* 141

Truman, Harry S., and, *1:* 139

Vietnam and, *1:* 141

Vietnam War and, *1:* 198

West Berlin and, *1:* 132; *2:* 237

World War I and, *1:* 135

World War II and, *1:* 134, 135–38

Elections

of 1932, *1:* 2, 64, 170

of 1944, *2:* 456

of 1948, *1:* 139; *2:* 389, 459, 460

of 1952, *1:* 128, 139–40, 143 (ill.); *2:* 301–2, 334, 356, 389, 461

of 1956, *1:* 141–42, 143

of 1958, *2:* 389

of 1960, *1:* 113, 197; *2:* 221, 358, 390

of 1964, *1:* 199–200; *2:* 358, 390

of 1968, *1:* 204; *2:* 257, 358, 390

of 1972, *2:* 259, 362, 390

of 1976, *1:* 55, 74; *2:* 390

of 1980, *1:* 55–56, 79; *2:* 251

of 1984, *1:* 56; *2:* 395

of 1988, *1:* 56; *2:* 399

of 1992, *1:* 60

of 2000, *1:* 61; *2:* 406

Carter, Jimmy, monitors, *1:* 80–81

in Chile, *1:* 19, 20–21

communism and, *1:* 162; *2:* 295

democracy and, *1:* 25–26, 42, 86, 127; *2:* 251, 271, 314, 385, 404, 426, 449

in France, *1:* 14

in Germany, *2:* 274

in Great Britain, *1:* 27, 28, 33, 40, 106, 107; *2:* 304, 305, 306, 308, 437

in North Korea, *2:* 247

in Poland, *1:* 36–37, 66, 171; *2:* 431

in Soviet Union, *1:* 41, 44, 45, 152–53, 157, 163, 166; *2:* 210–11, 232

Stalin, Joseph, and, *1:* 138
in United States of America, *1:* 25–26
in West Germany, *1:* 12, 15; *2:* 271
in Yugoslavia, *2:* 450
Elizabeth II, *1:* 100–101
Elsey, George, *1:* 111
Emergency Powers Act, *1:* 35
Energy, *1:* 76–77. *See also* Nuclear energy
Enrico Fermi Award, *2:* 377
Espionage. *See also* Reconnaissance
Eisenhower, Dwight D., and, *1:* 144; *2:* 308
Johnson, Lyndon B., and, *1:* 203
Khrushchev, Nikita, and, *1:* 144; *2:* 238, 308
Manhattan Project and, *1:* 191–92; *2:* 285, 287, 351
North Korea and, *1:* 203
nuclear weapons and, *1:* 191–92; *2:* 285, 287, 333, 351
space race and, *1:* 142
Watergate scandal and, *2:* 363, 364
Ethiopia, *1:* 50, 164
Europe
Brezhnev, Leonid, on, *1:* 41
economy of, *1:* 14, 30–31, 38; *2:* 308–9, 324–26
Marshall Plan and, *2:* 324–25
military and, *2:* 262
unification of, *2:* 269–70, 272, 273
European Advisory Commission, *2:* 210
European Common Market. *See* Common Market
European Defense Community (EDC), *1:* 12
European Economic Community (EEC). *See* Common Market
Execution. *See* Death

F

Fabian Society, *1:* 26
Facism, *1:* 185–86, 189–90
Fair Deal, *2:* 459

Farrell, Thomas, *2:* 372
FBI. *See* Federal Bureau of Investigation (FBI)
February Revolution, *2:* 347. *See also* Bolshevik Revolution
Federal Bureau of Investigation (FBI)
civil rights and, *1:* 187, 193
communism and, *1:* 186, 189–92
corruption and, *1:* 188
democracy and, *1:* 186, 189–90
facism and, *1:* 189–90
Great Depression and, *1:* 188–89
Hoover, J. Edgar, becomes director of, *1:* 187–88
Manhattan Project and, *1:* 191–92
organized crime and, *1:* 189
Prohibition Era and, *1:* 185
Red Scare and, *1:* 189–92
science and, *1:* 188
Watergate scandal and, *2:* 363
World War II and, *1:* 189–90
Federal Council of Churches of Christ in America, *1:* 126
Federal Republic of Germany. *See* West Germany
Federalism, *2:* 450
Felix, Antonia, *2:* 403, 404, 407
"Feminine factor," *2:* 439
Ferguson, Francis, *2:* 368
Fermi, Enrico, *2:* 284, 371, 375, 377
Fission, *2:* 284–85, 409
Ford, Gerald, *1:* 49 (ill.)
Brezhnev, Leonid, and, *1:* 48–49
Bush, George, and, *1:* 55
détente and, *1:* 49
election of 1976 and, *1:* 74
Kissinger, Henry, and, *2:* 264–65
Nixon, Richard M., and, *1:* 74; *2:* 364
nuclear weapons and, *1:* 166
Reagan, Ronald, and, *2:* 266, 390
Rockefeller, Nelson A., and, *1:* 55
Strategic Arms Limitation Talks and, *1:* 166
Ford Motor Company, *2:* 339, 342

Foreign Intelligence Advisory Board, *1:* 113
Foreign Service, *2:* 208
The Fountainhead, 2: 383
Four Modernizations, *2:* 320
France
  Adenauer, Konrad, and, *1:* 12, 14
  colonialism and, *1:* 177–78, 180
  Communist Party in, *1:* 178
  economy of, *1:* 12
  elections in, *1:* 14
  Great Britain and, *2:* 308
  Ho Chi Minh and, *1:* 177–78, 180; *2:* 257
  Indochina and, *1:* 177–78, 180
  Suez War and, *1:* 131–32, 142; *2:* 306
  Vietminh and, *1:* 180
  Vietnam and, *1:* 141, 177–78, 179, 180, 198; *2:* 257, 469
  West Germany and, *1:* 12, 13, 14
Franco, Francisco, *1:* 84
Franco-German Friendship Treaty, *1:* 14
Frankfurter, Felix, *1:* 2
Franklin Delano Roosevelt Freedom from Want Medal, *2:* 343
FRAP. *See* Popular Revolutionary Action Front (FRAP)
Freedom. *See also* specific freedoms
  Brezhnev, Leonid, and, *1:* 46, 47
  communism and, *2:* 250, 381
  Communist Party and, *2:* 434
  in Czechoslovakia, *1:* 47
  Helsinki Accords and, *2:* 264–65
  Ho Chi Minh and, *1:* 181–82
  KGB (Soviet secret police) and, *1:* 46
  Khrushchev, Nikita, and, *2:* 233, 234
  Mao Zedong and, *2:* 312, 314, 318, 320
  McNamara, Robert S., and, *2:* 337
  Reagan, Ronald, on, *2:* 387
  Red Scare and, *2:* 384

  Sakharov, Andrey, and, *2:* 408, 412
  Shevardnadze, Eduard, on, *2:* 416
  in Soviet Union, *2:* 233, 234, 408
  Thatcher, Margaret, and, *2:* 437, 442–43
  Tito, Josip Broz, and, *2:* 451
  in Vietnam, *1:* 181–82
  in Yugoslavia, *2:* 451
Freedom March, *2:* 222
Freedom of assembly, *1:* 193
Freedom of religion, *2:* 385, 389
Freedom of speech, *1:* 193
Fuchs, Klaus, *1:* 192; *2:* 287
Fusion, *2:* 409

G

Gamsakhurdia, Zviad, *2:* 422
Gang of Four, *1:* 119, 120; *2:* 320
GDR. *See* German Democratic Republic (GDR)
General Electric, *2:* 389
General Intelligence Division (GID), *1:* 187
Geneva Conference, *2:* 469
George Bush Presidential Library, *1:* 61
Georgia (USSR), *2:* 417, 422–23
German Democratic Republic (GDR). *See* East Germany
Germany. *See also* East Germany; West Germany
  Bush, George, and, *2:* 405
  Byrnes, James F., and, *1:* 67
  Christian Democratic Union in, *2:* 274
  containment and, *2:* 432
  division of, *1:* 12, 66, 105, 106–7, 138, 161; *2:* 224, 235, 268, 351–52, 432
  Eisenhower, Dwight D., and, *1:* 138
  elections in, *2:* 274
  Gorbachev, Mikhail, and, *1:* 58; *2:* 405
  government of, *1:* 138
  Harriman, W. Averell, and, *1:* 172
  Kennan, George F., and, *2:* 210
  Molotov, Vyacheslav, and, *2:* 348–50, 351

World War II and, *1:* 148
Yeltsin, Boris, and, *1:* 157; *2:*
  418, 419
Gorbachev, Raisa, *1:* 120 (ill.),
  151–52, 153, 156 (ill.), 157
Gore, Al, *1:* 61
Government Operations Com-
  mittee, *2:* 334
Great Britain. *See also* British
  Commonwealth of Nations;
  British Empire
  Acheson, Dean G., and, *1:* 2
  Attlee, Clement R., and, *1:* 25,
    27–32
  Bevin, Ernest, and, *1:* 33, 35–40
  Chamberlain, Neville, and, *1:*
    27
  China and, *1:* 39; *2:* 307
  colonialism and, *2:* 309–10
  Conservative Party in, *1:* 25,
    27, 102; *2:* 304, 439, 443
  Dockers' Union in, *1:* 34
  Dominican Republic and, *1:*
    203
  economy of, *1:* 28–29, 32, 38,
    39, 170; *2:* 305–6, 308–9,
    310, 439–40
  elections in, *1:* 36, 40; *2:* 304,
    305, 306, 308, 437
  European Common Market
    and, *2:* 308–9
  France and, *2:* 308
  Greece and, *1:* 29, 38, 112
  Independent Labour Party in,
    1: 26
  Israel and, *1:* 36–37
  Johnson, Lyndon B., and, *1:*
    203
  Kurchatov, Igor, and, *2:* 291
  labor in, *1:* 34
  Labour Party in, *1:* 25, 27
  Lend-Lease program and, *1:*
    170
  Liberal Party in, *1:* 102
  missiles and, *2:* 307
  Molotov, Vyacheslav, and, *2:*
    348–49
  nationalization in, *1:* 28–29
  North Atlantic Treaty Organiza-
    tion and, *2:* 441–42
  nuclear energy and, *2:* 284, 291
  nuclear weapons and, *1:* 31, 38,
    108; *2:* 307, 309, 440–41
  Palestine and, *1:* 36–37

Reagan, Ronald, and, *2:* 441–42
  Republic of China and, *2:* 307
  socialism in, *1:* 25, 28–29; *2:*
    439–40
  Soviet Union and, *1:* 35, 36–37,
    108; *2:* 307–8, 348–49,
    437–38
  Suez War and, *1:* 131–32, 142;
    2: 306
  Turkey and, *1:* 29, 38, 112
  Vietnam and, *1:* 141
  West Germany and, *2:* 308
  World War II and, *1:* 35, 100,
    102–7; *2:* 219, 348–49, 438
Great Depression
  Byrnes, James F., and, *1:* 64
  Carter, Jimmy, and, *1:* 71–72
  Federal Bureau of Investigation
    and, *1:* 188–89
  Johnson, Lyndon B., and, *1:*
    195–96
  MacArthur, Douglas, and, *2:*
    294–95
  Marshall, George C., and, *2:*
    323
  New Deal and, *2:* 455
  Oppenheimer, J. Robert, and, *2:*
    369–70
  Roosevelt, Franklin D., and, *1:*
    64; *2:* 295, 389
Great Leap Forward, *1:* 118–19; *2:*
  317–18, 470–71
Great Society, *1:* 197–98, 201
Great Terror
  Brezhnev, Leonid, and, *1:*
    42–43
  Communist Party and, *1:* 45
  execution during, *1:* 42–43; *2:*
    232, 236, 278, 412, 430,
    434–35
  Gorbachev, Mikhail, and, *1:*
    147–48
  Gromyko, Andrey, and, *1:* 160
  Kennan, George F., and, *2:* 209
  Khrushchev, Nikita, and, *2:*
    232, 236
  Kosygin, Aleksey, and, *2:*
    278–79, 279–80
  Molotov, Vyacheslav, and, *2:*
    348, 351, 352
  Sakharov, Andrey, and, *2:*
    409–10
  Stalin, Joseph, and, *2:* 278, 370,
    420, 430, 434–35

Oppenheimer, J. Robert, and, *2:* 375, 376
Sakharov, Andrey, and, *2:* 290, 375, 409, 410
testing of, *2:* 290, 307, 375, 410

I

J

Kennedy, John F., *1:* 112 (ill.), 174 (ill.); *2:* 218 (ill.), **218–29**, 222 (ill.), 224 (ill.), 228 (ill.), 340 (ill.)
Acheson, Dean G., and, *1:* 7
Adenauer, Konrad, and, *1:* 15
as author, *2:* 219
Bay of Pigs and, *1:* 87, 144; *2:* 223, 340
Berlin Wall and, *1:* 15; *2:* 218, 226, 275
Churchill, Winston, and, *1:* 101
civil rights and, *2:* 218, 221–22
Clifford, Clark M., and, *1:* 113
communism and, *2:* 340
Cuba and, *1:* 87, 88
Cuban Missile Crisis and, *1:* 7, 89–91; *2:* 218, 226–28, 238, 308
death of, *1:* 113, 194, 197; *2:* 218, 222, 228–29
Dulles, John Foster, and, *1:* 131
early life of, *2:* 218–19, 230–31
election of, *1:* 113, 197; *2:* 220, 221, 358, 390
Harriman, W. Averell, and, *1:* 173
honors for, *2:* 219
Hoover, J. Edgar, and, *1:* 192
imperialism and, *1:* 87, 88; *2:* 223, 226
inaugural address of, *2:* 222
Johnson, Lyndon B., and, *1:* 197; *2:* 221, 228
Kennan, George F., and, *2:* 215
Khrushchev, Nikita, and, *2:* 223–26, 227–28, 230
Kissinger, Henry, and, *2:* 256, 257
Macmillan, Harold, and, *2:* 225, 308–9
McCarthy, Joseph R., and, *2:* 220
McNamara, Robert S., and, *2:* 337, 339–40, 341
military and, *2:* 225
nuclear weapons and, *2:* 226–27, 227–28, 341
Operation Mongoose and, *1:* 88; *2:* 226
Oppenheimer, J. Robert, and, *2:* 377
peace and, *2:* 221

Peace Corps and, *2:* 221
Reagan, Ronald, and, *2:* 216
Rusk, Dean, and, *1:* 202
segregation and, *2:* 221–22
Soviet Union and, *2:* 227–28, 340
submarines and, *2:* 309
Truman, Harry S., and, *2:* 220
Ulbricht, Walter, and, *2:* 225
in U.S. Congress, *2:* 219–21
Vietnam War and, *1:* 198
West Berlin and, *2:* 224–25
World War II and, *2:* 219
Kennedy, Robert F., *1:* 204; *2:* 227, 228 (ill.), 358
Kent State University, *2:* 359
KGB (Soviet secret police), *1:* 46; *2:* 240, 433
Khomeini, Ayatollah Ruhollah, *1:* 79
Khrushchev, Nikita, *2:* 224 (ill.), 230 (ill.), **230–40**, 237 (ill.), 239 (ill.), 290 (ill.), 357 (ill.), 449 (ill.)
agriculture and, *2:* 238, 239
Berlin Wall and, *1:* 14; *2:* 225–26, 237, 275
Bolshevik Revolution and, *2:* 231
Brezhnev, Leonid, and, *1:* 43, 44–46; *2:* 238
Bulganin, Nikolay, and, *2:* 233, 234
Castro, Fidel, and, *2:* 223
character of, *1:* 46; *2:* 233–34
China and, *1:* 118; *2:* 235
communism and, *2:* 235, 236
Communist Party and, *2:* 231–32, 233, 234, 239–40
coup d'état and, *1:* 45–46
"Crimes of Stalin" speech and, *2:* 236, 291, 436
Cuban Missile Crisis and, *1:* 90–91; *2:* 226–27, 227–28, 230, 238
death of, *1:* 41; *2:* 240
Deng Xiaoping and, *1:* 118
de-Stalinization and, *1:* 118; *2:* 233, 236
East Germany and, *2:* 224–25
economy and, *2:* 239
Eisenhower, Dwight D., and, *1:* 141, 144; *2:* 230, 237, 238, 308

L

M

strength and, *2:* 409, 411

test bans and, *1:* 173; *2:* 238–39

testing of, *1:* 6, 31, 106, 108; *2:* 285, 287–88, 307, 333, 351, 366, 371, 372, 373, 375, 410, 434, 458

Thatcher, Margaret, and, *2:* 440–41

treaties concerning, *1:* 48, 50, 56, 58, 70, 77–78, 91, 155, 164–65, 166, 173, 204; *2:* 227–28, 238–39, 248, 255, 261–62, 265, 281, 309, 359, 360–61, 395–96, 420

Truman, Harry S., and, *1:* 3, 31, 108; *2:* 212, 288, 333, 351, 375, 458

U.S. Congress and, *1:* 108

use of, *1:* 3, 31; *2:* 285, 297, 371, 372, 409, 432, 458

West Germany and, *2:* 272–73

World War II and, *1:* 3, 31; *2:* 285, 297, 371, 409, 432, 458

Yeltsin, Boris, and, *1:* 58

Nuclear Weapons and Foreign Policy, *2:* 256

NYA. *See* National Youth Administration (NYA)

O

OAS. *See* Organization of American States (OAS)

Objectivism, *2:* 379, 382, 383, 384, 385

October Revolution, *2:* 347. *See also* Bolshevik Revolution

October War, *1:* 50; *2:* 262–63, 363

OEEC. *See* Organisation for European Economic Cooperation (OEEC)

Oil, *1:* 54, 76–77, 142; *2:* 262–63, 363

Olympics, *1:* 70, 78

One Day in the Life of Ivan Denisovich, *2:* 234

OPEC. *See* Organization of Petroleum Exporting Countries (OPEC)

"Open Skies" plan, *1:* 140–41

Operation Mongoose, *1:* 88; *2:* 226

Oppenheimer, J. Robert, *2:* 213–14, 283, 366 (ill.), **366–78,** 374 (ill.), 410–11

Order of Lenin, *1:* 149; *2:* 410

Order of Merit, *1:* 32

Order of Stalin, *2:* 410

Order of the Garter, *1:* 100–101

Order of the Red Banner of Labor, *1:* 149–50

Organisation for European Economic Cooperation (OEEC), *1:* 38; *2:* 325

Organization of American States (OAS), *1:* 60; *2:* 327, 377

Organization of Petroleum Exporting Countries (OPEC), *1:* 76; *2:* 363

Organized crime, *1:* 185, 189

Ortega, Daniel, *2:* 398

Ostopolitik, *1:* 15

Oswald, Lee Harvey, *2:* 228–29

P

Pace, Stephen, *1:* 72

Pahlavi, Mohammed Reza, *1:* 79; *2:* 391

Pakistan, *1:* 29

Palestine, *1:* 29, 36–37

Palestine Liberation Organization (PLO), *1:* 50

Palmer, A. Mitchell, *1:* 187

Palmer Raids, *1:* 187

Pan Am bombing, *2:* 399

Panama, *1:* 59–60, 77, 81

Panama Canal, *1:* 59, 77, 125

Partisans, *2:* 446

Pasternak, Boris, *2:* 234

Paul VI (pope), *1:* 164

Peace

Dulles, John Foster, and, *1:* 126

Eisenhower, Dwight D., and, *1:* 134

Johnson, Lyndon B., and, *1:* 200, 204

Kennedy, John F., and, *2:* 221

Khrushchev, Nikita, and, *2:* 352

Kirkpatrick, Jeane, on, *2:* 249

Kurchatov, Igor, and, *2:* 283, 289–91, 373

Nixon, Richard M., and, *2:* 359, 365

communism and, *1:* 3, 18, 26, 42, 82, 100, 110, 127, 150, 160, 168, 178, 186; *2:* 211, 223, 231, 278, 295, 312, 331, 340, 346, 366, 385, 389, 404, 410, 426, 445, 458, 464

democracy and, *2:* 426

Pulitzer Prize, *1:* 8

Purple Heart, *2:* 219

Putin, Vladimir, *2:* 419

Q

Quarantine, *1:* 90; *2:* 227, 238

R

Rabi, I. I., *2:* 375

Racism, *1:* 63, 68. *See also* Discrimination; Segregation

Radical Party, *1:* 18

Radio, *1:* 75; *2:* 334

Radio Free Europe, *1:* 75

Radio Liberty, *1:* 75

Rajk, Laszlo, *2:* 434

Rand, Ayn, *2:* 379 (ill.), **379–86,** 384 (ill.)

Rayburn, Sam, *1:* 195

Reagan Doctrine, *2:* 397–98

Reagan, Nancy, *1:* 156 (ill.); *2:* 389, 441 (ill.)

Reagan, Ronald, *1:* 156 (ill.); *2:* 252 (ill.), 387 (ill.), **387–400,** 391 (ill.), 394 (ill.), 397 (ill.), 441 (ill.)

as actor, *2:* 388–89

Afghanistan and, *2:* 392–93

Andropov, Yuri, and, *1:* 155

assassination attempt of, *2:* 392

as author, *2:* 399

Brezhnev, Leonid, and, *1:* 51

Bush, George, and, *2:* 391

Carter, Jimmy, and, *2:* 391–92

character of, *2:* 387

Cold War and, *2:* 387, 396

communism and, *2:* 251, 387, 389

containment and, *2:* 395, 395–97

Democratic Party and, *2:* 389

détente and, *2:* 390, 393

dictatorship and, *2:* 395–97

early life of, *2:* 387–88

economy and, *2:* 392

Eisenhower, Dwight D., and, *2:* 389

elections of, *1:* 55–56, 79; *2:* 251, 390–92, 395

Ford, Gerald, and, *2:* 266, 390

on freedom, *2:* 387

General Electric and, *2:* 389

Goldwater, Barry, and, *2:* 390

Gorbachev, Mikhail, and, *1:* 56, 57, 155–56; *2:* 395–96

as governor, *2:* 390

Great Britain and, *2:* 441–42

Grenada and, *2:* 395

Gromyko, Andrey, and, *1:* 166

Harriman, W. Averell, and, *1:* 175

health of, *2:* 399

honors for, *2:* 399

House Un-American Activities Committee and, *2:* 389

imperialism and, *2:* 395–97

Iran and, *2:* 399

Iran-Contra scandal and, *1:* 56, 60; *2:* 398

Kennan, George F., and, *2:* 216, 396

Kirkpatrick, Jeane, and, *2:* 251

Kissinger, Henry, and, *2:* 266, 390

Kohl, Helmut, and, *2:* 272

Korean Airlines tragedy and, *2:* 394

Libya and, *2:* 398–99

military and, *1:* 51; *2:* 392, 393

Nicaragua and, *2:* 398

Nixon, Richard M., and, *2:* 364, 390

nuclear war and, *2:* 394

nuclear weapons and, *1:* 56, 78, 155; *2:* 252, 392, 395–96, 418

as radio broadcaster, *2:* 388

Reagan Doctrine and, *2:* 397–98

Reaganomics and, *2:* 392

Red Scare and, *2:* 389

retirement of, *2:* 399

Screen Actors Guild and, *2:* 388–89

T

MacArthur, Douglas, and, *1:* 5,
40; *2:* 297, 298, 299–301,
327, 461
Marshall, George C., and, *2:*
324, 326–27
Marshall Plan and, *2:* 459
McCarthy, Joseph R., and, *1:*
140; *2:* 299–300, 334, 460,
461
middle initial of, *2:* 453
Molotov, Vyacheslav, and, *2:*
350–51
North Atlantic Treaty Organization and, *2:* 459
nuclear weapons and, *1:* 3, 31,
108; *2:* 212, 288, 333, 351,
375, 458
Oppenheimer, J. Robert, and, *2:*
373
Pendergast, Thomas, and, *2:*
454
political beginnings of, *2:*
454–55
popularity of, *2:* 459, 460, 461,
462
Potsdam Conference and, *1:*
65, 66; *2:* 351, 431, 457
presidency of, *2:* 452, 456–62
Reagan, Ronald, and, *2:* 389
Republic of China and, *1:* 39,
98, 118
retirement of, *2:* 461
Rio Pact and, *2:* 459
Roosevelt, Franklin D., and, *1:*
65; *2:* 455, 456
Rusk, Dean, and, *1:* 202
as senator, *2:* 455–56
Soviet Union and, *1:* 171–72; *2:*
288, 333
Stalin, Joseph, and, *2:* 351, 452,
457
Tito, Josip Broz, and, *2:* 448
transportation and, *2:* 455
Truman Committee and, *2:*
455–56
Truman Doctrine and, *1:*
29–30, 38, 112, 172; *2:* 212,
458–59
Turkey and, *1:* 29–30, 38; *2:*
326
United Nations and, *2:* 457
Wallace, Henry A., *2:* 461
World War I and, *2:* 454

World War II and, *1:* 106–7; *2:*
455–56, 457–58
Yalta Conference and, *1:* 65
Zhou Enlai and, *2:* 468–69
TUC. *See* Trades Union Congress
(TUC)
Tupolev, A. N., *2:* 290 (ill.)
Turkey, *1:* 3–4, 29–30, 38, 112; *2:*
326
26th of July Movement, *1:* 85

U

Ukraine, *1:* 58
Ulbricht, Walter, *2:* 225
UN. *See* United Nations (UN)
Union of Soviet Socialist Re-
publics (U.S.S.R.). *See* Soviet
Union
United Front, *1:* 96
United Fruit Company, *1:* 86
United Nations Security Council
Cuba and, *1:* 91
formation of, *1:* 161
United Nations (UN)
Attlee, Clement R., and, *1:* 28
Bush, George, and, *1:* 55, 60
China and, *1:* 98–99, 119; *2:*
313, 360, 469
Cuba and, *1:* 91
Deng Xiaoping and, *1:* 119
Dulles, John Foster, and, *1:* 127
formation of, *1:* 28, 105, 127,
161; *2:* 457
Gorbachev, Mikhail, and, *1:*
156
Grenada and, *2:* 395
Gromyko, Andrey, and, *1:* 161,
166
Khrushchev, Nikita, and, *2:*
233–34, 238
Kirkpatrick, Jeane, and, *2:* 249,
251–52, 253
Korea and, *2:* 243
Korean War and, *1:* 5; *2:* 243,
299
North Korea and, *2:* 247
nuclear energy and, *1:* 3; *2:* 373
October War and, *2:* 263
Panama invasion and, *1:* 60
proposal for, *1:* 161
Reagan, Ronald, and, *2:* 395

death in, *1:* 201; *2:* 258, 359
Democratic Party and, *2:* 358
economy and, *1:* 204
Eisenhower, Dwight D., and, *1:* 198
end of, *1:* 182; *2:* 260
Gulf of Tonkin Resolution and, *1:* 199
Harriman, W. Averell, and, *1:* 174–75
Ho Chi Minh and, *1:* 182
Hoover, J. Edgar, and, *1:* 192
Johnson, Lyndon B., and, *1:* 7–8, 109, 114, 174–75, 182, 183, 194, 198–203, 203–4; *2:* 281, 302, 342, 358, 359
Kennan, George F., and, *2:* 216
Kennedy, John F., and, *1:* 198
Kissinger, Henry, and, *2:* 255, 257–60, 261–62, 264, 359
Kosygin, Aleksey, and, *2:* 277, 281
MacArthur, Douglas, and, *2:* 302
McNamara, Robert S., and, *2:* 337–38, 341–43
Nixon, Richard M., and, *1:* 50, 175; *2:* 257, 259, 359–60, 362–63
opposition to, *1:* 175, 192, 201, 202, 204; *2:* 258, 342, 343, 358, 359, 390
peace and, *1:* 175, 204
Reagan, Ronald, and, *2:* 390
Rusk, Dean, and, *1:* 201, 202
Soviet Union and, *1:* 50; *2:* 261–62, 281
Tet Offensive, *1:* 114, 183, 203–4
U.S. Congress and, *1:* 199, 201
Vietcong and, *1:* 183, 203; *2:* 258
Vietnamization, *2:* 258, 359
Virgin Land program, *1:* 44; *2:* 238
Voice of America, *1:* 75; *2:* 334
Voorhis, Jerry, *2:* 355
Voting Rights Act of 1965, *1:* 198

W

Wagner, Robert, *1:* 127–28
Wallace, Henry A., *1:* 64; *2:* 456, 460, 461

Warren Commission, *2:* 229
Warsaw Pact, *1:* 47–48; *2:* 271, 274
Washington Dulles International Airport, *1:* 131
Watergate scandal, *1:* 55, 74; *2:* 262, 264, 363–64
We the Living, *2:* 383
Weapons, *1:* 42, 150, 190. *See also* Missiles; Nuclear weapons
Weinberger, Caspar, *1:* 60
Welch, Joseph N., *2:* 329, 335, 335 (ill.)
West Berlin, *1:* 132; *2:* 224–25, 235–37
West Germany
    Acheson, Dean G., and, *1:* 4–5
    Adenauer, Konrad, and, *1:* 9, 11–16
    Brandt, Willy, and, *1:* 15
    Brezhnev, Leonid, and, *1:* 47–48
    capitalism and, *2:* 268
    Christian Democratic Union in, *2:* 270, 271
    constitution of, *1:* 11–12
    democracy and, *2:* 268
    Dulles, John Foster, and, *1:* 131
    East Germany and, *1:* 15; *2:* 271–72
    economy of, *1:* 9, 12, 14; *2:* 272
    elections in, *1:* 12, 15; *2:* 271
    formation of, *1:* 4–5, 12, 138; *2:* 224, 235, 268, 432
    France and, *1:* 12, 13, 14
    Great Britain and, *2:* 308
    Gromyko, Andrey, and, *1:* 165
    independence of, *1:* 13
    North Atlantic Treaty Organization and, *1:* 12–14; *2:* 271–72, 273
    nuclear weapons and, *2:* 272–73
    Poland and, *1:* 15
    Soviet Union and, *1:* 13–14, 15, 47–48, 165; *2:* 271–72
Western Union, *2:* 208
Westmoreland, William C., *2:* 342
White Citizen's Council, *1:* 73
The White House Years, *1:* 144
"Whiz Kids," *2:* 339
Why England Slept, *2:* 219
Wiley, Alexander, *2:* 330–31
Will, George F., *2:* 345